Material Game Studies

Also Available from Bloomsbury

Fictional Games: A Philosophy of Worldbuilding and Imaginary Play, ed. Stefano
Gualeni and Riccardo Fassone
Game Play: Paratextuality in Contemporary Board Games, Paul Booth
Childhood by Design: Toys and the Material Culture of Childhood, 1700-Present,
ed. Megan Brandow-Faller
Video Games, Violence, and the Ethics of Fantasy: Killing Time,
Christopher Bartel

Material Game Studies

A Philosophy of Analogue Play

Edited by
Chloé Germaine and Paul Wake

BLOOMSBURY ACADEMIC
LONDON • NEW YORK • OXFORD • NEW DELHI • SYDNEY

BLOOMSBURY ACADEMIC
Bloomsbury Publishing Plc
50 Bedford Square, London, WC1B 3DP, UK
1385 Broadway, New York, NY 10018, USA
29 Earlsfort Terrace, Dublin 2, Ireland

BLOOMSBURY, BLOOMSBURY ACADEMIC and the Diana logo are trademarks of
Bloomsbury Publishing Plc

First published in Great Britain 2023
This paperback published 2024

Series design by Charlotte Daniels

Cover image: Brecht, Belgium – 28 July 2020: A hand of a person reaching out holding the
metal dinosaur pawn or game piece of a game of monopoly between the fi nger
(© Joeri Mostmans/Alamy Stock Photo)

A catalogue record for this book is available from the British Library.

Library of Congress Cataloging-in-Publication Data

Names: Germaine, Chloé, editor. | Wake, Paul, editor.
Title: Material game studies : a philosophy of analogue play / Edited by
Chloé Germaine and Paul Wake.
Description: New York, NY : Bloomsbury Academic, 2023. |
Includes bibliographical references and index.
Identifiers: LCCN 2022036546 (print) | LCCN 2022036547 (ebook) |
ISBN 9781350202719 (hardback) | ISBN 9781350202726 (paperback) |
ISBN 9781350202733 (pdf) | ISBN 9781350202740 (epub)
Subjects: LCSH: Games–Design. | Games–Philosophy. |
Board games–Social aspects. | Analog computer simulation–Social aspects.
Classification: LCC GV1230.M38 2023 (print) |
LCC GV1230 (ebook) | DDC 794.8/3–dc23/eng/20220825
LC record available at https://lccn.loc.gov/2022036546
LC ebook record available at https://lccn.loc.gov/2022036547

ISBN: HB: 978-1-3502-0271-9
PB 978-1-3502-0272-6
ePDF: 978-1-3502-0273-3
eBook: 978-1-3502-0274-0

Typeset by Deanta Global Publishing Services, Chennai, India

To find out more about our authors and books visit www.bloomsbury.com and
sign up for our newsletters.

Contents

List of figures   vii

List of contributors   viii

Acknowledgements   xi

Introduction: Material game studies *Paul Wake and Chloé Germaine*   1

I Provocations

1 Thinking the things we play with *Miguel Sicart*   21

2 Analogue games as infrastructure *Aaron Trammell*   32

II Materials

3 Component parts: Board games as architecture and performance *Paul Wake*   47

4 A queer touch of fantasy role-play *Jack Warren*   65

5 Lead fantasies: The making, meaning and materiality of miniatures *Mikko Meriläinen, Katriina Heljakka and Jaakko Stenros*   83

III Ideologies

6 'Men should try playing the woman's part to see what it feels like. Remember ~ it's only a game . . .': The representation of gendered experience in chance-based board games *Holly Nielsen*   105

7 Deterritorializing game boards: Mapping imperialism in *RISK* and modern board games *Jonathan Rey Lee*   123

8 'Nature' games in a time of climate crisis *Chloé Germaine*   143

IV Cultures

9 Contested spaces, velvet ropes, exclusion zones: The pleasures and dangers of face-to-face play in analogue gaming spaces *Tanya Pobuda*   165

10 'Hands, face, space': The material turn in board gaming during Covid-19 *Esther MacCallum-Stewart*   187

V Hybridity

11   The cult of new (stuff): Kickstarter's digital/material tensions
     Paul Booth   205
12   The logic of analogue adaptation *Nathan Altice*   222

Index   240

Figures

3.1	*Jenga* (Hasbro 1983)	53
3.2	The Ballinderry gaming board	59
3.3	Rune stone (Gs 19) (Ockelbo Kyrka - Replica)	60
4.1	Miniature gaming model	69
4.2	Role-playing mat	72
4.3	Paper character sheet	76
5.1	The experiential dimensions of object play	97
7.1	Diagramming the glance	126
7.2	A reproduction of the 1959 first edition of *RISK* staged to replicate the downward glance of a player seated over the game board	130
7.3	Images from the *Twilight Struggle* rulebook (top) and *Ideology* game (bottom), showing how the games map territorial control	136
7.4	A comparison of the networked maps on the *Pandemic* (left) and *Freedom* (right) boards, both of which train the player to direct their operational glance towards lines of flow rather than territories	139
9.1	What selection below best describes the length of your participation in the board gaming hobby?	171
9.2	The board gaming industry is dominated by white men	172
9.3	I have experienced homophobic remarks while participating in the board gaming hobby	179

Contributors

Nathan Altice is a writer, game designer and Teaching Professor of Computational Media at UC Santa Cruz. His research includes computing history, computational platforms and Japanese board and card game history. His first book, *I AM ERROR*, was published by MIT Press in 2015.

Paul Booth is Professor of Communication at DePaul University and the author or editor of fourteen books, including *Board Games as Media* (2021), *Game Play* (2015), *The Fan Studies Primer* (with Rebecca Williams, 2021), *Watching Doctor Who* (with Craig Owen Jones, 2020) and *Digital Fandom 2.0* (2016). He is co-editor, with Aaron Trammell, of the Tabletop Gaming series from the University of Michigan Press. He is currently enjoying a cup of coffee.

Chloé Germaine is Senior Lecturer in English at Manchester Metropolitan University and co-director of the Manchester Metropolitan Game Centre, with Paul Wake. In game studies, her research focuses on ecology and climate change in relation to tabletop games, including board games and role-playing games, and on LARP. She is a game designer and writes for the role-playing games *Cthulhu Hack*, the *Dee Sanction* and the *Codex* Magazine, which is published by the Gauntlet, as well as working on original games.

Katriina Heljakka, Doctor of Arts, is a researcher at Pori Laboratory of Play, University of Turku (digital culture studies). Her background is in toy research with a particular interest in adult toy play and character toys. Heljakka currently studies connected toys, playful tools, techniques and environments in the workspace, and the visual, material, digital and social cultures of play. Her main interests include the emerging toyification of culture, toy design, playful spaces and the hybrid and transgenerational dimensions of ludic practices.

Jonathan Rey Lee researches material play media, especially toys and board games. He has written several articles on board games, and his book *Deconstructing LEGO: The Medium and Messages of LEGO Play* was published by Palgrave Macmillan in 2020. Jonathan received his PhD in comparative literature from the University of California, Riverside, and currently teaches in Seattle.

Esther MacCallum-Stewart is Professor in the School of Digital, Technologies and Arts at Staffordshire University. Her work examines the ways in which players understand the worlds around them – as players, fans, producers and consumers. She has written widely on aspects of gaming including gender in games, representation and diversity, the ways in which players tell stories and understand narratives in games. Her work extends beyond the digital to examine gaming worlds such as role-playing, board games, fan communities and conventions.

Mikko Meriläinen (PhD) is a postdoctoral researcher at the Centre of Excellence in Game Culture Studies at Tampere University's Game Research Lab. In his work Meriläinen focuses on qualitative player research and is currently exploring youth gaming cultures, masculinities and gaming, and miniaturing.

Holly Nielsen is a postgraduate research student in the Department of History at Royal Holloway University of London studying British board games and play *c*. 1860–1960. She is a writer and narrative designer working in media and on games.

Tanya Pobuda is a board game academic, licensed drone pilot, artificial intelligence chatbot creator and virtual and augmented reality practitioner. Her research on the board games has been featured in *The New York Times*, the *Analog Game Studies* journal and various podcasts, including *Stuff Your Mom Never Told You About*, *The Spiel*, *Who What Why Podcast* and *Beyond Solitaire*. She gained her PhD from Ryerson & York University's Communication & Culture programme and has a 26-year background as a former journalist, certified project manager, digital storyteller with a background in public relations, communication, marketing and Web design.

Miguel Sicart is an Associate Professor at the Center for Computer Games Research, IT University of Copenhagen. He is the author of *Play Matters*. His research inquiries on the cultural, political, ethical and technical implications of playing with software. You can read more at miguelsicart.net and ridiculous. software.

Jaakko Stenros (PhD) is a University Lecturer in game studies working at the Centre of Excellence in Game Culture Studies at the Game Research Lab,

Tampere University. He has published nine books and over fifty articles and reports, and has taught game studies for a decade. Stenros has also collaborated with artists and designers to create ludic experiences and has curated many exhibitions at the Finnish Museum of Games.

Aaron Trammell is Assistant Professor of Informatics and Core Faculty in Visual Studies at UC Irvine. He writes about how *Dungeons & Dragons*, *Magic: The Gathering* and board games inform the lived experiences of their players. He is the editor-in-chief of the journal *Analog Game Studies* and the multimedia editor of *Sounding Out!*

Paul Wake is Reader in English literature at Manchester Metropolitan University and a co-director of the Manchester Metropolitan Game Centre. He has published on literary representations of casino games, 1980s Adventure Gamebooks and game design for communication. He also designs, uses and plays games to start conversations about important societal topics.

Jack Warren is a postgraduate researcher at Manchester Metropolitan University, a member of the Manchester Metropolitan Game Centre and an organizer of the Queer Research Network Manchester. Jack completed his MA in gender, sexuality, and culture at the University of Manchester and now researches new materialisms, role-play and queer theory.

Acknowledgements

The editors would like to thank all the contributors for their efforts in putting together this volume and for the shared conversations from which the concept of material game studies emerged. We would also like to thank our colleagues in the Manchester Metropolitan Game Centre for providing such a vibrant research community in which to work. We furthermore acknowledge the field-defining work of the *Analog Game Studies* journal and thank the editors for providing a forum for the development of research on analogue games and play. Likewise, we have benefitted from the support of Asmodee Research and Game in Lab in providing a network through which to develop ideas with researchers across the globe. Chloé would like to thank Paul for the collaboration that made this volume possible. Paul would like to thank Chloé for the collaboration that made this volume possible.

We offer our thanks for the inclusion of Figure 3.2, which was reproduced courtesy of the Royal Irish Academy; Figure 7.2, which was reproduced courtesy of Winning Moves Games; Figure 7.3, which was reproduced courtesy of GMT Games LLC; and Figure 7.4, which was provided courtesy of Academy Games.

Introduction

Material game studies

Paul Wake and Chloé Germaine

What happened to the material turn?

Writing in 2012, Thomas H. Apperley and Darshana Jayemanne announced an emerging material turn in game studies, noting an increasing engagement with the material context of digital games, the relationship between technology and the body, and with gaming as a situated cultural practice. Despite this announcement of game studies' material turn in 2012, there has been no subsequent sustained attempt to address the concept of materiality in relation to games, and while scholars such as Sky LaRell (2017), Brendan Keogh (2018) and Miguel Sicart (2021) have written in response to Apperley and Jayemanne's provocation, work on the topic, often pursuing productive lines of enquiry, has tended to be sporadic and scattered through the discipline. Despite these notable contributions in the study of games, and the fact that scholars working in isolated fields of enquiry have continued to investigate the themes identified by Apperley and Jayemanne, there has yet to be an expansive articulation of what is at stake in game studies' material turn. Almost a decade later, *Material Game Studies* takes up the call to attend to the material turn in the study of games and play. This introduction begins the important work of exploring the material turn by sketching the parameters, concerns and approaches for what we call 'material game studies'.

In addition to drawing together distinct strands of enquiry in game studies that attend to the material dimensions of games and play, our formulation of 'material game studies' responds to a wider turn in critical thought that has seen calls for a materialist theory of politics or agency and a 'reconfiguring of our very understanding of matter' (Coole and Frost 2010: 2). Over the past decade, this material turn has shaped enquiry in disciplines across the humanities as scholars have sought to push back against constructivist epistemologies, including the cultural and linguistic turns of the late twentieth century, which hold that 'immaterial' things, such as (human) consciousness, subjectivity, mind, language and meaning, are fundamentally different to matter. Following the philosopher Jane Bennett, who argues that paying attention to the vibrancy of materiality requires cultivating playful attitudes (2010: 15), we offer *Material Game Studies* as a way of exploring the ways in which games and game playing puncture the 'constructivist' idea that matter is passive and inert. Through *Material Game Studies*, we suggest that games and play disclose a reality in which humans exist within an assemblage of myriad material agencies whose intra-actions co-constitute the world. Constructivist approaches continue to be valuable for material game studies, since games are, of course, culturally specific and embedded in human social and linguistic processes. However, we contend that games cannot only be understood as social or cultural constructions, because they reveal the 'generativity and resilience of material forms within which social actors interact' (Coole and Frost 2010: 26). That is, material game studies as we conceive it considers games as specific modes of intra-action between a range of agencies and co-actors (human and otherwise).

Material Game Studies positions play as a material-discursive site requiring inter- and multi-disciplinary interrogations, which consider games as material objects, investigate the material conditions of production and consumption, study the embodied experience of gameplay and theorize the more-than-human dimensions of play. Such interrogations would surely include, as Apperley and Jayemanne contend, a focus on the material technologies that facilitate digital games. However, this volume limits itself to overtly *material* games, that is, games that are played through and as material objects: board games, tabletop games and role-playing games. It is our hope that the focus on such obviously *material* games will allow for a distinct attention to materiality and to the ways in which human play is embedded within and co-constitutive of materiality, rather than an idealism that is superimposed upon the world as mere background. Moreover, the work in this volume, focused as it is on tabletop games, is infused with the sense that its insights apply to games more generally, be they digital or otherwise, and it is our hope that the term offers an umbrella under which we can begin to bring together formerly disparate aspects of game studies into dialogue, including closing the gap between 'digital' and 'analogue' game studies through a consideration of the materiality that undergirds both.

Our introduction to the volume scopes potential areas of enquiry within material game studies, elaborating conceptual and theoretical tools that we feel will extend game studies beyond the limits of constructivist epistemologies and theories. Areas of study that emerge in the volume include the distinct practices and cultures of analogue games; the materials of games, such as tokens, miniatures, maps, boards; and the embodied aspects of game playing in its different forms. We also seek to invert dominant anthropocentric perspectives that have tended to dominate in the humanities and social sciences despite the challenges brought into those disciplines through such discourses as posthumanism. Material game studies shifts focus from the human agent to the play of materiality itself, thinking through the agency of nonhuman actors and players that co-constitute games. The more-than-human scope of material game studies leads us to suggest that play is not only a human cultural activity but an example of the ways in which humans co-constitute themselves and the world as part of more-than-human entanglements and assemblages.

Analogue, digital, material

Our emphasis on what has been called the 'analogue' as the medium of play through which to formulate material game studies responds to and builds upon a history of calls within game studies to pay attention to board games and other 'analogue' forms of play. The formulation of material game studies is related to, then, and also distinct from, what has become known as 'analogue game studies'. Nonetheless, the work in *Material Game Studies* is indebted to scholars such as Rafael Bienia, Paul Booth, Shelly Jones, Greg Loring-Albright, Esther MacCallum-Stewart, Nicholas Mizer, Evan Torner, Aaron Trammell, Emma Leigh Waldron and Stewart Woods, to name but a few, who have worked to develop and promote the study of analogue games, including board games, tabletop role-playing games and live action role-playing games (LARP), in the face of a tendency in game studies to prioritize digital technologies.

Those taking up the cause of analogue games have done so in the context of the origins of the discipline in video game studies (Aarseth 2001). Important responses to the dominance of video games in game studies include the inaugural issue of *Analog Game Studies* in which the editors state their commitment to 'support the critical analysis, discussion of design, and documentation of analog games' (2014: n.p.). Arguing that 'game studies can no longer afford to primarily focus on computer games in an era where the world has become so digitally mediated that the nomenclature ceases to carry the same weight that it once did' (2014: n.p.), their focus on what they call 'analog games' emerges from a belief that games might produce social change. For Aaron Trammell,

Emma Leigh Waldron and Evan Torner, then, 'analog games' can 'make clear
the rulesets that govern behavior within games and, in doing so, reveal the
biological and cultural rules which have forever governed our society' (2014:
n.p.). Our formulation of material game studies concurs with this assessment of
the imbrication of analogue games with social and political change, combining
this with theoretical interest in the part played by materiality in the context of
such social and political concerns. More recently, Douglas Brown and Esther
MacCallum-Stewart's collection of essays, *Rerolling Board Games*, continues
the work of 'transporting games beyond the digital' (2020: 1), focusing on what
they describe as specific 'ludic complexities arising from the physicality of board
games as a played entity' (2020: 4). Building on the work in that volume, *Material
Game Studies* offers a variety of ways of investigating such complexities. We
agree with Brown and MacCallum-Stewart's suggestion that while board games
are 'critical texts in their own right', they should not be seen as 'paving new
theoretical pathways entirely separate from the rest of game studies' (2020: 4).
While there are, of course, points at which video games and board games invite
and benefit from distinct modes of critical attention, such points of divergence
are sites of productive mismatches that reveal the play of materiality common to
both. Thus, we suggest that although a focus on board and tabletop games helps
make explicit the need to investigate the materiality of play, by engaging in this
study it becomes evident that all game studies are, in fact, material game studies.

It is this contention that leads us to prefer the word 'material' to the word
'analogue' in describing the endeavour that impels material game studies. In
common parlance, 'analogue' has come to mean tangible, touchable stuff: 'real'
things. It is in this sense that David Sax uses the word in his book *The Revenge
of Analog: Real Things and Why They Matter* (2016). There, Sax nostalgically
contrasts things people can hold and touch with digital or 'virtual' objects and
cultures. And so, vinyl records are bundled up with a discussion of, among other
things, paper, film, board games, retail, work and summer. The temptation to
connect the analogue with the physical world and the digital with the virtual
shapes Sax's book, in which those who turn to vinyl records and Moleskine'
notebooks are afforded a countercultural aspect that is ultimately unhelpful.
Granting a form of countercultural, even subcultural, social capital to analogue
items in this way suggests a kind of nostalgic and uncritical mode of consumption
and positions the analogue as that which precedes, and so has been superseded
by, the digital, upholding a false binary between the retro and the modern, the
real and the virtual, the authentic and the fake. We suggest that this sentiment,
while seductive, relies on an artificial construction that says little about either the

analogue or the digital. To connect the analogue with real things and the digital to the purely virtual is to misunderstand both. Accordingly, while the work of those in analogue game studies informs this introduction and several chapters in the volume, the formulation material game studies allows us to sidestep a problematic and unhelpful divide between the digital and the analogue, shifting focus to the material affordances, contexts and ontologies of games in a broader sense.[1] Analogue, we contend, is not a synonym for material. It would be entirely possible for there to be a material turn in analogue game studies: the analogue and the material are not, as it were, analogous.

As we have suggested, our formulation of material game studies responds to attempts to define a material 'turn' within game studies discussed by Apperley and Jayemanne (2012). In contrast to those scholars calling for the inclusion of the analogue within game studies, Jayemanne and Apperley evoke the notion of materiality in relation to the study of digital culture and video games. In so doing, they hope to nudge game studies beyond the 'formalised and calcified structures' (2012: 7) that have dominated since the inception of the field in 2001. Jayemanne and Apperley identify two strands in game studies' material turn: the study of game technologies and situated analyses of play and players. These strands further break down into three methodological tendencies in game studies: (1) ethnographies that consider the lives and experiences of players; (2) platform studies that consider the material technologies which undergird video games (see, for example, Baldwin and Woodard 2008; Montfort and Bogost 2009); and (3) concerns with the ways in which play intersects with digital labour. This taxonomy provides a useful diagnostic of the ways in which the material has been a concern to scholars working in digital games. This work has been taken forward in analogue game studies, too, where even 'platform studies', a mode of study unambiguous in its attachment to the digital, has led to examples of fertile cross-hybridization between the study of 'digital' and 'analogue' games (see Altice 2014; Bellomy 2017; Hubble 2021; Švelch 2016). Indeed, such methodologies and concerns arise in this volume, with authors turning attention to the hybrid modes of play that developed during a time of social distancing (MacCallum-Stewart, Chapter 10) and to the effects of digital platforms such as Kickstarter on board game production (Booth, Chapter 11).

Alongside these concerns we seek to draw attention to materiality as the ground for better understanding how play makes meaning in the world and exists as a site for ontological and ethical investigations. To do this, we draw on the theoretical insights and challenges of the so-called new materialisms and challenge the dominance of the idealist and constructivist tendencies that inhere in game studies. Indeed, we contest the way in which materiality in Apperley and Jayemanne's analysis tends to conflate the materiality of games with the idea that games are objects. While they praise the fact that the material turn in game studies asks scholars to understand games as 'objects that exist in the world' (2012: 15), we contend that considering games as objects upholds constructivist conceptions of reality as hierarchically divided into subjects and objects. Such a conception construes materiality, including games as material objects, as 'passive and immutable' (Barad 2003: 801), deriving its potentiality from human intentionality, language and culture. Material game studies, by contrast, intends on upsetting this kind of ontological division and emphasizes the agency of games as co-actors in the production of meaning and social realities.

In considering games as co-actors in the production of realities, social or otherwise, this volume builds on existing investigations of materiality in game studies, which are concerned with the 'stuff' of analogue play and are pushing at the humanist constraints of game studies. At the intersection of analogue and digital game studies, Melissa Rogerson, Martin Smith and Wally Gibbs's ethnographic work on board game cultures builds on Stewart Woods's germinal work on player communities in his book *Eurogames* (2012), identifying materiality as one of four significant factors in the player experience of tabletop gaming (2016). They give examples of the importance of miniatures and other game components, such as board game boxes, and physical gaming environments, to players. While Rogerson, Smith and Gibbs consider such materials in the context of human player experience and gaming practices, their work provides important context for more theoretical considerations of the role of material components in gaming.

Theoretically oriented work in this area includes Rafael Bienia's (2016) ground-breaking work on role-playing game materials which brings Bruno Latour's actor network theory into game studies. Bienia's contention is that it is 'insufficient to understand role-playing as a mindset or a social process' (2016: 3) that occurs between players alone. Rather, he takes up Latour's call to 'follow the actors', aiming to show how 'materials collaborate with narrative and ludic actors', studying the 'interrelational processes and the networks of rpgs' (Bienia 2016: n.p.). Responding to Bienia's prompts, Paul Wake's *Analog Game Studies* article 'Token Gestures: Towards a Theory of Immersion in Analog Games' also accounts 'for the affordances of analog game platforms', arguing 'that their tactile mechanics facilitate immersive gameplay' (2019: n.p.). However, as Wake suggests, more work is needed to further consider the implications of his ontological claims made about the relation of players and the pieces with which they play. The materials that comprise analogue games have also been considered by Chloé Germaine (writing as Germaine Buckley) in a different context through her work on props in LARP, which likewise brings theories from the material turn in philosophy into game studies, drawing specifically on Jane Bennett's concept of vibrant matter and Graham Harman's articulation of object-oriented ontology. Germaine Buckley argues, contra the humanist impulse of much game studies scholarship, that the props of LARP disclose the agency of 'the unhuman nature of reality' (2020: 392), contesting a constructivist notion that humans impose meaning on materiality.

As well as building on this body of emerging scholarship and drawing together new work on the materiality of games, *Material Game Studies* is also interested in teasing out discussions of materiality that are already baked into discussion of games and play. The concept of the 'magic circle' provides a good example of a latent concern with materiality that has persisted since the origins of game studies. As Johan Huizinga put it, in a passage made (in)famous by Katie Salen and Eric Zimmerman in their *Rules of Play* (2004):

> All play moves and has its being within a play-ground marked off beforehand either materially or ideally, deliberately or as a matter of course. [. . .] The arena, the card-table, the magic circle, the temple, the stage, the screen, the tennis court, the court of justice, etc., are all in form and function play-grounds, i.e. forbidden spots, isolated, hedged round, hallowed, within which special rules obtain. (Huizinga 1955: 10)

The magic circle has been seen by some (and criticized by many: see Copier 2005; Zimmerman 2012; and Stenros 2014) as placing games beyond the reach of material concerns, defining play, as Roger Caillois suggests, 'as action denuded of all material interest' (2001: 5). While Huizinga's concern is with the 'form and function' of the space of play it is notable that the playgrounds he describes (both in this famous passage and in the volume as a whole), card tables, temples, stages, and tennis courts, are material spaces. If, then, the magic circle is understood in terms of negotiations that separate the 'real' and the 'game' world rather than describing the spaces themselves it is clear that these negotiations are informed by material concerns. Thus, when Juul asks, rhetorically, in 'The Magic Circle and the Puzzle Piece' (2008), 'surely it cannot matter whether the player smokes cigarettes?' his response, a quotation from Beth Dillon's account of a roundtable at the 2005 Austin Games Conference, is telling, 'the Internet café-dominant MMO play setting in Asia must be solo friendly. Simple "point & click" design is also essential in the café environment, because players often hold a drink or cigarette in one hand' (2008: 62). For Juul, this confirms the ways in which games fit, like puzzle pieces, culture. For us, the account of the role of cafés, drinks and cigarettes confirms that the negotiations of the 'magic circle' are themselves embodied and material, and that these negotiations take place between human and nonhuman agents.

Theorizing materiality in game studies

We contend that there is both a latent and emerging engagement in game studies with a wider material turn already established in critical theory and philosophy. Serenella Iovino and Serpil Opperman helpfully summarize this material turn as comprising a variety of new 'ways to analyse language and reality, human and nonhuman life, mind and matter, without falling into dichotomous patterns of thinking' (2014: 2). For Coole and Frost, the 'material turn' challenges 'some of the most basic assumptions that have underpinned the modern world, including its normative sense of the human and its belief about human agency, but also regarding material practices, such as the ways we labor [*sic*] on, exploit and interact with nature' (2010: 4). *Material Game Studies* responds to these challenges and provocations, applying the theoretical tools developed as part of this material turn to games. We also suggest synergies between existing concepts and approaches in games studies and the material turn and offer games, and play, as particularly rich topics through which we might engage with materiality.

Material Game Studies understands play not as a solely human activity that imposes meaning on a passive material background, or environment, but as a mode of engagement with what Jane Bennett calls the 'vibrant matter' of the world. Bennett's work has been particularly influential in the material turn, and her propositions are particularly resonant for game studies. Indeed, her work prompts Miguel Sicart to reconsider the 'things we play with' in his provocation for this volume. His discussion of the material affordances of play discloses what Bennett describes as 'a turbulent, immanent field in which various and variable materialities collide, congeal, morph, evolve and disintegrate' (2010: xi). Here we further consider Bennett's exhortation for scholars to puncture the 'quarantines of matter and life' in terms of material game studies' attention to the 'lively powers of material formations' (2010: vii), whether this be the 'gyre' of role-playing game materials as discussed in Jack Warren's chapter in this volume or the pull material objects exert even in a time of physical distancing and online play, as described in Esther MacCallum-Stewart's chapter on board gaming during the pandemic. Material game studies suggests that games are an 'enchanted mode' through which human players encounter a vibrant materiality, pointing to 'the agency of the things that produce effects in human and other bodies' (Barad 2010: xii). Games are cultural, yes, but, as Bennett suggests, 'cultural form are themselves powerful, material assemblages' (2010: 1).

Material game studies' sympathy with Bennett's account of vibrant matter requires an alternative critical approach to the study of games to those that have tended to dominate during the first two decades of game studies, and which emphasize human action and the human social domain. One such approach is 'posthuman performativity' expounded by Karen Barad (2003). For Barad, posthuman performativity offers a contestation of the excessive power that has been granted to language to determine what is real; it 'allows matter its due as an active participant in the world's becoming' (2003: 803). Understood in this way, performativity describes not only the coming into being of the human subject via the human body and associated socio-political discourses but comprises the material-discursive interactions of human and nonhuman bodies, with matter itself playing an active role. We think the study of games is a particularly rich means of providing 'a robust account of the materialisation of all bodies – "human" and "non-human" – and the material-discursive practices by which their differential constitutions are marked' (Barad 2003: 810). Sicart's recent work echoes this idea, also drawing on Barad to describe play as 'the meeting point in which human agency, human experience, technological agency, and materiality become entangled in a process of ontogenesis' (2021: 7). Elsewhere, Conor McKeown has applied Barad's 'agential realist' approach to develop a 'performative' account of video games (2018). Following this emerging interest in Barad's ideas, material game studies draws on the idea of posthuman performativity to suggest that games are not brought into being by human minds and actions but that there is a much more complex material-discursive entanglement at work from which human players are not separate.

As the word 'entanglement' suggests, material game studies emphasizes relational ontologies of games. Relational ontologies suggest that reality is composed not of subjects and objects, nor of matter and minds, but of relational processes through which material assemblages come into being. Moreover, thinking of reality as relational prompts a consideration of the ethical ground that underlies the political and social dimensions of play. Here we evoke the idea of 'entanglement' as elaborated by Barad (2007) through her discussion of the Copenhagen Interpretation of quantum physics and Niels Bohr. Barad expands on Bohr's theories to expound an ontology based on phenomena, not objects.

Phenomena produce contingent objects and subjects through shifting and specific intra-actions within entanglements (Barad 2007: 128). In the science of quantum physics, this means that the properties of matter are only determinate given specific experimental arrangements (Barad 2007: 261). This implies that there are no pre-existing objects; rather, objects emerge from what Barad calls 'intra-actions' (Barad 2007: ix) – the term 'interaction' implies a separability that Barad suggests the science rejects. Sicart applies these ideas to play and games in his recent work on 'playthings' (2021), developing his relational account of play as an entangled process that brings into being new 'things' in his chapter for this volume. Elsewhere, in his account of literature and games in nineteenth-century America, Douglas A. Guerra suggests that the interpretation and analysis of games 'requires an approach that probes for meaning at persistently unsettled boundary lines between content and form, production ethos and reception aesthetics, subjects and objects' (2018: 2). Guerra considers reading games as an act that 'slides freely between material and conceptual domains of knowledge' (2018: 1). In line with Guerra's thinking, we suggest Barad's notions of phenomena and intra-action illuminate the unsettled boundaries between the material and discursive that any study of games necessarily involves.

In addition to the concepts of entanglement and intra-action, we also suggest Stacey Alaimo's (2010) concept of 'transcorporeality' as particularly generative for theorizing materiality in game studies, particularly in relation to existing work on the body in gaming. Building on the Baradian notion of entanglement, Alaimo offers transcorporeality as a theoretical site for understanding movement across human corporeality and nonhuman nature, a project that demands attention to the material and discursive, natural and cultural, biological and textual (2010: 3). For Alaimo, then, the human body is a site of transit, a mediating membrane, which is generative of a 'tangible sense of connection to the material world' (2010: 15–16). Material game studies suggests that games make space for the recognition of this connection and of the porous nature of the human body as it connects with the props, objects and environments that comprise play across the tabletop. Wake's chapter in this volume, for example, offers the evocative example of depictions of players merging with their games, while Warren draws out the queer potential of the porous nature of the human body as they meet the 'leaky' materials of role-play.

Following the material turn in critical thought, material game studies also asks scholars to consider the ethical dimension of games. According to Barad, 'entanglements are relations of obligation' (2010: 265) and, so, attention to games as material assemblages and intra-actions requires thinking about the responsibilities, obligations and vulnerabilities that inhere in play. Barad's is an 'ethics of worlding' grounded in a relational conception of intersubjectivity, and which refuses a neat separation between being, knowing and ethics (Barad 2007: 392). Material game studies is alert to this entanglement of dimensions as it navigates human player experiences, analyses cultural practices and embodied experiences of those practices and considers the materiality of games, including the technologies, props and objects that generate play. At every turn there are ethical questions about 'cuts' of inclusion and exclusion that comprise the assemblages that emerge in play, about the ways in which the material affordances of games direct ethical attention to some actors while eliding others, and about the shifting and provisional power relations that structure games and our experiences of play. We suggest here, then, that game playing is a particular kind of entanglement that produces contingent and provisional actors, including human players, who may, for the duration of the game, take account of the worlding which is taking place. In this volume, Tanya Pobuda's chapter on diversity in gaming cultures suggests that such a taking account of, and responsibility for, worlding in games is particularly necessary and urgent, especially for those people who have been marginalized or excluded, or else who face discrimination.

Material Game Studies draws on the ethical dimension of the material turn to suggest that game studies is implicated in the broader context of global social, climate and ecological crises that define the contemporary moment. It is such crises that have prompted such theories as Alaimo's 'transcorporeality' and Bennett's 'vibrant matter', providing game studies with essential theoretical and methodological tools to address its role in these crises. Those working in game studies are already responding to this important challenge. Alenda Chang's ground-breaking *Playing Nature* (2019) proposes that games are (inter) mediations of ecological problems, concepts and ethics and provides a series of case studies to explore these affordances in a time of climate crisis. Kira Voss Apperley and Jayemanne's piece in 'Ecocomposition: Writing ecologies in digital games', arguing that some games, such as Mojang's *Minecraft*, might work to reconcile 'putative antagonisms between nature and technology' (2014: 221). Following such interventions, we make a political and ethical argument for the necessity of material game studies, with its attention to the materiality of games and play, as one way in which the study of games can be responsive and responsible. As Bennett states, 'the image of dead or thoroughly instrumentalized matter feeds human hubris and our earth-destroying fantasies of conquest and consumption. It does so by preventing us from detecting (seeing, hearing, smelling, tasting, feeling) a fuller range of the nonhuman powers' (2010: ix). Germaine's chapter in this volume suggests that games might pay attention to the subjectivity of nonhuman actors and materials that have been consigned to the domain of 'Nature' and so intervene to puncture anthropocentric perspectives usually privileged in play. In her work, we see that games accord with the material turn in that both might provide what Iovino and Opperman describe as a more 'ontologically generous' picture of reality, 'a material-semiotic network of human and nonhuman agents incessantly generating' the world (2014: 3). Games have the potential to disclose this more ontologically generous reality, particularly through the ways in which they disclose the subjectivity of the more-than-human world, not only in the material actors that generate play but in their representations of more-than-human agents in games and their invitation for players to inhabit such subject positions. That is, material game studies asks scholars to examine the ways in which games 'hybridize human and nonhuman matters' (Iovino and Opperman 2014: 5) and so might puncture anthropocentric notions of mastery, the denial of agency and subjectivity to the more-than-human world, and fantasies of endless growth and consumption that are fuelling habitat destruction and climate crisis.

Summary of chapters

The chapters that comprise this volume offer insights into some of the ways game studies scholars might take up the concerns we have highlighted in this introduction. Not all the chapters engage directly with the material turn in philosophy, though each interrogates the materiality of tabletop games in some form. Our contributors hail from distinct disciplines and so draw on different methodologies. We consider this a strength and suggest that material game studies going forward be open to the insights that might be generated by cross- and interdisciplinary dialogue and collaboration.

This volume is organized into five parts. Part I, 'Provocations' contains two short chapters that set up the many questions that this volume seeks to address. Chapter 1, Miguel Sicart's 'Thinking the things we play with', describes play as a mode of being in the world that sets in motion an entangled process of becoming through which objects in the world, like sticks, balls or software, become the things we play with. Chapter 2, Aaron Trammell's 'Analogue games as infrastructure', offers a historical and critical narrative about the way in which the discipline of analogue game studies has formed against the discursive grain of game studies, exploring the division of the analogue from the digital and questioning the relationship between analogue game studies and game studies more broadly. Taken together, the two chapters generate a dialogue with our provocation in this introduction that 'material' might be a more fitting word than 'analogue' to describe this work and our contestation that all game studies are material in some way.

Part II, 'Materials', address the first of the provocations in their attention to the objects that enter into play during games. Responding to Sicart's call for relational thinking that 'situates ontology not on things, or in the human, but in the relations between agents and the material world', Wake's 'Component parts: Board games as architecture and performance' offers an ontology of board games that places Roman Ingarden's work in dialogue with that of Barad and Bennett. Figuring game objects not as the foundations of play but rather as elements that construct players as components, Wake argues that game performances entail an intra-action that aligns human and nonhuman components in the mutable and temporary networks. Jack Warren, in his chapter 'A queer touch of fantasy role-play', extends this reading to the intra-action of players and game objects (identified as gaming miniatures, gaming mats and character sheets for *Dungeons and Dragons*), figuring role-playing as a form self-touch that elicits ambiguity, undecidability, indeterminacy and radically queers notions of subjectivity. Concluding this part, Mikko Meriläinen, Katriina Heljakka and Jaakko Stenros explore the relationships between players, wargaming and role-playing figurines through a qualitative survey in their chapter, 'Lead fantasies'. Meriläinen, Heljakka and Stenros coin the term 'miniaturing' to describe in detail the complex and varied relations players have with miniatures that are variously objects, artworks, toys, playing pieces and props for imagining.

Part III, 'Ideologies', explores the social and political implications of the material turn in games. Holly Nielsen's chapter, 'Men should try playing the woman's part to see what it feels like', investigates the ways in which chance-based board games have been used to explore gendered experience. Through three illuminating case studies – *Pank-a-Squith* (1909), *The Ladder of Academic Success* (1951) and *Womanopoly* (1970s) – Neilsen demonstrates the ways in which games about women's experience have used purely chance-based mechanics to explore ideas of inevitability, lack of control and unfairness. These games were sites of protest, satire, celebration and education. Jonathan Rey Lee's chapter considers the role of modern game boards in mapping imperialism. His work builds on a growing postcolonial critique of board games which shows how board games often invoke and replicate a colonialist narrative through their mechanics and components. Lee investigates the material dimensions of this claim, arguing that, as spaces to be traversed, game boards present world views, inviting players into virtual yet material worlds that are constructed from the perspectival logic of maps. Drawing on the longstanding cultural intertwining of war and tabletop games and perspectival theories such as Martin Heidegger's theory of the 'world picture' and Rey Chow's theory of the 'world target', Lee theorizes and deconstructs the colonial logic of *RISK*-style game boards, proposing ways in which critical game design might work to deterritorialize war games. In the final chapter of this part, Germaine turns attention to the role of games in the ecological and climate crisis, arguing that in the face of the climate crisis and failed globalization, ecological thought must reorient itself towards the 'terrestrial' and become mired in earthly matters (Latour 2018; Haraway 2016). Her assessment of a plethora of recent nature-themed board games, many of which imply eco-friendly ethics, points to the problems and possibilities that inhere in the ways that board games engage human players with nonhuman subjects. From this she derives an eco-ethical framework that challenges board game designers to transcend some of the mechanical constraints that have become embedded in contemporary board games.

Part IV, 'Cultures', considers players and player communities, themselves material (as Warren makes clear in Chapter 4). Tanya Pobuda's important work draws attention to the pleasures and dangers of embodied play in gaming spaces through a careful analysis of data that makes clear the barriers surrounding gaming spaces for players who are not white or men. Esther MacCallum-Stewart's chapter in this part, '"Hands, Face, Space" – The Material Turn in Board Gaming during Covid-19', considers the impact of mass lockdowns during the coronavirus pandemic on the ways in which we play, exploring the ways in which the play of board and role-playing games was rapidly reconfigured through a pivot to online gaming technologies, exploring, as Paul Booth does in Chapter 11, what we might call the 'fetishization' of physical artefacts in gaming, and the link between this and the digital platforms that both promote and make possible such materiality.

Part V, 'Hybridity', responds directly to Aaron Trammell's suggestion that the analogue and the digital enjoy a mutually constitutive relationship. Paul Booth's chapter considers the tensions and possibilities that emerge in the use of digital platforms in the promotion and sale of analogue games. Building on Stefan Werning's work on Kickstarter (2017) with rich ethnographic data gathered from a survey of over 900 board gamers, Booth explores the impact of the crowdfunding platform on the material reality – what he calls the 'ludo-textuality' (Booth 2021) – of board games. Arguing that games are a ludo-textual combination of material physicality and immaterial play experience, Booth's analysis of what he describes as the digital infrastructure of analogue games indicates the complex motivations traded on and instigated by a distribution model that emphasizes the production of material elements and tangible, game-related goods. This volume concludes with Nathan Altice's 'The Logic of Analogue Adaptation', which reverses the expected trajectory (analogue to digital) through an account of the remediation of games from the digital to the analogue. His analysis of various adaptations in this direction offers insight into the affordances of both the digital and the analogue, suggesting an entangling inherent in the infrastructure described by Trammell.

Closing remarks: Future directions for material game studies

These chapters represent the opening moves of material game studies, and we hope that the provocations, concerns and methods developed in these chapters prompt scholars to take up the challenge to further develop the material turn, which remains, we suggest, nascent in the study of both digital and analogue games. The chapters herein offer examples of the kind of work that developing a robust material turn might require, but they are not proscriptive. There is a multiplicity of ways in which scholars might continue to investigate the material entanglements that are games and, conversely, to think about how games and play reveal the material entanglements that are the world. It is this multidirectional interrelation that concerns *Material Game Studies* and which suggests the study of games and play as a site for ontological and ethical thinking and speculation with implications that reach beyond only thinking about game technologies, gaming culture, or game design. With such broader concerns in mind, scholars might follow *Material Game Studies* and take up a material ecocritical approach to games of all kinds, considering the ways in which the material production of games is imbricated with the climate and ecological crises, as well as further developing the eco-ethical framework we advocate in this volume. We also consider the urgent need to grapple with the ways in which theorizing the material might contribute to a decolonizing of the discipline of game studies. Not only are the material conditions of gaming and play often exclusionary, as work in this volume suggests, but the discipline as a whole tends to uncritically perpetuate the philosophical and scholarly paradigms of the Global North, particularly those rooted in Cartesian and Idealist modes of thought. As eco-material philosophers point out, such paradigms are responsible for the social and ecological crises now engulfing the globe. Thus, *Material Game Studies* asks scholars to think critically about the modes of thought which undergird approaches to games and play, to cultivate methodologies and theories that push beyond humanist approaches and to consider the political ramifications of their work.

References

Aarseth, E. (2001), 'Computer Game Studies, Year One', *Game Studies*, 1 (1). Available online: http://gamestudies.org/0101/editorial.html (accessed 29 October 2021).

Alaimo, S. (2010), *Bodily Natures: Science, Environment, and the Material Self*, Bloomington, IN: Indiana University Press.

Altice, N. (2014), 'The Playing Card Platform', *Analog Game Studies*, 1 (4). Available online: http://analoggamestudies.org/2014/11/the-playing-card-platform/ (accessed 4 November 2021).

Apperley, T. H. and D. Jayemanne (2012), 'Game Studies' Material Turn', *Westminster Papers in Communication and Culture*, 9 (1): 5–25. Available online: https://doi.org /10.16997/wpcc.145 (accessed 2 November 2011).

Baldwin, C. Y. and C. J. Woodard (2008), 'The Architecture of Platforms: A Unified View', Harvard Business School Finance Working Paper No. 09-034. Available online: http://dx.doi.org/10.2139/ssrn.1265155 (accessed 24 October 2021).

Barad, K. (2003), 'Posthumanist Performativity: Toward an Understanding of How Matter Comes to Matter', *Signs*, 28 (3): 801–31.

Barad, K. (2007), *Meeting the Universe Halfway: Quantum Physics and the Entanglement of Matter and Meaning*, Durham, NC: Duke University Press.

Barad, K. (2010), 'Quantum Entanglements and Hauntological Relations of Inheritance: Dis/continuities, SpaceTime Enfoldings, and Justice-to-Come', *Derrida Today*, 3 (2): 240–68.

Bellomy, I. (2017), 'What Counts: Configuring the Human in Platform Studies', *Analog Game Studies*, 4 (2). Available online: https://analoggamestudies.org/2017/03/what -counts/ (accessed 4 November 2021).

Bennett, J. (2010), *Vibrant Matter: A Political Ecology of Things*, Durham, NC, and London: Duke University Press.

Bienia, R. (2016), *Role Playing Materials*, Berlin: Zauberfeder Verlag.

Booth, P. (2021), *Board Games as Media*, London: Bloomsbury.

Bohunicky, K. M. (2014), 'Ecocomposition: Writing Ecologies in Digital Games', *Green Letters*, 18 (3): 221–35.

Brown, D. and E. MacCallum-Stewart, eds (2020), *Rerolling Boardgames: Essays on Themes, Systems, Experiences and Ideologies*, Jefferson, NC: McFarland & Company Inc.

Caillois, R. (2001), *Man, Play and Games*, trans. M. Barash, Urbana and Chicago, IL: University of Illinois Press.

Chang, A. Y. (2019), *Playing Nature: Ecology in Video Games*, Minneapolis, MN: University of Minnesota Press.

Coole, D. H. and S. Frost (2010), *New Materialisms: Ontology, Agency, and Politics*, Durham, NC: Duke University Press.

Copier, M. (2005), 'Connecting Worlds. Fantasy Role-Playing Games, Ritual Acts and the Magic Circle', in *Proceedings of DiGRA 2005 Changing Views: Worlds in Play*. Available online: http://www.digra.org/dl/db/06278.50594.pdf (accessed 2 November 2021).

Germaine Buckley, C. (2020), 'Encountering Weird Objects: Lovecraft, LARP, and Speculative Philosophy', in M. Rosen (ed.), *Diseases of the Head: Essays on the Horrors of Speculative Philosophy*, 361–94, Santa Barbara, CA: Punctum Books.

Guerra, D. (2018), *Slantwise Moves. Games, Literature, and Social Invention in Nineteenth-Century America*, Philadelphia, PA: University of Pennsylvania Press.

Haraway, D. (2016), *Staying with the Trouble: Making Kin in the Chthulhucene*, Durham, NC: Duke University Press.

Hubble, M. (2021), 'Wooden Flows and Cardboard Algorithms: Abstracting the Human in *Pax Transhumanity*', *Analog Game Studies*, 8 (1). Available online: https://analoggamestudies.org/2021/03/wooden-flows-and-cardboard-algorithms -abstracting-the-human-in-pax-transhumanity/ (accessed 2 November 2011).

Huizinga, J. ([1955] 2016), *Homo Ludens: A Study of the Play-Element of Culture*, Kettering, OH: Angelico Press.

Iovino, S. and S. Opperman (2014), *Material Ecocriticism*, Bloomington, IN: Indiana University Press.

Juul, J. (2008), 'The Magic Circle and the Puzzle Piece', in S. Günzel, M. Liebe, and D. Mersch (eds), *Conference Proceedings of the Philosophy of Computer Games 2008*, 56–67, Potsdam: University Press, 2008.

Keogh, B. (2018), *A Play of Bodies: How We Perceive Videogames*, Cambridge, MA: MIT Press.

LaRell Anderson, S. (2017), 'Watching People Is Not a Game: Interactive Online Corporeality, Twitch.tv and Videogame Streams', *Game Studies*, 17 (1). Available online: http://gamestudies.org/1701/articles/anderson (accessed 2 November 2011).

Latour, B. (2018), *Down to Earth: Politics in the New Climatic Regime*, trans. C. Porter, Cambridge: Polity Press.

McKeown, C. (2018), 'Playing with Materiality: An Agential-Realist Approach to Videogame Code-Injections', *Information Communication and Society*, 21 (9): 1234–45.

Montfort, N. and I. Bogost (2009), *Racing the Beam: The Atari Video Computer System*, Cambridge, MA: MIT Press.

Rogerson, M. J., M. Gibbs and W. Smith (2016), "'I Love All the Bits": The Materiality of Boardgames', *CHI '16: Proceedings of the 2016 CHI Conference on Human Factors in Computing Systems*, May, 3956–69. Available online: https://doi.org/10.1145 /2858036.2858433 (accessed 29 October 2021).

Salen, K. and E. Zimmerman (2004), *Rules of Play: Game Design Fundamentals*, Cambridge, MA: MIT Press.

Sax, D. (2016), *The Revenge of Analog: Real Things and Why They Matter*, New York: PublicAffairs.

Sicart, M. (2021), 'Playthings', *Games and Culture*, May. Available online: https://doi.org /10.1177/15554120211020380 (accessed 2 November 2021).

Stenros, J. (2014), 'In Defence of a Magic Circle: The Social, Mental and Cultural Boundaries of Play', *Transactions of the Digital Games Research Association*, 1 (1). Available online: https://doi.org/10.26503/todigra.v1i2.10 (accessed 29 October 2021).

Švelch, J. (2016), 'Platform Studies, Computational Essentialism, and Magic: The Gathering', *Analog Game Studies*, 3 (4). Available online: https://analoggamestudies .org/2016/07/platform-studies-computational-essentialism-and-magic-the -gathering/ (accessed 4 November 2021).

Wake, P. (2019), 'Token Gestures: Towards a Theory of Immersion in Analog Games', *Analog Game Studies*, 6 (3). Available online: https://analoggamestudies.org/2019 /09/token-gestures-towards-a-theory-of-immersion-in-analog-games/ (accessed 1 October 2021).

Werning, S. (2017), 'Conceptualizing Game Distribution, *Kickstarter* and the Board Game "Renaissance"', *La Valle Dell'Eden. Semestrale Di Cinema e Audiovisivi*, 31: 65–82.

Woods, S. (2012), *Eurogames: The Design, Culture and Play of Modern European Board Games*, Jefferson, NC: McFarland & Co.

Zimmerman, E. (2012), 'Jerked around by the Magic Circle – Clearing the Air Ten Years Later', *Gamasutra*, 7 February. Available online: http://www.gamasutra.com/view/ feature/6696/jerked_around_by_the_magic_circle_.php (accessed 21 Oct 2021).

I

Provocations

1

Thinking the things we play with

Miguel Sicart

The Strong National Museum of Play, United States, is responsible for the 'National Toy Hall of Fame', an initiative that highlights, documents and preserves what the museum curators consider to be the most important toys. The list of inductees is extensive, and it includes dolls like Barbie, board games like *Candy Land* (Abbott 1948) and even the venerable Atari 2600. It is a surprising collection that combines the analogue and the digital, games and toys, and commercial items with more surprising selections. For example, among the inductees we have the ball, the cardboard box and the stick. Intuitively, these decisions make sense. A cardboard box is an excellent toy, a vessel for the imagination that, as the text on the Hall of Fame's website states, transports players 'to a world of his or her own, one where anything is possible' (The Strong 2005: n.p.). The cardboard box is also an excellent example of a cross-species toy, as anybody with a cat knows. The ball is another excellent example of a toy we can all agree upon and another case of a phenomenal plaything for interspecies play. But the National Toy Hall of Fame inductee that fascinates me the most is the stick. First inducted in 2008, the stick is acknowledged on the website as perhaps being 'the world's oldest toy' (The Strong 2008: n.p.), capable of mediating pretend play, exploration play, free play, interspecies and animal play and even artistic expressions. The stick is also an excellent object to think the things we play with.

In this chapter I will use the stick as a starting point to inquire into the relation between materiality and play. More specifically, I want to reflect on the processes that take place when a stick becomes a toy, and what these processes tell us about the activity of play. The study of toys and their position in culture and society is an old topic of play and game studies (Giddings 2016; Heljakka 2016; Sutton-Smith 1986). In this chapter I want to ride the wave of materialist game studies (Apperley and Jayemanne 2012) to provide a new materialist reading of the activity of play. This reading wants to draw game studies closer to the tradition of materialist media theory (Coole and Frost 2010; Parikka 2012).

Drawing on Karen Barad's philosophy (Barad 2003, 2007) and following its applications in game studies (Fizek 2018; McKeown 2018), this chapter will sketch an understanding of material play as a relational engagement with objects and things (Ingold 2012), an entanglement of agencies and materialities that leads to the reconfiguration of the nature of objects and the world. Ingold's distinction between objects, which are 'completed forms that stand over and against the perceiver and block further movement' (Ingold 2012: 439); and 'things', which are 'gatherings of materials in movement' (Ingold 2012: 439), allows addressing materiality as a dynamic process that is the result of an engagement with *things*. To understand the ontology of that engagement, Barad's ontoepistemology is an essential perspective. In Barad's work, things come into being; things begin mattering when agential cuts stabilize 'phenomena into doings' (Barad 2007: 139–42). In other words, the ontology of things, in Ingold's sense, comes to being when there is an agential engagement with them, when things start *mattering*.

Relationality is one of the key concepts in a general epistemological trend that continues the displacement of anthropocentric thinking. Relational thinking situates ontology not on things or in the human but in the relations between agents and the material world. This is an essential displacement of anthropological thinking because it de-centres the way knowledge is constructed. From ethics (Coeckelbergh 2021; Lee 2004) to aesthetics (Bishop 2004), relationality implies inquiring not on what things are but on what relations they establish, and the nature of these relations are openings towards inclusive, ecocritical thinking. By de-centring ontology and situating humans as part of a network of relations that are not always anthropocentric, or in which humans do not always have a central hierarchical position, ecocritical thinkers are formulating novel ways of engaging with the problems of the Anthropocene, as they come up too with new potential ways of addressing these problems that do not take exclusively (Western, male) human beings for granted (Bennett 2010; Tsing 2015). The material turn in game studies should also be interpreted as a relational turn. Rather than focusing on the nature or content of games, materialist game studies situates play in the relation between agents who play, human and nonhuman, and the things and objects around them.

With this chapter I want to first highlight how this relational understanding of play is part of the history of play, as seen through the objects we play with. And second, I want to sketch the possible avenues of research that relational material game studies can conduct, with a focus on the ethics and politics of play, more specifically as they relate to current ecocritical thinking around games (Backe 2017; Chang 2019).

When a stick becomes a toy

When I think about playing with a stick, my immediate response is embodied. My hands feel the weight of the stick, its length, whether it is coarse with bark or smooth after having been washed ashore. There are good sticks for playing and bad sticks for playing. If I want to use it to hit things, the stick needs to provide a certain resistance, or it has to be rotten enough that it will surrender to my will for chaos and shatter into thousands of pieces. If I want to use it to build something, it has to be sturdy for support or flexible for bending at the right places. A stick can keep others away, but it can also pull us together. All of these material characteristics of the stick are present in the object, whether that which we find in the floor of the woods or the one we rescue from the ocean or river waters. But the stick is not a toy until we play with it. Before that, it is something in the world, an object towards which we do not relate. Sticks become toys when we engage with them and when we relate to them.

My embodied response to the stick as a toy is part of the activity of play. As phenomenologists of games have already identified (Keogh 2018; Sudnow 1983), our relation with games and other play technologies starts with the body. The research on game feel (Pichlmair and Johansen 2021) is a design-driven inquiry on how to make things *feel*, that is, be experienced as, games or other forms of playable media. Feel is a point of entry to understand relational play and materiality. Philosophers of materiality and experience have inquired about the role of the material things that mediate our experience of the world (Heidegger 1971; Ihde 1990; Verbeek 2006). Within this tradition, play could be understood as a relational strategy (Rosenberger 2014) that stabilizes the mediation of things and what effects it has in the world-as-experienced. That is, phenomenology would look at the stick-as-toy as part of the extended experiential gestalt. When playing, the stick would become a toy so that it can extend our capacity to play in specific ways.

However, classic phenomenology as well as post-phenomenology can be said to continue an anthropocentric tradition in Western thinking. The things that mediate the experience of the world are perceived as tools, instruments or extensions of human agency but not necessarily as agents themselves. The world can be understood to be inert unless humans, and more specifically men, engage with it. But sometimes it is things that want to play, that display agency and that force us, humans, to renegotiate what we can and cannot do. Being in the world is not imposing human agency to things but negotiating – relating human agency to the world.

We need, then, a different approach to understand what happens when a stick becomes a toy. The argument that objects have agency is not new (Harman 2018; Latour 1992, 2008; Winner 1986), and in fact it is shaping not only humanistic theory but also the fields of design and human–computer interaction (Frauenberger 2019). New materialism allows for observing the processes of entanglement between agencies while taking into consideration their materiality. The new materialist argument I propose is simple: a stick is an object that becomes a toy when it entangles with agency that comes into being by playing.

The concept of entanglement has been used in game studies to address the complexities of making sense of the interfaces, agencies and communities that constitute video game play (Taylor 2009). This understanding of entanglement has drawn from science and technology studies (Latour 2008), as well as from the intersection between that field and philosophy (DeLanda 2019). However, my understanding of entanglement draws closer to Barad's new materialism: it is only in an entanglement of agencies and matter that we can talk about ontology (the nature of *things*) and epistemology (how can we construct knowledge about those things). In other words, what we study when we study the materials of play is the ontology of an entanglement of materiality and agency.

There is nothing immanent in the ontological category of 'toy'. The nature of the things we play with is a consequence of a materially based entanglement between the agency of the thing and the activity of play, which itself creates forms of agency. I started this section by thinking about the embodied experience of the stick and how the way it felt was important to reflect on what makes a piece of wood a toy. The stick becomes a toy when I become a player, when my agency comes into being in the form of a player. When I act as a player, I look for ways of engaging with the world that are appropriative, expressive and pleasurable in and of themselves (Sicart 2014). When playing, the materiality of the stick becomes significant for my agency as player: the weight of the wood, its texture, its strength. The materiality of the stick is part of what facilitates my entanglement with it. And when I become entangled with the stick by playing, its agency is part of what I become related with: what it allows me to do, how it lets itself be appropriated and how it appropriates me. What I can do with a stick while playing is partially a result of the agency of the stick.

What happens to wood when it becomes a stick is part of a relational process that involves agency, material properties and cultural settings. Being a toy is not as simple as it sounds; it is the result of a process of entanglement between the material and the biological, in a cultural and historical context. From a piece of wood, a new world comes into being.

Wood is a stick is a toy

Playing is creating new subjectivities, a new 'self' that becomes an agent in a ludic activity. Goffmanian understandings of play (Deterding 2009; Goffman 1961; Stenros 2015) understand this approach and provide a solid, empirical foundation of this phenomenon. Goffman describes the self as a construction that takes place in social contexts. In the case of games, for example, the rules and the materials of the game help create the individual and collective selves of the players. When we play, we construct a particular self and perform that particular self too, because play is performance. However, understanding what happens to wood when it becomes a stick when it becomes a toy goes beyond understanding playing as a human activity. Humans play, as do animals. But things play too: video games are forms of software agency that are created to play (Boluk and Lemieux 2017; Kunzelman 2014). To understand material play we need to understand how things play. This leads inevitably to the question of agency.

In contemporary social sciences and humanities, it is commonplace to think that nonhuman objects have agency. What interests me is to specify that assumption: what happens to objects when we play with them? Material play is not just the activity of engaging with objects, it is a more complex process of negotiation of agencies and acknowledgement of materialities. The focus on materiality reveals the importance of play as a form of relating to objects, others and the world. To understand what it means to take a relational approach, we need to start by playing. And I will do so by embracing Maria Lugones's philosophy of playfulness. For Lugones, playing is a form of world travelling that allows us to meet others, to identify 'with them [. . .] because by travelling to their "world" we can understand what it is to be them and what it is to be ourselves in their eyes' (1987: 17). Playing as world travelling is establishing a relation to others, in which we also understand and construct ourselves.

What makes playing a unique mode of relating to others is 'openness to surprise, [. . .] to being a fool, [. . .] to self-construction or reconstruction and to constriction or reconstruction of the 'worlds' we inhabit playfully' (Lugones 1987: 17). Playing is also characterized by 'uncertainty, lack of self-importance, absence of rules or as not taking rules as sacred, a not worrying about competence and a lack of abandonment to a particular construction of oneself, others and one's relation to them' (Lugones 1987: 17). While Lugones's theory is broader than a focus on materiality, it provides a good starting point to understand what happens to things when we play with them.

A piece of wood becomes something else when we approach it with the intention of playing, of having fun, of wanting to use it for something that is silly, not self-important, with rules that are created for the particular material characteristics of that piece of wood. When picking up wood to play with it, we acknowledge in its material properties a particular world and a particular agency – what I described as my physical experience of it. When the piece of wood is picked up and it becomes a stick, we engage in a relational process that is, following Barad's new materialist theory, a 'specific worldly configuration [. . .] in the sense of materially engaging as part of the world in giving it specific material form' (2007: 91). When a piece of wood becomes a stick, it is being 'mattered' (Barad 2007: 148), that is, it becomes a particular reconfiguration of its materiality in relation to my agency. But also, my own agency as player, both materially and experientially, is mattered by the stick – what it allows me to do, what it forbids me from doing. In that double process of mattering, a relation between two agencies comes to being, and a toy emerges.

This is pretty abstract philosophy, so let me try to explain the implications of it through the stick and a game. Playing is a way of acting in the world, a particular form of agency. Sometimes that agency takes place together with a material element, like a piece of wood. The piece of wood has a series of material properties that allows it to do certain things. That is a form of agency. Playing with a piece of wood is relating to its agency, figuring out what we can do with it and becoming related to it.

In *Metagaming* (2017), Stephanie Boluk and Patrick LeMieux write about speed running as a form of metagaming, a way of playing with the type of software called 'video game'. Speed running is also a good example of relational play as a way of creating an entanglement between human and nonhuman agencies by playing. The software called 'video game' is designed to act in particular ways, sometimes on its own, sometimes as a response to players' actions. A speed runner is a player who has a playful relation to the rules of the original game. The purpose is to beat the game as fast as possible, sometimes with little respect for the way the game wants to be played. Great speed runners change the way they play, their agency, to match as perfectly as possible the requirements that the software agency has to receive input. Sometimes, speed runners glitch or break parts of the software's agency to achieve even better times, often by engaging with a material understanding of how, for example, the physical memory of a computer works and how it allocates resources in it. Speed running is playing as world travelling: adjusting who we are as players to who the software as agent is in order to playfully explore boundaries.

Understanding play in the context of the human and the nonhuman requires a new materialist approach: a perspective that does not subordinate the material to the will of man, but that sees playing as a way of engaging and establishing relations with the things and the world around us, and letting those things and that world shape who we want to be. When wood becomes a stick and a stick becomes a toy, it is not just the material that becomes something else: we also change, our agency and our bodies transformed by the things we play with, in a mutual process of understanding and becoming.

The worlds of play

In *Vibrant Matter* (2010), Jane Bennett explores the political and ethical implications of new materialist theory. She defines her understanding of new materialism as 'vital materialism', as her interests are centred on the politics of mattering. If we are to consider that every *thing* is an agent, how should we treat them? What are the politics of a world that needs to acknowledge the power of the things in it? While this form of new materialist thinking is powerful and evocative, it sometimes requires to be specified, to describe in particular how a politics or an ethics of a world of *things* can take place.

Play can be accused of being similarly vague. In the Western world, the tradition of thinking about play that Schiller started and Huizinga continued sometimes sees the ludic activity as something mostly positive, that will make people free, that will allow for pleasure and the addressing of conflicts in orderly ways, in simplified manner. Play is supposed to help us learn, become better people and entertain us. These possibilities are often realized through forms of learning that take the structure of games to reward certain behaviours or to communicate certain ideas. This idea of play as an instrument for change, while useful, might also be unambitious.

Thinking about the things we play with, thinking about the materiality of play, opens up the possibility of novel forms of the politics and ethics of play. Lugones observes how 'the agonistic attitude' of Huizinga and Gadamer's theories of play is 'inimical to travelling across "worlds". The agonistic traveller is a conqueror, an imperialist' (1987: 15). Her idea of play as world travelling is an idea of moving towards others, understanding them while we also understand ourselves. A new materialist understanding of world travelling implies that others can be nonhuman: they can be wood, electrons, plastic, cardboard and complex forms of agency embodied in different material possibilities.

From this perspective, our relation to the materials of the world through play is based on world travelling. We relate to the materials of the world as if they were agents in our play, inquiring what they can do, adapting to the way they let us act while we also change them so they can be better at playing with us. When the stick becomes a toy, we travel to its world, we relate to the potential it has to play together with us. It is a form of material acknowledgement, an understanding of the thing power it has and how we should relate to it. And that 'how' is by playing, but trying to understand it, by becoming entangled with it in the practice of the silly, fun, pleasurable experience of play.

Playing is a meeting of agencies that is rooted in materiality. Playing is related to the things in the world, how they can act, how they are constituted as agents. Focusing on material play grounds the possibilities that emerge in the activity of play – the worlds that are created, the experiences that take place. Playing is an acknowledgement of materiality, an entanglement with it and a practice of relating to other agencies. In *Play Anything* (2016), Ian Bogost proposes a materialist theory of play, drawing on object-oriented ontology (OOO) (Harman 2018) to explain that playing is a way of approaching the things around us. Bogost's ideas are close to the ones I sketch in this chapter. However, a main point of divergence is that it is unclear whether Bogost's position of object-oriented ontology implies a separation between things and humans, a critique sometimes levied against OOO (Frauenberger 2019). Adopting Barad's new materialist perspective avoids this issue, since she explicitly claims that ontology is relational. In other words: there is no human-stick but an agential combination of human and stick that comes to being when playing.

Why, then, is material play important? The nonhuman turn in social sciences and the humanities has revealed that a world full of things is also a world full of agents. This new ecology has de-centred the human, complicated the idea of 'man' (*sic*) as the centre of 'creation' or 'knowledge' and forced us to understand that the current climate crisis and the arrogance of the biased technologies we have developed are in part a consequence of our incapacity as humans to meet and entangle with the material world in other terms than our imperialist, colonialist and extractive ways.

Precisely here is where material play brings new possibilities to the table, especially if we embrace Lugones's ethos of loving world travelling as a form of play. Playing is becoming entangled with other material agents. Not make them instruments but playmates, allowing them to change our agency so we can have fun together. The stick lets us play with it, and it changes how we play. We also select the right sticks to play. In that process of mutual acknowledgement, material play creates new worlds, new possibilities and new hybrid agencies.

Material play is, then, a way of letting us think about how we can better relate to the world around us and how we can better respect, enjoy and inhabit its multiplicity while we also have fun doing it. Material play is then by definition ecocritical: an understanding that the things in the world are not there to serve us but are there with us so we can together coexist, or play. In his essay 'What Is the Point If We Can't Have Fun?' David Graeber writes: 'The play principle can help explain why sex is fun, but it can also explain why cruelty is fun [. . .] but it gives us ground to unthink the world around us' (2014: n.p.). Material play is a way of unthinking the world as a place serving human will. Material play is a way of understanding how wood can become a stick and can become a toy, and in doing so it changes from what is to what it could be. My understanding of material play is about those possibilities, about being reduced not to thinking that things are instruments for action or extraction but to see the world as a place full of agents, all ready to play with us.

References

Apperley, T. and D. Jayemanne (2012), 'Game Studies' Material Turn', *Westminster Papers in Communication and Culture*, 9 (1): 5–25.

Backe, H. J. (2017), 'Within the Mainstream: An Ecocritical Framework for Digital Game History', *Ecozon@: European Journal of Literature, Culture and Environment*, 8 (2): 39–55.

Barad, K. (2003), 'Posthumanist Performativity: Toward an Understanding of How Matter Comes to Matter', *Signs: Journal of Women in Culture and Society*, 28 (3): 801–31.

Barad, K. (2007), *Meeting the Universe Halfway: Quantum Physics and the Entanglement of Matter and Meaning*, Durham, NC: Duke University Press.

Bennett, J. (2010), *Vibrant Matter*, Durham, NC: Duke University Press.

Bishop, C. (2004), 'Antagonism and Relational Aesthetics', *October*, 110: 51–79.

Bogost, I. (2016), *Play Anything: The Pleasure of Limits, the Uses of Boredom, and the Secret of Games*, New York: Basic Books.

Boluk, S. and P. LeMieux (2017), *Metagaming: Playing, Competing, Spectating, Cheating, Trading, Making, and Breaking Videogames*, Minneapolis, MN: University of Minnesota Press.

Candy Land (1948), [board game], Designer: E. Abbott, USA: Hasbro.

Chang, A. Y. (2019), *Playing Nature*, Minneapolis, MN: University of Minnesota Press.

Coeckelbergh, M. (2021), 'How to Use Virtue Ethics for Thinking About the Moral Standing of Social Robots: A Relational Interpretation in Terms of Practices, Habits, and Performance', *International Journal of Social Robotics*, 13 (1): 31–40.

Coole, D. H. and S. Frost (2010), *New Materialisms: Ontology, Agency, and Politics*, Durham, NC: Duke University Press.

DeLanda, M. (2019), *A New Philosophy of Society: Assemblage Theory and Social Complexity*, London: Bloomsbury Publishing.

Deterding, S. (2009), 'The Game Frame: Systemizing a Goffmanian Approach to Video Game Theory', *Breaking New Ground: Innovation in Games, Play, Practice and Theory. Proceedings of DiGRA 2009*. Available online: http://www.digra.org/wp-content/uploads/digital-library/09287.43112.pdf (accessed 4 October 2021).

Fizek, S. (2018), 'Automated State of Play: Rethinking Anthropocentric Rules of the Game', *Digital Culture & Society*, 4 (1): 201–14.

Frauenberger, C. (2019), 'Entanglement HCI The Next Wave?', *ACM Transactions on Computer-Human Interaction*, 27 (1): 1–27.

Giddings, S. (2016), *Gameworlds: Virtual Media and Children's Everyday Play*, London: Bloomsbury.

Goffman, E. (1961), *Encounters. Two Studies in the Sociology of Interaction*, Indianapolis, IN: Bobbs-Merrill.

Graeber, D. (2014), 'What's the Point If We Can't Have Fun?', *The Baffler*. Available online: https://thebaffler.com/salvos/whats-the-point-if-we-cant-have-fun (accessed 31 May 2021).

Harman, G. (2018), *Object-Oriented Ontology: A New Theory of Everything*, London: Pelican Books.

Heidegger, M. (1971), *Poetry, Language, Thought*, New York: Harper & Row.

Heljakka, K. (2016), 'Contemporary Toys, Adults and Creative Material Culture: From Wow to Flow to Glow', in A. Malinowska, K. Lebek (eds), *Materiality and Popular Culture: The Popular Life of Things*, 237–49, London: Routledge.

Ihde, D. (1990), *Technology and the Lifeworld: From Garden to Earth*, Bloomington and Indianapolis, IN: Indiana University Press.

Ingold, T. (2012), 'Toward an Ecology of Materials', *Annual Review of Anthropology*, 41 (1): 427–42.

Keogh, B. (2018), *A Play of Bodies*, Cambridge, MA: The MIT Press.

Kunzelman, C. (2014), 'The Nonhuman Lives of Videogames', MA diss., Georgia State University, Atlanta. Available online: https://scholarworks.gsu.edu/communication_theses/110 (accessed 4 October 2021).

Latour, B. (1992), 'Where Are the Missing Masses? The Sociology of a Few Mundane Artifacts', in W. E. Bijker and J. Law (eds), *Shaping Technology/Building Society: Studies in Sociotechnical Change*, 225–58, Cambridge, MA: The MIT Press.

Latour, B. (2008), *Reassembling the Social: An Introduction to Actor-Network-Theory*, Oxford: Oxford University Press.

Lee, R. G. (2004), *The Values of Connection: A Relational Approach to Ethics*, Christchurch: Gestalt Press.

Lugones, M. (1987), 'Playfulness, "World"-Travelling, and Loving Perception', *Hypatia*, 2 (2): 3–19.

McKeown, C. (2018). 'Playing with Materiality: An Agential-Realist Reading of SethBling's Super Mario World Code-Injection', *Information, Communication & Society*, 21 (9): 1234–45.

Parikka, J. (2012). 'New Materialism as Media Theory: Medianatures and Dirty Matter', *Communication and Critical/Cultural Studies*, 9 (1): 95–100.

Pichlmair, M. and M. Johansen (2021), 'Designing Game Feel. A Survey', *IEEE Transactions on Games*. Available online: https://doi.org/10.1109/TG.2021.3072241 (accessed 4 October 2021).

Rosenberger, R. (2014), 'Multistability and the Agency of Mundane Artifacts: From Speed Bumps to Subway Benches', *Human Studies*, 37 (3): 369–92.

Sicart, M. (2014), *Play Matters*, Cambridge, MA: The MIT Press.

Stenros, J. (2015), 'Playfulness, Play, and Games: A Constructionist Ludology Approach', PhD thesis, University of Tampere, Tampere. Available online: https://researchportal.tuni.fi/en/publications/playfulness-play-and-games-a-constructionist-ludology-approach (accessed 4 October 2021).

Sudnow, D. (1983), *Pilgrim in the Microworld*, New York: Warner Books.

Sutton-Smith, B. (1986), *Toys as Culture*, New York: Gardner Press.

Taylor, T. L. (2009), 'The Assemblage of Play', *Games and Culture*, 4 (4): 331–9.

The Strong (2005), *Cardboard Box*, National Toy Hall of Fame. Available online: https://www.toyhalloffame.org/toys/cardboard-box (accessed 31 May 2021).

The Strong (2008), *The Stick*, National Toy Hall of Fame. Available online: https://www.toyhalloffame.org/toys/stick (accessed 31 May 2021).

Tsing, A. L. (2015), *The Mushroom at the End of the World*, Princeton, NJ: Princeton University Press.

Verbeek, P. P. (2006), *What Things Do*, Pennsylvania, PA: Pennsylvania State University Press.

Winner, L. (1986), *The Whale and the Reactor: A Search for Limits in an Age of High Technology*, Chicago, IL: University of Chicago Press.

2

Analogue games as infrastructure

Aaron Trammell

'You want to play a board game? Like *Monopoly*?' We've all heard some variation of this phrase when attempting to introduce the latest greatest board game to a group of uninitiated friends or family. The suggestion frames board games as nostalgic, antiquated and a quaint reminder of a time long since past, when games were played over the holidays on tables rather than daily on consoles. The tricky thing about understanding analogue games – modern board games, card games, role-playing games, escape rooms, LARPs and interactive theatre experiences – is to overcome this sepia-toned aura and thus recognize that analogue games are not the past: they are the future.

Since the development of the personal computer in the 1970s, the arc of progress has bent alongside developments in digital technology: smaller, cheaper, faster. These values have stoked the embers of a race in the tech industry for decades now. Each new generation of computer hardware is itself an improvement and iteration upon the last. But what is a screaming fast computer without a killer app? Digital games have long been the carrot at the end of the computational stick. Games are software that allow end users to grok the capabilities of their new PC. Thus, our discourse of futurity, with its peculiar focus on the development of new and more powerful digital technologies, has actually been understood and apprehended through the digital games that have in turn helped to sell computers. *Rogue* was packaged with UNIX when the operating system was originally distributed, IBM paid Sierra On-Line almost a million dollars to develop *King's Quest* so that the PCjr could use it as a tech demo in 1984, *Final Fantasy VII* popularized disc-based game consoles with its state-of-the-art video rendering, the rollout of a massive broadband infrastructure coincided with the development and sales of *World of Warcraft* the first massively popular MMORPG. The list goes on.

Set against the backdrop of these technological developments, it becomes clear how analogue games might seem like something of a throwback. They don't sell computers, after all. And they are mostly sold in hobby stores – present only in a specialized retail network assumed to cater to men with idiosyncratic tastes. Given the obvious importance of computing to everyday life today, as well as the massive popularity of the video games industry – which now pulls in more money on an annual basis than the film industry and music industries combined (Saltzman 2021) – one might wonder as to the significance of analogue games against this backdrop. What could their cultural significance be when so many other games are so much more popular?

For the purposes of this chapter, the answer is simple. I argue that there is a deep interrelatedness between analogue games and digital games and that one cannot be adequately understood without the other. Any theory of the digital that neglects the analogue is akin to a theory of light that neglects shadows, a theory of capital that ignores gifts or a theory of computing that disregards hardware. The analogue exists alongside the digital: it always has. And, what's more, understanding this interrelatedness is fundamental to theorizing games in the future as analogue games come into their own as an industry and begin to share the spotlight with digital games as popular modes of media in the twenty-first century.

Analogue and digital game studies

Analogue game studies as a discipline is predicated upon the notion that board games, role-playing games, performance art, card games, improvisational theatre and more help to inform the study of digital games, play and media more broadly. In our introduction to the inaugural issue of *Analog Game Studies*, co-editors Evan Torner, Emma Leigh Waldron and I summed up the importance of pivoting towards analogue games:

> Game studies can no longer afford to primarily focus on computer games in an era where the world has become so digitally mediated that the nomenclature ceases to carry the same weight that it once did. Furthermore, analog games are notably detached from many cultural attitudes prevalent in the computer game industry, and can offer an insight into the ways that games work to produce social change. They make clear the rulesets that govern behavior within games and, in doing so, reveal the biological and cultural rules which have forever governed our society. (2014: n.p.)

Perhaps we expressed a bit too much wide-eyed optimism about the importance of analogue games in a digitally mediated world, but we were writing in 2014 and conversations in digital game studies were beginning to get serious. We alluded to the cultural attitudes of the computer game industry because Gamergate (a group of misogynist Redditors who argued that game journalism was becoming less objective) saturated the moment's zeitgeist, and we wanted to address the elephant in the room – that the digital game industry was itself the by-product of toxic masculinity within the tech industry more broadly. In analogue games we saw the opportunity to resist the oppressive feedback loops of the digital. In the analogue game industry the barriers to participation were far lower – anyone could be a designer, regardless of technological proficiency, access to technology or access to the wealthy networks of investors that make silicone dreams come true.

Of course, the analogue game space was not without its own problems for both players and designers. As Tanya Pobuda points out in her ground-breaking essay on representation in modern board games (2018: n.p.) and her chapter in this volume, the hobby game industry overwhelmingly caters towards white male sensibilities in the design of their games. Not only are women and Black, Indigenous, and People of Colour (BIPOC) underrepresented on the boxes and artwork of board games, but this gap in representation is even more exacerbated among designers. Analogue games have historically been the province of suburban white men – but perhaps in spite of this, the fanbase of analogue games has managed to diversify. Today the work of a broad and intersectional coalition of activists has begun to push the needle. Perhaps reinforcing our original hypothesis that the lack of barriers to participation in the analogue game industry allows the scene to imagine itself as thriving and diverse, in a way that the digital game industry cannot. Specifically, I'm arguing here that, despite its recent growth, the analogue game industry remains small and agile compared to the digital game industry. Because of this difference in size, it is easier for key actors in the analogue game industry to reconfigure their practices in order to support the participation of a more diverse set of up-and-coming designers and reviewers. The digital game industry, in contrast, relies on hundreds of specialists to create AAA games, and thus progressive change is slower to come and more out of reach.

These limitations to the growth and utility of game studies are well known to many of the ludologists who established the field today. In a retrospective on the first twenty or so years of game studies, Espen Aarseth wrote an editorial for *Game Studies* entitled 'Just Games'. In this editorial, Aarseth tried to put some of the unsaid and informal gatekeeping practices within the field in the past. Key among these divisions was an assumed binary between digital and non-digital (or as I term them – analogue) games. 'To exclude the study of *D&D* (and war games, role-play, board games, mechanical arcade games, card, dice, and gambling games) from this journal (and the field) does not make good, academic sense' (2017: n.p.). Of course, the good academic sense to which Aarseth refers to in this context bespeaks the field's blind spots. How can a field grow if its every instinct is to dig deeper into defining its object of study? If we take Aarseth's lamentations seriously, do analogue games offer a way out of the bunker that game studies has holed itself into?

I think they do. In what remains of this short chapter, I will suggest ways we might go about bridging this gap. In game studies and information studies more broadly, there has been a somewhat coy disconnect between a recent ten-to-twenty-year fascination with the digital, as it inundates our scholarship and a simultaneous drive to avoid defining what the digital is due to a number of argumentative pitfalls. Lev Manovich, for instance, refers to it as a 'myth' in his book *The Language of New Media*. He argues that few qualities of digital technology are 'new'. And while that observation is certainly true, 'newness' is itself a spurious rationale for intellectual inquiry, and perhaps, more tellingly, is a tip of the hat towards a system of values focused on what is trending as opposed to the boring grey infrastructural make-up of our world.

In information studies, scholars such as Susan Leigh Star and Geof Bowker have shown how the dull invisible infrastructural make-up of the world can inform the lived politics of the everyday. They call for a sensitivity to the invisible power relations that infrastructure constitutes (2002: 151–2). To loop back to the 'digital', I argue that one of the reasons the term has been so vexing is that it is often used in a way that neglects its infrastructure. The early critique of 'screen essentialism', for example, spoke to how the complex mechanical and algorithmic infrastructures of digital technology was neglected by scholars who looked only at the representative characteristics of digital media. In this sense, in order to understand what digital does, we must also understand what analogue is. Analogue is not an opposition to the digital, it is, in fact, its infrastructure. This chapter traces the many valences of both the analogue and the digital in an effort to situate and explain that the interrelatedness of the two terms stems from the fact that analogue games are, in fact, the infrastructure upon which digital games are built.

Analogue

The future is analogue. In 1959, John W. Campbell, the editor of *Astounding Science-Fiction*, was at a crossroad. His once lauded science-fiction magazine had been acquired by Condé Nast following a series of price hikes by the prior publisher Street and Smith. Never fond of the sensational moniker, 'Astounding', Campbell renamed the magazine *Analog Science Fact and Fiction* in a series of changes that were rolled out over the course of 1960. Campbell felt the new title would help to ground the publication in a less fictional space of scientific reasoning. As Trevor Quachri describes, '[Campbell] chose "Analog" in part because he thought of each story as an "analog simulation" of a possible future, and in part because of the close analogy he saw between the imagined science in the stories he was publishing, and the real science being done in laboratories around the world' (n.d.: n.p.). For Campbell, the analogue is juxtaposed against the computerized work of simulation that was being carried out in military and para-military think tanks like the RAND Corporation, MIT Center of International Politics and Hudson Institute. In this context the analogue sits alongside computer simulations as another technique for peering into the future, as opposed to retreating from it.

Analogue, like digital, is a historically situated term. And as such its meanings and connotations change over time. Similar to how the term 'digital' is often used but rarely defined, definitions of the analogue are also scarce. The term is most frequently addressed in scholarship as a counterpoint to discussions about the digital, or as a shorthand for things non-digital, but what happens when we take an approach that sees the analogue as infrastructure and foreground the invisible labour of maintaining the analogue?

As Campbell's use of the term shows, analogue was once seen as a term used to distinguish short stories from computer simulations. At this point in the late 1950s computers inhabited large rooms and were comprised of wires, tubes and other hallmarks of early electronics. The analogue work of computing in this valence speaks to the creative and design work that went into developing simulations as well as the invisible and often gendered work that went into maintaining this 1950s series of tubes.

The analogue is always already in dialogue with the ways digits are abstracted and understood – it is infrastructure. As the previous example shows, before coding or even soldering digital simulations, researchers often turn to analogue mock-ups first. This was the case in the scientific circles that Campbell hails in his writing, it is the case for musicians hacking out their songs on acoustic guitars and pianos early in the creative process, and it is the case for game designers today who work with paper prototypes before inscribing their work within machines with ones and zeroes.

Etymologically, 'analogue' (US spelling 'analog') is derived from the word 'analogous', meaning 'proportionate'. It holds a second and now prevalent connotation stemming from 1946 that intones a computational valence, 'in reference to operating with numbers represented by some measurable quantity (as a slide-rule does; opposed to *digital*)' (The Online Etymology Dictionary). These etymological distinctions help to make clear the term's relevance within technological discourse. To the extent that simulations are understood as computerized digital experiments, analogue simulations accomplish the same thing but without numbers.

There are also many technical connotations to the term 'analogue'. In his book *The New Analog*, Damon Krukowski offers some simple but intuitive definitions of the digital and the analogue. He explains that the digital is on and off, start and stop, while the analogue is a continuum and gradient, 'Here, analog refers to a continuous stream of information, whereas digital is discontinuous' (2017: 15). Krukowski, a public intellectual and drummer of the band Galaxy 500, speaks to the ways analogue technology is commonly disambiguated from digital technology in the music industry. As musical instruments and recording technology embraced new digital technologies as conduits for recording, performance and playback, some vintage 'analogue' gear presented a more accurate or authentic path for the emulation or recreation of popular tones. Thus, Krukowski's perspective is informed by the many recording consoles with mechanical, analogue, knobs and sliders that he watched the industry update to digital over the course of his career.

Where Campbell theorized the analogue to work alongside and supplement the limits of the digital, Krukowski is significantly more nostalgic. Krukowski connects the analogue to a conception of authenticity that he feels digital technologies are threatening. This definitional breach pulls into focus some of the stakes of this discussion, as it reveals how intricately connected are the different technological paradigms to professional craft and identity.

Krukowski links the digital and the analogue to cultural patterns of taste, and questions what has been lost in an era that has become reliant on digital technology (2017: 20). The discontinuity of the digital has specific implications for the trained ear. As Jonathan Sterne points out in *MP3*, digital audio technology – specifically sound compression algorithms, but to some extent digital audio samplers as well – work by breaking sound waves down into tens of thousands of discreet bits per second and then playing them back so quickly that one's brain fills in the perceptual gaps (2012: 1–2). At its root, analogue technology offers a distinctly different phenomenological experience than digital technology, yet for most, these differences mean very little.

In games the phenomenological differences between analogue and digital experience grow even more stark and obvious. The stakes of both conversations are clearly grounded in questions of embodiment. Compare Sterne's research on listening to the clear experiential difference between playing a digital game with a controller on a TV and console alone and playing a board game around a table with friends, or a live action role-play in a park. Not only are the industries that produce analogue and digital games dissimilar, but they produce fundamentally different instances of play, interaction and engagement as well.

Lived experience, however, never fails to complicate. And while Sterne describes how digital technologies exploit our perceptual gaps through the discontinuity of their technological structures, science and technology scholars Trevor Pinch and Frank Trocco reveal that musicians often regard the digital as too perfect. They relate interviews with Jon Weiss and Brian Eno, who describe a longing for the 'personality' and messiness of analogue synthesis. Particularly telling is their quote from Jon Weiss, who worked with analogue synthesis pioneer Bob Moog:

> There were . . . certain inaccuracies in the equipment that resulted in wonderful and bizarre events . . . in that sense it was an instrument, it wasn't a machine. A machine would have created no inaccuracies and I think that's maybe why these computer digital generated sounds are not as interesting as the analog sounds. . . . Accuracy like that doesn't exist in our lives, nature is never accurate, there are always weird concussions of sound waves, and overlapping and so on. (Pinch and Trocco 2004: 318)

Weiss aligns the digital with crisp, machinic, perfection and the analogue with the messy, natural, perhaps even authentic realm of the human. These dichotomies are of course, and perhaps tellingly, classic ideological hallmarks of nineteenth-century philosophy, like that of the transcendentalists, which often contrasted machine with nature as it grappled with the implications of a rapid industrialization in Western society. Of course, like the provocations of Krukowski earlier, these are romantic and nostalgic notions of technology, which situate the analogue almost combatively against an almost colonial theorization of the digital.

There are a variety of ways that the analogue is defined, but chief among them is a persistent opposition to a concept of digital technology. I argue that this comparison, far from an opposition, bespeaks a far deeper infrastructural connection. If we look at the example of *Analog Science Fiction*, we can see a different theorization of the analogue that is less attached to a combative and nostalgic yearning for a time before the digital. Indeed, Campbell's work helps us to see how the analogue may have always been an infrastructural base of digital technology and vice versa. In analogue games we see again not only the potential for a wide and diverse participation in the industry but also the wild, exciting proliferation of ideas that would be too financially risky to commit to the development cycle of the digital game industry.

Digital

Let's return to game studies, as its star rose alongside the turn of the millennial investment in digital technology. In the mid-1990s, there was a tremendous enthusiasm in literature and the arts for approaches that better understood the structure and affordances of interactive media. It was within this churn of enthusiasm that game scholarship was able to make itself visible and distinct. This excitement was certainly due to the rapid mobilization of technological infrastructure outside of the academy. It was no coincidence that early game studies scholarship emerged during the dot com boom and early days of the consumer internet. Not only did writing and research about hypertext speak to the aesthetic potential of digital technology, it also spoke clearly to the forking everyday experiences of the millions who were dialling into internet portals globally.

The rapid transition to a web-based network society can be described as the digital turn. And although game studies was a manifestation of how that turn was articulated within literary studies, human–computer interaction, and the arts, scholars from a variety of disciplines were quickly becoming enamoured with the ways that digital technology was reconfiguring society. Accordingly, there are many different ways that the digital is known, configured and understood. The digital is the work of digits. It is, as Jack Bratich describes, both the algorithmic space of computerization and technology as well as the human, crafty space of hand-work, be it woven, stitched or typed (2010: 303). In our world today, this resonates well with its most common-sense definition, the ever-resonant moments where digit meets digit on keyboard and screen everywhere. The digital is the space where everyday life takes place. Even when it is not present as a phone in someone's hand, it is interpreting and interpolating one's lived reality. It is the silent capture of satellite surveillance or the invisible hand of Google guiding and sculpting traffic patterns. The digital is the culture that we live, breathe, take for granted and inhabit.

As I have noted earlier, definitions of the digital are scarce. The term is often taken for granted in academic and popular press writing. In other writing it is generally characterized in two main ways. These ways epitomize different discourses within scholarship broadly. The first discourse uses a definition that foregrounds the technological aspects of the digital. Succinctly, this approach argues that the digital is a set of qualities that an object possesses. Here, as popularized by Manovich (2002: 49–65), the digital is a formal and structural quality of technology that understands the digital as numerical, modular, automated, variable and for lack of a better term, interactive. The second discourse prioritizes the cultural impact of the digital and expresses the digital as a form of culture or subjectivity that is produced by the ubiquity of computers and computerization in our everyday life. As opposed to digital technology, which foregrounds digital objects, digital culture is a subjectivity – a way of understanding and approaching the world.

The digital is rarely defined when it is invoked as an object of study. It is either taken as common sense or sidestepped. In media studies, the binary construction that juxtaposes digital and analogue media was unfruitful. As an emerging field, the terminology of 'new media' became a prevalent shorthand for digital technologies and was popularized by scholars such as Manovich in *The Language of New Media* (2002) and Noah Wardrip-Fruin and Nick Montfort in their collection *The New Media Reader* (2003). It was an adaptive shorthand as it allowed the field to avoid critiques of 'screen-essentialism' that read the digital as an interactive space that took place predominantly on screens, thus allowing theorists the flexibility to investigate more than just the representational aspects of emerging media.

As I noted, Manovich refers to the digital as a myth. In *The Language of New Media*, new media is said to be numerical, modular, automated, variable and transcode-able. The digital, in contrast, is strictly defined by its technical characteristics. If, for instance, the digital is simply the rapid parsing of ones and zeroes, signal and noise, then Morse code is clearly a digital technology. Manovich sees little novelty in digital technology and thus chooses to emphasize the newness of media instead. Thus, he argues that the myth of the digital is the very idea that it is ground-breaking and new.

But why discount the mythic? When McKenzie Wark describes digital subjectivity, she suggests that *Katamari Damacy* (2004) – a game for the PS2 – be read as a myth. She explains that the game's protagonist, the Prince, is a hero for digital times, comparable to how Odysseus from Homer's *Odyssey* was a hero for the analogue days of yore. The plural, intuitive and messy interpretations of myth are part of Wark's take on digital subjectivity insofar as they epitomize what is lost in the shift towards digital culture. For Wark, the digital and the analogue always stood in relationship to one another, but it is only in the twenty-first century that the analogue has become truly subordinate to the digital. Make no mistake, she is cynical, 'Everything the military entertainment complex touches with its gold-plated output jacks turns to digits. Everything is digital and yet the digital is as nothing. No human can touch it, smell it, taste it. It just beeps and blinks and reports itself in glowing alphanumerics, spouting stock quotes on your cell phone' (Wark 2007: 6). For Wark, digital subjectivity means embracing the logic of binary metrics. Points, win/loss states, militaristic competition and ecology of objects that can be clustered and understood through their individual, quantifiable, attributes.

Katamari Damacy is the ur-myth of digital subjectivity because of how analogue control is subordinate to the game's digital logic. Players control the Prince with the Playstation's analogue sticks, which translate the analogue haptics of control into a digital logic of ones and zeroes that animate the Prince's body on the screen. The metaphor cuts even deeper. The Prince rolls a katamari – which is a sticky ball – on the screen. As it rolls over objects, it grows. This growth is tracked in real time, quantified and abstracted in a representation in the corner of the screen. Eventually, when this perfectly digital ball exceeds an exact numerical threshold in size, the player has won, and the katamari becomes a star in the new digital cosmos (Wark 2007: 63–4). The myth of the digital is that thresholds are truth, that they are not socially constructed, and that all continuums can be represented through binary logics.

I agree with much of Wark's empirical assessment yet I disagree with a good deal of her cynicism. Where Wark imposes a frame of dominance and subordinance upon technological paradigms, I argue that an infrastructural lens is more apt when approaching this phenomenon. By understanding the present relationship between analogue and digital technology as one of infrastructure and superstructure, we can better glimpse the implications of both terms. Additionally, this relationship provokes a conversation that is better attended to a set of materialist feminist concerns around lived experience as opposed to the situationist and spectacular critiques to which Wark alludes. For instance, tuning into the analogue realm of game design encourages us to think about who is doing the creative work of design. How much time and labour go into spreadsheets, emails, artistic mock-ups, prototypes and more? Even more importantly, who is in charge of managing this creative work and are they adequately compensated for this labour?

A third approach to 'the digital' synthesizes insights from the approaches discussed earlier and presents it as a knowledge domain. Alan Liu addresses how the impact of the digital stems from its place as an epistemology. For Liu, digital technologies work alongside material technologies. Just as the library now is abstracted within a digital database, the earth is abstracted in a digital database owned by Google Maps. An approach to the digital that reads it as an epistemology recognizes the unique affordances of digital materiality – the consequences of an epistemology built upon an infrastructure of discreet units or bits – as well as the ways that this infrastructure is inhabited. In other words, whether the code that allows our technological infrastructure to function is known by people, it allows people to inhabit a new subjectivity or way of being. In this way we must consider 'the digital' a social change (2014: 3).

Among the definitions of the digital I have listed earlier, this chapter is most partial to Wark's because it grapples concretely with the power relations that the term invokes. Additionally, the invocation of digital subjectivity addresses how the digital hangs above and around us in a cultural milieu. Recognizing how digital technologies impact our perception of the world is key to understanding the importance of discussing the relevance of analogue games today.

Conclusion

Analogue games offer the opportunity to reimagine what the field of game studies might be when the invisible work of infrastructure is foregrounded and not erased. Analogue games exist in an immanently playable, readily mod-able and inherently teachable context that eschews many of the expert trappings that constitute the video game industry. What is more, the design thinking of analogue games is universal, meaning that the lessons learned in their design can be used to build the computer games of tomorrow.

The argument that analogue is infrastructure should resonate in this sense, as it is broadly an argument for understanding the complex ecosystem of game design. Digital games are not produced in a vacuum, nor are analogue games. Game designers are omnivorous, often playing any game that they can get their hands on with hopes of unearthing some precious new inspiration for their next project. The historical account of the popularization of the term 'analogue' is true to this point. From its roots in speculative science fiction, analogue technologies have always been a fast and gritty way to get ideas down on paper quickly. The original paper computer was analogue, affording thought experiments in science the opportunity to command space in the imaginations of its readers.

This chapter aimed to situate analogue games as the infrastructural layer of digital games research. I did this by characterizing the use of the terms 'analogue' and 'digital' and contextualizing their general use within emerging scholarship. Having established and defined these terms, the chapter then situated them within game studies scholarship more broadly. Having spent this work on historically situating analogue games, it is important to take a moment to acknowledge my active role in shaping the field. The journal I edit, *Analog Game Studies*, was developed specifically as a means to address these blind spots that I and other like-minded game studies scholars were frustrated with. Along with Evan Torner and Emma Leigh Waldron, we founded the journal as a publication pathway for analogue game research broadly construed. The analogue game studies community has since become a popular clearinghouse for analogue games research of all sorts, even previewing the work of some designers who have later found mainstream success. For example, Elsa Sjunneson-Henry, author of 'Reimagining Disability in Role-Playing Games', won a Hugo award in 2019; Cole Wehrle, author of 'Affective Networks at Play: *Catan*, Coin, and the Quiet Year', has received many accolades for his board game *Root*; and Tanya Pobuda's essay 'Assessing Gender and Racial Representation in the Board Game Industry', has been cited by many media outlets, including the *New York Times*. The essays published in *Analog Game Studies* are very much a product of their time, foregrounding the critical themes of third-wave game studies within the analytic presentation of analogue games research.

It is my hope that the work in this chapter offers a rationale for why research on analogue games is urgent and necessary. Analogue games mirror the design schemas of digital games and fill in essential context around game design and usability that is sorely lacking in game studies research. The object of this chapter is to bridge this gap and to bring the co-constitutive aspects of analogue games into focus within the broader discourse of game studies. To begin this mending, I needed to better explain how these niche divisions had been built into the field in the first place. It is my hope that with this context aside, the following chapters will offer jumping-off points for researchers in the future hoping to bridge the two and even contextualize the present analogue media boom more broadly within the context of research on digital media.

References

Aarseth, E. (2017), 'Just Games', *Game Studies*, 17 (1). Available online: http://gamestudies.org/1701/articles/justgames (accessed 5 October 2021).

'analogue (n.)', *The Online Etymology Dictionary*. Available online: https://www.etymonline.com/word/analogue (accessed 5 October 2021).

Bratich, J. (2010), 'The Digital Touch: Craft-work as Immaterial Labour and Ontological Accumulation', *ephemera*, 10 (3/4): 303–318.

Krukowski, D. (2017), *The New Analog*, New York: The New Press.

Liu, A. (2014), 'Theses on the Epistemology of the Digital: Advice for the Cambridge Centre for Digital Knowledge', *Alan Liu*. Available online: http://liu.english.ucsb.edu/theses-on-the-epistemology-of-the-digital-page/ (accessed 5 October 2021).

Manovich, L. (2002), *The Language of New Media*, Cambridge, MA: The MIT Press.

Pinch, T. and F. Trocco, (2004), *Analog Days: The Invention and Impact of the Moog Synthesizer*, Cambridge, MA: Harvard University Press.

Pobuda, T. (2018), 'Assessing Gender and Racial Representation in the Board Game Industry', *Analog Game Studies*, 5 (4). Available online: https://analoggamestudies.org/2018/12/assessing-gender-and-racial-representation-in-top-rated-boardgamegeek-games/ (accessed 5 October 2021).

Quachri, T. (n.d.), 'History of Analog Science Fiction and Fact', *Analog Science Fiction and Fact*. Available online: https://www.analogsf.com/about-analog/history/ (accessed 5 October 2021).

Saltzman, M. (2021), 'E3 2021: Video Games are Bigger Business than Ever, Topping Movies and Music Combined', *USA Today*, 16 September. Available online: https://www.usatoday.com/videos/tech/2021/06/10/e-3-2021-video-games-big-business-topping-film-and-music-combined/7637695002/ (accessed 5 October 2021).

Star, S. and G. Bowker (2002), 'How to Infrastructure', in L. Lievrouw and S. Livingstone (eds), *Handbook of New Media*, 151–162, London: SAGE Publications, Ltd.

Sterne, J. (2012), *MP3: The Meaning of a Format*, Durham, NC: Duke University Press.

Torner, E., A. Trammell and E. L. Waldron (2014), 'Reinventing Analog Game Studies', *Analog Game Studies*, 1 (1). Available online: https://analoggamestudies.org/2014/08/reinventing-analog-game-studies/ (accessed 5 October 2021).

Wardrip-Fruin, N. and N. Montfort (2003), *The New Media Reader*, Cambridge, MA: The MIT Press.

Wark, M. (2004), *Gamer Theory*, Cambridge, MA: Harvard University Press.

Wark, M. (2007), *Gamer Theory*, Cambridge, MA: Harvard University Press.

II

Materials

3

Component parts

Board games as architecture and performance

Paul Wake

In everyday discourse one understands by board game a real thing, made of card, paper, wood or plastic, accompanied by a printed rulebook and presented in a box. The game might be packed away on a shelf or arranged on a table with its various components distributed to the advantage of its players. However, the game in play, what I will call the game performance, is not identical with this material object. This thing is simply the objective, real condition of an encounter with the game, while various subjective conditions must also be fulfilled if the game is to be given to us in the sense of ludic performance.

These opening lines draw directly on Roman Ingarden's prefatory note to 'The Picture' in his *Ontology of the Work of Art* (1989), a book that, along with his earlier *Cognition of the Literary Work of Art* ([1937] 1973) and *The Literary Work of Art* ([1960] 1973), inspires this exploration of the ways in which players act alongside and as component parts of games. Put in Ingarden's terms, the two questions I am trying to answer are these: How is the board game structured? And, how do we cognize, though perform might emerge as a more appropriate term, the game presented in the form of the board game (in, say, the collection of written rules, printed cards, tokens and blocks)? Put simply, what kind of things (texts?) are board games? And what happens when we play with them? In addressing these questions, questions that might come to be seen as rather imperfectly expressed, this chapter is an attempt to account for the nature of the board game both as a static text (the 'board game') and as multiple individual ludic performances.

This investigation begins, in the mode of Ingarden's own analyses, with some basic assertions about the essential structure of analogue games (and, again following Ingarden's method, these assumptions might be revisited in the following analysis):

1. A game consists of a set of rules (verbal or written), which (a) set out the goal towards which players work (collectively or independently), (b) seek to constrain the possible actions by which players might achieve these goals and (c) include the possibility of various outcomes.

2. Analogue games are distinguished (from digital or purely imaginative) games by the inclusion of one or more material components; these might include, but are not limited to, game boards, tokens, playing cards and dice. These components are integral to game play and (a) make play possible in the manner of props or cues to action; (b) convey information (Järvinen 2007) or mediate communication (Wasserman 2020) during game play, recording the 'state of play' during the unfolding of the game; (c) contribute to the generation of game environments, guiding and configuring player interactions (Järvinen 2007: 67); and, (d) take part in the game itself as material actors alongside human interactors who in turn become component parts of the game performance.

3. Analogue games are 'more than half real': as Jesper Juul suggests (2005), games are both real in their determination of actual outcomes in relation to actual rules and fictional in that they are realized in imagined gameworlds. Complicating Juul's formulation, in analogue games these two elements share the connecting tissue of the real ontic foundations that make play possible and which remain steadfastly real *in and as* the imagined spaces they create.

4. The game system should be distinguished from its performances (what Ingarden might term 'concretizations'), which arise from individual instances of play. It is through these performances, which take in a temporal structure, that the indeterminacies of the game come to be resolved. Each performance of a game is an individual process and therefore also a temporal object, which is clearly situated in time and space.

The parallels between this initial outline of analogue games and the various works of art as they are described by Ingarden (specifically literature, music and architecture) are deliberate. Like literary works, board games are complex objects depending for their existence on the intentional acts of their designers (or more properly, team of designers) and players (again, best seen in the plural), but not identical with these acts. As I shall go on to discuss, board games are characterized by, if not defined according to, their *'spots of indeterminacy'* [italics in original] (Ingarden 1973b: 246), and like literary works they are necessarily intersubjective, dependant on the interaction (or as I will go on to suggest intra-action) of multiple agencies. Like musical works, games at play are unique performances tied to specific spatiotemporal locations and non-identical with either the material 'board game' or other instances of the game at play. Finally, like the architectural works that Ingarden discusses in the third essay in *Ontology of the Work of Art*, these performances are dependent on the specifics of their material foundations.

Games as performance: Indeterminancy and intersubjectivity

In its discussion of spots of indeterminancy – those points of ambiguity that make it possible for a single work to be concretized in multiple unique ways – Ingarden's work comes close to formal definitions of games in which variable outcomes regularly feature (for a summary, see Salen and Zimmerman 2004: 71–83). These spots of indeterminancy in games, as in literature, are 'not accidental' (Ingarden 1973a: 51), they are characteristic of what Umberto Eco describes as 'open' texts, which deliberately employ 'syntactic-semantico-pragmatic device[s] whose foreseen interpretation is a part of its generative process' (1984: 3). Dynamic by design, games are an example of the open text par excellence. Spots of indeterminancy, and the associated schemes and structures of the literary work that support readerly concretizations, become in games carefully structured *invitations to determine*. Wolfgang Iser's critique of Ingarden in *The Act of Reading* (1978) is instructive in the thinking through of this apparent parallel. Noting the distinction Ingarden makes between true and false concretizations, Iser suggests that Ingarden's position is too limiting in accounting for the dynamic relation that pertains between text and reader. For Iser, the act of reading becomes too passive if, as he puts it, summarizing what he finds in Ingarden, 'the work unfolds as a schematic structure in a series of determinant acts stimulated by the empty portions of each schematised aspect' (1978: 171). While Iser overemphasizes Ingarden's use of the word 'appropriate' – in this I follow Menachem Brinker's (1980) reading of Iser – the 'regulated process' or 'code' (Iser 1978: 173) he finds in Ingarden seems appropriate in the transportation of that work to games where rules, even as they work in the service of multiple possible outcomes, are indeed proscriptive. Indeed, it is telling that game genres are often discussed in terms of types of interactivity rather than in terms of narrative or visual properties (King and Krzywinska 2002; Apperley 2006). In other words, the well-mannered player, the player who accepts the contract instituted by rules and components, agrees to a set of conventions that limit their actions in the service of the game.

As Aki Järvinen puts it, 'Game design is a practice where designers more or less deliberately direct players into patterns of behaviour that can be anticipated' (2007: 83). In such an account, games come close to what Roland Barthes, in literary studies, calls 'readerly' texts (1974: 5), those texts whose codes and conventions construct and constrain the encounter of reader and text. Of course, such anticipation can only ever be partial. When George Skaff Elias, Richard Garfield and K. Robert Gutschera write, in their influential *Characteristics of Games*, 'if we had to pick one ingredient that was necessary (although not sufficient) for something to be a game, uncertainty of outcome would probably be it' (2012: 137), this uncertainty encompasses outcomes that designers could not anticipate, making possible aberrant forms of play, metagaming, rules lawyering, hacking and modding (see Consalvo 2007; Boluk and Lemieux 2017). Games then, despite their formal properties, prompt a playful exuberance, *jouissance* in Barthes's terms, both goading and guiding players into action.

The centrality of uncertainty in games suggests a strong connection to literature as it is described by Ingarden and, more clearly still, to theories of reader response as put forward in the works of critics such as Iser and Eco. Accordingly, and in line with literary studies, while it is possible to study games on a purely formal level, attending to the logical and mathematical systems on which they depend, or indeed, as collections of material objects (attending, say, to the analysis of imagery, or to the environmental impacts of their production), a focus on individual performances is common in game studies. What I am calling the game performance, a term that echoes Ingarden's work on music and which pre-figures the turn to theatre later in this chapter, has been variously described in terms of 'experience' (Schell 2008); 'game play' (Salen and Zimmerman 2004); 'metagame' (Garfield 2000; Boluk and Lemieux 2017); 'play session' (Stenros and Waern 2011; Booth 2021); 'performance activity' (Fernández-Vara 2019; Fritsch 2021); and 'aesthetics' (Hunicke, LeBlanc and Zubek 2004). As Melanie Fritsch writes: '[o]n a phenomenological level, a game (be it digital or otherwise) only manifests itself during the current act of play, the unique event, as a unique ephemeral structure (the *Aufführung*) that can be perceived and interpreted by a competent recipient' (2021: 248).

Central to discussions of games as performance is a distinction between the game (as object or system) and play (the interaction with those objects or systems). Stephanie Boluk and Patrick LeMieux draw attention to the conflation of these two things in their book *Metagaming*, noting the 'reduction of play as a pure possibility to a class of consumer goods' and asking '[w]hen did the term game become synonymous with hardware warranties, packaged products, intellectual property, copyrighted code, end user licences, and digital rights management?' (2017: 8, 3). Not to be conflated with the objects with which and alongside which it takes place, play is an activity, made possible by game systems, and making possible the concretization of the possibilities of those systems. As Bernard De Koven writes in *A Playful Path*, 'playfulness . . . allows you to transform the very things that you take seriously into opportunities for shared laughter, the very things that make your heart heavy into things that make you rejoice, it turns junk into toys, toys into art, art into celebration' (2014: 31). Play, according to such a reading, is a transformative interaction with the material foundations, the junk, toys and art, that act as 'enablers' or 'vehicles' (Sicart 2014: 42). Accordingly, the game performance, an act of 'aesthetic apprehension' (Ingarden 1973a: 53), fleshes out the schematic structure of the work, the game system, revealing the aesthetic value that is present in the work in potential form. As Ingarden's work shows, there are essential correlations between kinds of objects and the modes of cognition by means of which they can be known. As such, this investigation of cognition runs in parallel with an investigation of the nature of game components that are well described as intersubjective rather than being seen as aesthetic objects in and of themselves.

Material ontic foundations

While games might have their origin in the creative acts of consciousness of their designers (whose names are only now beginning to appear on game boxes with any frequency), it is necessary to recognize that they also have an ontic basis in their material foundations, the various components that facilitate and, as I will go on to argue, enter into play. It does not seem possible to say of analogue games, as Ingarden says of literary texts, that '[t]he print (the printed text) does not belong to the elements of the literary work of art itself . . . but merely constitutes its physical foundation' (1973a: 14). This proves to be a point at which the literary work as described by Ingarden and analogue games diverge. While both rely on material objects to make possible their continued existence after the conscious acts of the author have run their course, board games enjoy a level of materiality, as both objects of play and in their performances, that sets them apart from the works of literature. In responding to this distinction, Ingarden's essay 'The Architectural Work' proves useful in the attention it pays to texts whose material foundations prompt individual (spatiotemporally specific) performances. That the meanings of literary works also emerge in concert with their material forms – as Roger Chartier tells us, '[r]eaders are never confronted with abstract or ideal texts detached from all materiality' (1994: 3) – is an argument that must be set aside for want of space (for discussions of this, see Emerson 2014; Kirschenbaum 2016; Mak 2011; and McKenzie 1999).

'The Architectural Work', written in 1928 as a supplement to *The Literary Work of Art*, is significant in distinguishing its object of study from purely intentional objects such as literature, music and painting, giving careful consideration to the role of the independent objects that act as their foundations. While remaining dependant on these real spatiotemporal objects the architectural work of art is, like the literary work of art, intersubjective, relying on the intentions of architects and the reconstructive acts of their viewers: 'as a consequence of such acts of consciousness there arises certain intentional property of appropriate real objects that results from their becoming the ontic foundation of a new object' (1989: 261). To illustrate this point, Ingarden offers an account of the Cathedral of Notre-Dame in Paris, which is figured as both a 'building' ('a determinately ordered heap of building materials') and as a place of worship. The distinction is significant for Ingarden, who goes on to argue that 'a determinately ordered heap of building material is precisely what a "church" is not, although this heap serves as its real basis (its bearer) and forms the point of departure of the act of consecration' (1989: 259). In other words, what Ingarden terms the 'building', a real thing with physical properties such as extension and position in space, 'ontically independent of acts of consciousness' (1989: 258) is transformed, becoming a cultural object with qualities and functions that it previously did not possess.

Brought into the context of game studies, Ingarden's account of the 'consecration' of Notre-Dame recalls Johan Huizinga's discussion of play and ritual in *Homo Ludens*.

> The sacred performance is more than an actualization in appearance only, a sham reality; it is also more than a symbolical actualization – it is a mystical one. In it, something invisible and inactual takes beautiful, actual, holy form. . . . The rite produces the effect which is then not so much *shown figuratively* as *actually reproduced* in the action. The function of the rite, therefore, is far from being merely imitative; it causes worshippers to participate in the sacred happening itself. [italics in original] (2016: 14–15)

Play, according to this analysis, is performative, an act of will that transforms the 'ordinary', 'actualizing' new realities through the adoption of appropriate attitudes and behaviours. These accounts of the attitudes necessary in creating new objectivities (in buildings, games and rituals) find perhaps their clearest expression in Bernard Suits's determination that players adopt an appropriate 'lusory attitude' in order that play might commence – 'such obedience is a necessary condition for my engaging in the activity such obedience makes possible' (1978: 33). Accordingly, while games, like buildings, are actualized by the intentional acts of those who encounter them, these acts bring players (Huizinga's worshippers) into being through participation.

To think through these ideas as they apply to analogue games, I offer here a brief case study of Leslie Scott's block-stacking game *Jenga* (Hasbro 1983), a game with a similarly ordered (if soon disordered) heap of building materials (Figure 3.1).

In and of themselves *Jenga*'s fifty-four wooden blocks are real objects. They are slightly irregular in shape (Scott 2020: n.p.), carry a certain weight, change size as temperatures rise and fall and are capable of being stacked. They have six planar

Figure 3.1 *Jenga* (Hasbro 1983). Image by Guma89, via Wikimedia Commons licensed under CC BY-SA 3.0. (https://commons.wikimedia.org/wiki/Category:Jenga#/media/File:Jenga_distorted.jpg)

surfaces suitable for the embossing or printing of text or symbols, an affordance used for branding in classic *Jenga* and which makes possible variations such as Amanda Birkinshaw's *Jenga: Truth or Dare* (Hasbro 2001), they are smooth to the touch and make a range of sounds, themselves dependent upon the nature of the playing surface, when they fall. For all these qualities, the blocks do not, in and of themselves, constitute the game. From a commercial point of view this is of great importance to Scott, the game's designer, and to Hasbro, the game's publisher, both of whom invested in the game's identity in terms of intellectual property and as a marketable product. When Scott writes, in *About Jenga*, '[c]hildren at play have probably piled block-like objects, one on top of the other, to create tower-like structures ever since block-like objects existed . . . no game even remotely similar to *Jenga* existed before the early seventies' (2009: 5–6), she is concerned with the game as intellectual property, making an implicit division between 'block-like objects' and the 'game'. Scott is, to use Ingarden's terms, the game's architect whose intentional acts are transmitted in the form of the game's rules and component parts. As real things, *Jenga*'s rules and blocks become the 'bearers' or 'ontic foundation' (Ingarden 1989: 260) of this intention, making possible the transformation into new objects that they become through the individual performances of the game's players.

Like the work of architecture, then, the game performance is a 'doubly founded' (Thomasson 2020: n.p.) object that 'refers back not only to the creative acts of the architect and the reconstructive acts of the viewer, but also to its ontic foundation in a fully determined real thing shaped in a particular way' (Ingarden 1989: 263). However, while the significance given to the ontic foundations of the building proves useful in thinking through the roles of the material objects of board games as they relate to the attitudes of designers and players, Ingarden's insistence on the fully determined, extra-temporal nature of the building is the point at which the link to architecture begins to unravel. While for Ingarden the 'work of architecture consists only in its simple changeless duration as a whole' (1989: 282), the ontic foundations of analogue games engage in dynamic and networked transactions that include not only designers and players but also the things of play themselves. Rather than being the fully determined self-contained objects that their shrink-wrapped boxes might suggest, board games inaugurate new assemblages. Named for the tables on which they are often placed – '"Board" derives from a word originally meaning "plank" and secondarily "table", as in the phrase "bed and board"' (Parlett 2018: 5) – games require surfaces on which to be played (transforming tables, bedroom floors, gardens and knees into playgrounds). Sundry items such as pencils, paper, food and light become performers (Bienia 2016) alongside the players the game calls into being. Players become variously hosts and guests, teammates and adversaries. The question it therefore becomes necessary to ask is, What is the nature of this foundation as it is found in the components of board games? And, further to this, what is the nature of the transaction between these components and the intersubjective acts of designers and players?

Rather than seeing game components as foundations (or interfaces) that mediate between different realities – as 'occasion[s] to intend and intuitively apprehend a new object' (Ingarden 1989: 275) – they are better understood as 'props' that both initiate and participate in play. The term 'prop' is used here in the sense intended by Kendall Walton (1990) and brought into game studies by Chris Bateman (2011) to describe objects that prescribe imaginings and which make propositions true in make-believe worlds. Walton's account of props affords the possibility that the role of props extends beyond prescribing imagining into the imaginings themselves – 'Props are often prompters or objects of imagining also; even all three' (1990: 38) – an idea that becomes clearer when props are understood in the more familiar sense of the theatrical where the term denotes '[a]ny portable object (now usually other than an article of costume) used in a play, film, etc., as required by the action; a prop' (*OED*). In this theatrical sense, props retain Walton's sense of prescribing (or rather mediating) imaginings; as Andrew Sofer notes, 'the prop in performance is not a static or stable signifier whose meaning is predetermined by the playwright. Rather, the prop's impact is mediated both by the gestures of the individual actor who handles the object, and by the horizon of interpretation available to historically situated spectators at a given time' (2003: 61). At the same time, in participating in the theatrical production, props take on identities other than that of lifeless aspects of stage scenery, of owned objects (the 'properties' of theatre companies), becoming, as Eleanor Margolies has shown in her book *Props*, closer to Tadeusz Kantor's 'bio-objects' (1993: 240) than to inert portable properties, as part of the play performances that they both cue and constitute. Game components as props perform alongside players, operating not as 'threshold objects that take you in and lead you out of the experience' (Murray 2017: 134) but as 'autonomous objects', 'partners in performance' and 'protagonists' (Margolies 2016: 1, 23).

The sense that board game components accompany players in the move from 'thing/text' to performance (both material spaces) can be thought through in relation to the board game tokens: the wooden, metal, plastic or card avatars that represent players in game worlds that Järvinen calls 'components-of-self' (2007: 63). The standee is a stand-in – 'One who fills the place of or substitutes for another' (*OED*) – that 'functions', as Daniel Kromand writes of video game avatars, 'as the protagonist of the gameplay and also becomes the mediator of the fiction to the player' (2007: 400). The double role of board game avatars is experienced at a fundamental level in dexterity games such as Scott Frisco and Steven Strumpf's *Rhino Hero: Super Battle* (HABA 2017). In Frisco and Strumpf's game, players take on the role of superheroes, building a skyscraper from folded cards and placing their wooden avatars onto the increasingly precarious structure in a race to the top. The game's challenge is derived from the disjunction between player and playing piece, emerging in the awkwardness of an interface that trades on the shifting positions afforded to players who are kept, literally and figuratively, at arm's length from the material spaces they are simultaneously invited to occupy.

As Järvinen has suggested, in physical games, '[t]he self becomes the component, and one's own attributes – such as abilities and skills – become part of the information in the game system' (2007: 64), a claim that is borne out in reviews of dexterity games which repeatedly turn attention to players' bodies. Reviewing *Rhino Hero: Super Battle* on *Shut Up & Sit Down*, Leigh Alexander writes of her 'trembling thumb' (Smith and Alexander 2017: n.p.), Dale Yu, writing of Jay Cormier and Sen-Foong Lim's *Junk Art* (Pretzel Games 2016), tells us that 'the only thing that I can blame is my old-age tremor' (2016: n.p.), Tom Vasel remarks in his review of Naotaka Shimamoto and Yoshiaki Tomioka's *Tokyo Highway* (Asmodee 2018) 'if you have big clumsy fingers and stuff you'll have as much problem with this as any other game' (2018: n.p.), and Michael Heron gives *Rhino Hero* an F for Physical Accessibility on *Meeple Like Us*, noting that 'those with impairments in terms of fine or gross motor skills will be unable to play' (2017: n.p.).

The experience of playing games such as *Rhino Hero: Super Battle*, in which the touch of the game's card and wood pieces (cool, gently yielding and smooth, but also resistant, uncooperative and precarious), acts as a physical reminder of the distinct worlds of player and playing piece while simultaneously alerting us to the co-constituting nature of the game's components, both human and non-human. As Maurice Merleau-Ponty puts it in *The Visible and the Invisible*,

> my body is made of the same flesh as the world (it is perceived) . . . this flesh of my body is shared by the world, the world *reflects* it, encroaches upon it and it encroaches upon the world (the felt at the same time the culmination of subjectivity and the culmination of materiality), they are in a relation of transgression or of overlapping. (1968: 248)

A consciousness of self as both subject and object, Merleau-Ponty's body-subject, is felt in the doubled touch instituted by the board game piece, marking game objects as meeting points connecting (and overlapping) the mutually constituting worlds of players and the spaces of the games they play.

The materiality of analogue game components is in no way limited to dexterity games or to those games with elements of 'physical action' (Engelstein and Shalev 2020: 135) such as the classic card game *Snap!* It is, though, most obvious in games where players' bodies are factored into the design. In many cases, perhaps the majority of cases, the performative materiality of games operates in ways that are so familiar that they go unnoticed. Game boards, for example, traditionally flat two-dimensional objects, signify the boundaries of game spaces, establishing the relative position of in-game assets (houses and hotels in *Monopoly* for example), and often prompt specific (themed) imaginings in their players. In addition to the bearing much of the cognitive load (Rogerson, Gibbs and Smith 2020: 88–108) and the providing of narrative cues, game boards work to situate players in terms of proximity (games literally bring players together), sequence (managing and mediating turn order) and in-game relationships (opposition and alignment).

The *Monopoly* board, to take a well-known example, manages the game space by indicating the locations of each player's in-game avatar (the hat, the boot, the iron) and the ownership of any property, while gesturing from the abstract game space to the geographically and historically specific world of the players (Atlantic City in the original US version, London in the UK version). Simultaneously the *Monopoly* board works to situate its players who traditionally sit in a 'circle' around the square board. The board anticipates this, its text facing the four sides and its logo, chance and community chest spaces positioned diagonally. In this way, the board institutes a spatiotemporal sequence in which play continues clockwise, following the direction of the arrow on the 'GO' space and drawing players into the game's inescapable cycle of acquisition and exchange.

Other game boards, particularly those of two-player board wargames, establish more obviously adversarial positions, situating players opposite one another across the play space as is the case, for example, in Richard Borg's *Commands & Colors: Napoleonics* (GMT Games: 2012), in which this oppositional positioning aligns players and playing pieces with the historical geopolitical spaces towards which the game map gestures. By way of contrast, Jeremy Stoltzfus's *A War of Whispers* (Galakta: 2019) has a circular board around which players, taking on the role of a secret council, sit. In its lack of oppositional spaces, the circular board works to unsettle the clear-cut notion of 'sides', recalling the politics of the famous round table of Arthur's court at which, according to its early chroniclers Wace and Layamon, all sat as equals (Madden 1847: 383). *A War of Whispers* is a game of veiled competition, in which, as at Arthur's table, intrigue and power masquerade as comradeship and equality.

In tandem with these organizing principles, game boards remind us that play is an intimate experience. Drawing players together in a shared space, the traditional *Monopoly* board is just 20" across, facilitating the passing of things between players (dice, cards, currency, food, drink). *Monopoly* is not quite *Twister*, but almost certainly fingers will touch in the play of this game. This proximity, the intimate connection of players and playthings, central to the understanding of games advanced here, is ingrained in the boards of board games but is something to which players have become so habituated that it goes unnoticed.

Conclusions: Intimate networks

To revitalize our sense of the invisible-because-familiar transactions that connect game things and players, it is necessary only to look back in gaming's rich history to games made unfamiliar by the passage of time, recognizing, as Bill Brown does in his essay 'Thing Theory', that '[w]e begin to confront the thingness of objects when they stop working for us' (2001: 4). The early medieval game of Hnefatafl, a family of Nordic and Celtic games whose name comes from the Old Norse *tafl*, meaning table or board, prompts just such considerations. In asking, as Hencken *et al.* do, 'for what game was the board made' (1935: 186), or in attempting, as Eddie Duggan does, the 'unravelling the mystery of tafl games' (2020: 116), we are once again confronted by the work undertaken by the things with which we play. In the encounter with these artefacts, with the specifics of performance left only to surmise, we are, then, returned to a materiality that recalls the presence and actions of board game boards. Studies of two key examples, the Ballinderry gaming board and the Ockelbo Runestone, reveal the intimate connection that board games enact in calling players to the table.

The incorporation of what appear to be handles into the design of the tenth-century Ballinderry game board (Figure 3.2) – one a pointed human face, the other 'a beast of prosaic though indefinable type' (Hencken et al. 1935: 180) – suggesting that it was intended to be held by and between its players. We see this connection of board and players again in the eleventh-century Ockelbo Runestone (Figure 3.3), an early depiction of a game performance which

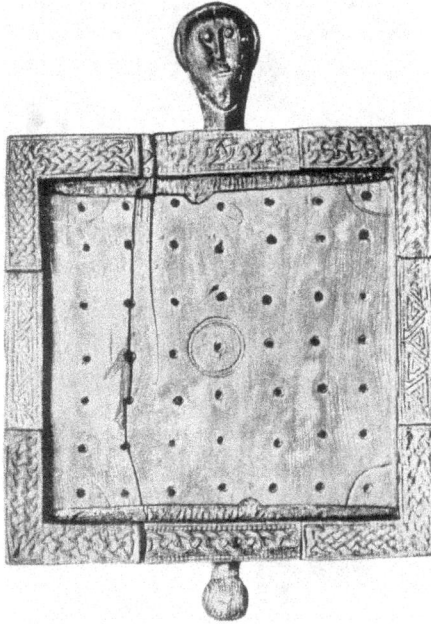

Figure 3.2 The Ballinderry gaming board. Image from Hencken et al. (1935), reproduced courtesy of the Royal Irish Academy.

shows two figures playing what is likely a game of tafl, sitting across from one another with the board balanced across their knees. Faded by time, the image, a twentieth-century reproduction of the lost original, sees the line between hand and board dissolve in a peculiarly intimate merging of human and nonhuman components.

While the specifics of the historical performances of games on the Ballinderry board and the Ocklebo Runestone remain inaccessible, both draw attention to the intimate connection of players and game objects, locating these performances in temporary and mutable constellations of objects and suggesting the co-constitutive relation between component parts. In this aspect, board game components are not so much threshold objects in the sense intended by Murray, as they are manifestations of what she describes as 'participatory environments' (2017: 138). Rather than situating the components as 'points of departure' (1989: 259), it becomes necessary to envisage the game performance as a reciprocal encounter akin to what Karen Barad describes as intra-action, a formulation which '*signifies the mutual constitution of entangled agencies*' [emphasis in the original] (2007: 33). These intra-actions, 'causally constraining nondeterministic enactments through which matter-in-the process-of-becoming is sedimented

Figure 3.3 Rune stone (Gs 19) (Ockelbo Kyrka - Replica). Image courtesy of Wikipedia licensed under CC BY 2.5. (https://commons.wikimedia.org/wiki/File:Gs _19,_Ockelbo.jpg)

out and enfolded in further materializations' (2003: 816), suggest the bringing into being of the game performance as a new, and unique, object (distinct from its component parts) while articulating the ways in which this process entails the bringing into being of the player (also a component part) through the interpenetrating and mutually transforming interplay of a network of other component parts (both human and nonhuman). Rather than figuring game objects as the foundations (starting points) of play, then, it is necessary to recognize their role in constructing the player as component – an intra-action or overlapping that aligns human and nonhuman components in the mutable and temporary network that I have called the game performance.

References

Apperley, T. H. (2006), 'Genre and Game Studies: Toward a Critical Approach to Video Game Genres', *Simulation and Gaming*, 37 (1): 6–23.

A War of Whispers (2019), [Board game], Designer: J. Stoltzfus. Poland: Galakta Games.

Barad, K. (2003), 'Posthumanist Performativity: Toward an Understanding of How Matter Comes to Matter', *Signs*, 28 (3): 801–31.

Barad, K. (2007), *Meeting the Universe Halfway: Quantum Physics and the Entanglement of Matter and Meaning*, Durham, NC: Duke University Press.

Barthes, R. (1974), *S/Z*, trans. Richard Miller, Oxford: Blackwell.

Bateman, C. (2011), *Imaginary Games*, Winchester: Zero Books.

Bienia, R. (2016), *Role Playing Materials*, Berlin: Zauberfeder Verlag.

Boluk, S. and P. Lemieux (2017), *Metagaming: Playing, Competing, Spectating, Cheating, Trading, Making, and Breaking Videogames*, Minneapolis, MN: University of Minnesota Press.

Booth, P. (2021) *Board Games as Media*, London: Bloomsbury.

Brinker, M. (1980), 'Two Phenomenologies of Reading: Ingarden and Iser on Textual Indeterminacy', *Poetics Today*, 1 (4): 203–12.

Brown, B. (2001), 'Thing Theory', *Critical Inquiry*, 28 (1): 1–22.

Chartier, R. (1994), *The Order of Books: Readers, Authors, and Libraries in Europe between the Fourteenth and Eighteenth Centuries*, trans. L. G. Cochrane, London: Polity Press.

Commands & Colors: Napoleonics (2012), [Board game], Designer; Richard Borg, USA: GMT Games.

Consalvo, M. (2007), *Cheating; Gaining Advantage in Videogames*, Cambridge, MA: MIT Press.

De Koven, B. (2014), *A Playful Path*, Halifax, Nova Scotia: ETC Press.

Duggan, E. (2020), 'A Game on the Edge: An Attempt to Unravel the Gordian Knot of Tafl Games', *Board Game Studies Journal*, 15: 99–132.

Eco, U. (1984), *The Role of the Reader: Explorations in the Semiotics of Texts*, Bloomington, IN: Indiana University Press.

Elias, G. S., R. Garfield and K. R. Gutschera (2012), *Characteristics of Games*, Cambridge, MA: MIT.

Emerson, L. (2014), *Reading Writing Interfaces: From the Digital to the Bookbound*, Minneapolis, MN: University of Minnesota Press.

Engelstein, G. and I. Shalev (2020), *Building Blocks of Tabletop Game Design: An Encyclopedia of Mechanisms*, Boca Raton, FL: CRC Press.

Fernández-Vara, C. (2019), *Introduction to Game Analysis*, 2nd edn, London: Routledge.

Fritsch, M. (2021), 'Game – Music – Performance: Introducing a Ludomusicological Theory and Framework', in M. Fritsch and Summers, T. (eds), *The Cambridge Companion to Video Game Music*, 238–62, Cambridge: Cambridge University Press.

Garfield, R. (2000), 'Metagames', in J. Dietz (ed.), *Horsemen of the Apocalypse: Essays on Roleplaying*, 14–21, Charleston, IL: Jolly Roger Games.

Guma89 (2012), 'Jenga', *Wikimedia Commons*. Available online: https://upload.wikimedia.org/wikipedia/commons/6/6b/Jenga_distorted.jpg (accessed 21 September 2021).

Hencken, H., G. Harrington, H. Movius, A. Stelfox and G. Roche (1935), 'Ballinderry Crannog No. 1', *Proceedings of the Royal Irish Academy. Section C: Archaeology, Celtic Studies, History, Linguistics, Literature*, 43: 103–239.

Heron, M. (2017), 'Rhino Hero (2011) – Accessibility Teardown', *Meeple Like Us*. Available Online: https://www.meeplelikeus.co.uk/rhino-hero-2011-accessibility -teardown/ (accessed 14 September 2021).

Hunicke, R., M. Leblanc and R. Zubek, (2004), 'MDA: A Formal Approach to Game Design and Game Research', AAAI Workshop – Technical Report.

Huizinga, J. (2016), *Homo Ludens: A Study of the Play-Element in Culture*, Kettering, OH: Angelico Press.

Ingarden, R. (1973a), *The Cognition of the Literary Work of Art*, trans. R. A. Crowley and K. R. Olson, Evanston, IL: Northwestern University Press.

Ingarden, R. (1973b), *The Literary Work of Art*, trans. G. G. Grabowicz, Evanston, IL: Northwestern University Press.

Ingarden, R. (1989), *Ontology of the Work of Art: The Musical Work, The Picture, The Architectural Work, The Film*, trans. R. Meyer with J. T. Goldthwait, Athens: Ohio University Press.

Iser, W. (1978), *The Act of Reading: A Theory of Aesthetic Response*, Baltimore and London: The Johns Hopkins University Press.

Järvinen, A. (2007), 'Games Without Frontiers: Theories and Methods for Game Studies and Design', PhD thesis, University of Tampere, Tampere.

Jenga (1983), [Dexterity game], Designer L. Scott, USA, Hasbro.

Junk Art (2016), [Dexterity game], Designers: J. Cormier and S.-F. Lim, USA: Pretzel Games.

Juul, J. (2005), *Half-Real: Video Games between Real Rules and Fictional Worlds*, Cambridge, MA: The MIT Press.

Kantor, T. (1993), *A Journey Through Other Spaces: Essays and Manifestos, 1944–1990*, ed. and trans. M. Kobialka, Berkeley and Los Angeles: University of California Press.

King, G. and T. Krzywinska (eds) (2002), *Screenplay: Cinema/Videogames/Interfaces*, London and New York: Wallflower Press.

Kirschenbaum, M. (2016), *Track Changes: A Literary History of Word Processing*, Harvard, MA: Harvard University Press.

Kromand, D. (2007), 'Avatar Categorization', *Situated Play, Proceedings of DiGRA 2007 Conference*, 400–6.

Madden, F. (1847), *Layamon's Brut, Or Chronicle of Britain; A Poetical Semi-Saxon Paraphrase of The Brut of Wace, Volume 3*, London: The Society of Antiquaries of London.

Mak, B. (2011), *How the Page Matters*, Toronto: University of Toronto Press.

Margolies, E. (2016), *Props: Readings in Theatre Practice*, London: Palgrave.

McKenzie, D. F. (1999), *Bibliography and the Sociology of Texts*, Cambridge: Cambridge University Press.

Merleau-Ponty, M. (1968), *The Visible and the Invisible*, ed. C. Lafort, trans. A. Lingis, Evanston, IL: Northwestern University Press.

Murray, J. (2017), *Hamlet on the Holodeck: The Future of Narrative in Cyberspace*, Updated Edition, New York: The Free Press.

Parlett, D. (2018), *Parlett's History of Board Games*, Brattleboro, VT: Echo Point Books.

'prop, n.6', *OED Online*. Available Online: https://www-oed-com.mmu.idm.oclc.org/ view/Entry/152851?rskey=QHrN08&result=7 (accessed 14 September 2021).

Rhino Hero: Super Battle (2017), [Dexterity game], Designers: S. Frisco and S. Strumpf, Germany: HABA.

Rogerson, M., M. Gibbs and W. Smith (2020), 'More than the Sum of their Bits: Understanding the Gameboard and its Components', in D. Brown and E. MacCallum-Stewart (eds), *Rerolling Boardgames: Essays on Themes, Systems, Experiences and Ideologies*, 88–108, Jefferson, NC: McFarland & Co.

Salen, K. and E. Zimmerman (2004), *Rules of Play: Game Design Fundamentals*, Cambridge, MA: The MIT Press.

Schell, J. (2008), *The Art of Game Design: A Book of Lenses*, San Francisco, CA: Taylor & Francis.

Scott, L. (2009), *About Jenga: The Remarkable Business of Creating a Game that Became a Household Name*, Austin, TX: Greenleaf Book Group Press.

Scott, L. (2020), 'Jenga: A Tale of Randomness and Design', *Oxford Science Blog*. Available Online: https://www.ox.ac.uk/news/science-blog/jenga-tale-randomness -and-design (accessed 14 September 2021).

Sicart, M. (2014), *Play Matters*, Cambridge, MA: The MIT Press.

Smith, Q. and L. Alexander (2017), 'Rhino *Hero Super Battle*: The Clambering Proletariat, Doomed Societies, The Duality of Heroism, Monkeys', *Shut Up & Sit Down*. Available online: https://www.shutupandsitdown.com/review-rhino-hero -super-battle/ (accessed 14 September 2021).

Sofer, A. (2003), *The Stage Life of Props*, Ann Arbor, MI: University of Michigan Press.

'stand-in, n.', *OED Online*. Available Online: https://www-oed-com.mmu.idm.oclc.org/ view/Entry/188986?rskey=1aQt5S&result=3 (accessed 14 September 2021).

Stenros, J. and A. Waern (2011), 'Games as Activity: Correcting the Digital Fallacy', in M. Evans (ed.), *Videogame Studies: Concepts, Cultures and Communication*, 11–22, Oxford: Oxford Interdisciplinary Press.

Suits, B. (1978), *The Grasshopper: Games, Life, and Utopia*, Toronto: University of Toronto Press.

Thomasson, A. (2020), 'Roman Ingarden', in E. N. Zalta (ed.), *The Stanford Encyclopedia of Philosophy*. Available Online: https://plato.stanford.edu/archives/fall2020/entries/ ingarden/ (accessed 14 September 2021).

Tokyo Highway (2018), [Dexterity game], Designers: N. Shimamoto and Y. Tomioka, France: Asmodee.

Twister (1966), [Physical game], Designer: Charles Foley, USA: Hasbro.

Vasel, T. (2018), 'Tokyo Highway Review - with Tom Vasel', *The Dice Tower*. Available
    online: https://www.youtube.com/watch?v=HU98BeZ9_Yg (accessed 14 September
    2021).
Walton, K. L. (1990), *Mimesis as Make-Believe: On the Foundations of the
    Representational Arts*, Cambridge, MA: Harvard University Press.
Wasserman, J. A. (2020), 'Materially Mediated: Boardgames as Interactive Media', in D.
    Brown and E. MacCallum-Stewart (eds), *Rerolling Boardgames: Essays on Themes,
    Systems, Experiences and Ideologies*, 71–87, Jefferson, NC: McFarland & Co.
Wikipedia (2007), 'Rune Stone (Gs 19) (Ockelbo Kyrka - Replica)', *Wikipedia*. Available
    online: https://upload.wikimedia.org/wikipedia/commons/0/05/Gs_19%2C
    _Ockelbo.jpg (accessed 21 September 2021).
Yu, D. (2016), 'Review of *Junk Art*', *The Opinionated Gamers*. Available online: https://
    opinionatedgamers.com/2016/09/05/dale-yu-review-of-junk-art/ (accessed 14
    September 2021).

4

A queer touch of fantasy role-play

Jack Warren

In analogue and role-playing game studies, there is a determination to centre queerness in the face of a community, praxis and product often rife with prejudice (Biswas 2019; Sihvonen and Stenros 2019; Stokes 2017; Vist 2018). Much of this work presents a queer remapping of the history of games, shows how structures of power can be resisted through play and playfully reveals the inherent queerness of games. Jaakko Stenros and Tanja Sihvonen, whose work focuses on remapping the history of role-playing games, scoured sourcebooks for traces of (predominately white) queer sexualities, finding, across three decades of material, that queer representation has 'moved from the complete darkness of dungeons out into the open' (2015: n.d.). The increasing visibility of queer lives should be celebrated, and it is vital to recognize that queerness is found even in the most heterosexist of spaces. However, this 'straight' line of progress obscures the rich and messy lives of queer folks and neglects the queer potential of the designed, technical and mechanical elements of games (Ruberg 2019). Instead, in furthering this project of queering games, touching becomes a way to feel the queerness of matter and of play. Exploring the embrace of play, this chapter asks how we might crawl between the space of a touch and become so intimate with the materials of the game that it brings them as close as the self.

To role-play is to engage in passionate sincerity and amateurism. Amateurism is no insult; rather it eschews notion of mastery, signalling instead an emphasis on process and becoming (Muñoz 2009). In eschewing mastery, role-playing centres intimacy and touch. It becomes a sensuous feeling-through of fantastical gameworlds: 'Touching, not mastering' declares Laura U. Marks (2002: xii). To play a tabletop role-playing game is to gather around a table, mixing objects, bodies, characters, affects, media and imaginations together, the pressure of each an upswell of sensation. The game has core rules that ground its physics and mechanics, but the game is meant to shift and morph as players perform as their characters in a constantly developing adventure and setting. Role-play is intimate. Between the dance of agencies, entities and forces around the table, there is a necessity to open oneself up to other performances as players work in tandem to create and play. Players might question whether their ideas and performance are congruent besides a fantastical world. Like many intimate moments, there is umming and ahhing, and shared apprehensions, yet in this remains pleasure and excitement when the material and immaterial circulate. Shaka McGlotten writes that intimacy is 'a *feeling* of connection or a *sense* of belonging; embodied and carnal sensuality, that is, *sex*' (2014: 1). This sensuous intimacy can be traced in role-play, the touch of it all, how objects pull, and push on, bodies, media caresses each other and imaginations massage the senses.

Intimacy and touch are always potentially queer. Tim Dean's (2009) *Unlimited Intimacy* explores the queer subcultural practice of 'barebacking', the deliberate abandonment of prophylactics during sex, which has become a queer subcultural site of eroticism. In eschewing condoms, barebacking is an experience of intimacy that is 'unfettered' by rubber or latex. Barebacking as erotic preference and subculture is commonplace in queer vernacular; however, Dean seeks to broker barebacking with a wider understanding of overcoming boundaries between persons.[1] He asks, '[w]hat might happen if we were a little more promiscuous about promiscuity itself, if we defined it more broadly, permitting promiscuity to affect all forms of attention, all those moments when our regard approaches and touches something else' (Dean 2009: 5)? Take, for instance, lead miniature gaming models that leave residues of lead upon the skin that might leech into the blood: Are the players and the miniature gaming models barebacking? Dana Luciano and Mel Y. Chen (2015), writing on queer inhumanisms, contend that when there is an intimacy between the nonhuman, they rub on, and against each other, generating friction and leakage. Being promiscuous with promiscuity exemplifies this intimacy and allows attention to be paid to nonhuman actors, the queerness and promiscuity of matter can be felt and touched as it touches and feels in return, a circulating system of response.

This chapter is enmeshed with the speculative and material turns of twenty-first-century philosophy to undo the understanding of matter as passive, inert and inanimate. New materialisms are not sentimental about skin; some bodies bend under the weight of a hand, and others do not. There are many tensions gathered around the table when playing tabletop role-playing games, and to role-play is to pluck, caress and grind them. As such, the material and affective collaborators of role-play require the same attention as their human partners. In mapping an ecology of role-play that entangles objects and players, this chapter is a response to Rafael Bienia's call for researchers to reconsider the relationship between materials and humans in role-play. He claims that when 'materials collaborate in tabletop role-playing games, materials role-play, too' (2016: 160). Bienia lends a voice to the nonhuman, to tell their stories alongside their human companions. These provocations parallel Donna Haraway's (2016a) foundational notion of 'worlding', which invites us to imagine and challenge, it tells us to play with works, inhabit new or different ecologies, radically combine knowledge practices and, with this, tell new stories. Jeffrey J. Cohen (2015) warns us, however, that any speaking for the nonhuman is a translation and therefore bound with errors, guesswork and inclined towards the fantastical. Yet, he notes, stories will always remain to intensify relations and make connections with the nonhuman.

It is important to note that there is no universal session of tabletop role-play, the embrace of all gathered can be manifold, yet the materials present are often very similar. For example, the popular game *Dungeons & Dragons* (Wizards of the Coast 2014). Upon a table is a screen, or sometimes a laptop, behind which a Dungeon Master, also understood as a storyteller and referee, is sitting, the screen concealing their notes. Players sit around the table too, dice in hands – eager. In front of each player is a character sheet adorned with stats, names with forgotten context, clues, drink stains and perhaps doodles. A vinyl role-playing mat lies upon the table, its grid pattern obscured by the remains of a marker pen that belie past adventures and battles. Upon the mat are miniature gaming models of fantastical creatures, perhaps painted, although often not. In touching and feeling the materiality of role-play, the vector of meaning, affect, imagination and media are similarly entangled with matter. This entanglement makes role-play possible, and so, to properly position all its dynamisms, role-play is understood as a gyre, an endless system of circulating materials and imaginings.[2] Queer intimacy and touch become a way to feel through role-play as it, in turn, grinds at discrete distinctions between the human, the object, the imaginary and the mediatic.

Props, tokens, ephemera and pieces of detritus are the matter of study for much role-play and analogue games scholarship (Bienia 2016; Cox 2018; Germaine Buckley 2020; Wake 2019). Following this existing work, this chapter centres on three objects: a miniature gaming model, a role-playing mat and a paper character sheet, each of which are common companions when playing *Dungeons & Dragons*. These objects guide the chapter, prompting questions about how we experience, understand and imagine sensuous forces and agencies with, outside and athwart to our skin. The first section, 'Touching/feeling', through the help of a miniature model finds what materials, media, worlds and textures delight at the touch of role-play, and how those forms grind together in an entanglement of sensuality. This leads to the next section, 'Leaking/sticking', which that holds when forces and entities touch, they leave residues of themselves after the embrace. Guided by a role-playing mat, friction and leakage are seen through the sticky residues of ink upon the mat that signify the bleeding of media between objects and media.

The final section and conclusion, 'Self/touch', expands the queer conceptual trajectory of Karen Barad's (2012) notion of self-touching understood through quantum field theory. For Barad, touch is an exploration of indeterminacy where virtuality circulates, and so the residues and leaks of role-play must be apprehended from the material and virtual world. Materiality and virtuality are not separate substances, and more virtuality is immanent potentiality; it is the 'indwelling force of things waiting, pressing, ready to act' (McGlotten 2014: 1). A character sheet guides us here, or more specifically, the doodles drawn upon a character sheet, where the virtual springs forth. Doodles, like a self-touch, signify an entanglement of virtual and actual. The self-touch of role-play does likewise, signifying role-play as a gyre of objects, bodies, characters, affects, media and imaginations that circulates and involutes in the intimate touch of a game.

Touching/feeling

At first glance of the image in Figure 4.1, viewers will notice a character unmistakably humanoid yet fantastical. The character is clad in plate armour, adorned with runes and gold embellishments, and sporting a thick red beard that reaches to their knees. It is a miniature gaming model, composed of several plastic components fused together with glue. The figure's steadfast and staunch demeanour becomes juxtaposed with the hand that gently holds it in this photograph. The rigidity of its form is made evident by the supple skin that it presses into, marking both as sensory and textured bodies. You might initially connect with the hand that senses the weight, firmness and pressure of the model. Yet in this embrace, the model enlivens the proximity of other more fantastical worlds. Cohen (2015) tells us that things can apprehend and act and be insistent and energetic in doing so. Things participate in relation-making and ignite connections.

'A Dwarf!' you might note, recognizing the character's beard and stout figure. You might recall the Nibelung from Richard Wagner's (1876) opera cycle *Der Ring des Nibelungen*, a story from Germanic heroic legend. Rather, you might see J. R. R. Tolkien's (1937) company of Dwarves heading to the Lonely Mountain,

Figure 4.1. Miniature gaming model. Photograph taken by the author.

led by the indomitable Thorin Oakenshield. Or perhaps, you see Peter Jackson's (re)imagining of Tolkien's *The Lord of the Rings* (2001–3), recalling Gimli, son of Glóin. Staring back at you might be a Dwarf from the *Warhammer* universe (Games Workshop, 1983–) and so perhaps the face of High King Thorgrim Grudgebearer of Karaz-a-Karak emerges. Or, quite possibly, a Dwarf from *World of Warcraft* (Blizzard, 2004–) is before you, and as such, you behold a denizen of Ironforge. When you look upon this model some remains of fantasy's mediatic past will always flit by. Riding the regenerative currents of media, the figure before you bears the traces of oral tradition, literature, film, theatre, photography and games both analogue and digital. Between the sensuality of hand on plastic, of plastic on hand, contact with the model brings these residues of fantasy media as close as the contact itself.

 Jean-Luc Nancy holds that all communication culminates as figurations of weighing. He writes that our world inherited the world of gravity; '[a] body doesn't have weight: [...] it *is* weight' (2008: 93). Bodies weigh, grind, rub, caress, entwine and embrace each other; they counterweigh and buttress. In each of these weighings, there is an arousal and exchange of sensation. On touching, Barad writes, '[w]hen two hands touch, there is a sensuality of the flesh, an exchange of warmth, a feeling of pressure, of presence, a proximity of otherness that brings the other nearly as close as oneself. Perhaps closer' (2012: 206). To permit oneself to touch is to apprehend and invite in sensation: sensation of the self and sensations of the other. As Jacques Derrida writes, touching is a reciprocal act; it is 'touching what one touches, to let oneself be touched by the touched, by the touch of the thing' (2005: 276). There is potency and intensity in a touch (Chen 2012). To touch, and be touched, is to feel the warmth, pressure, presence and otherness of the thing in relation to yourself. Touch always goes (at least) two ways, it is an exchange, letting oneself be touched entails a touching from another. In complicating these matters, Barad explains that touch is a communicative dance of electromagnetic interaction. To touch is to feel the repulsive force of negatively charged electrons pushing against the negatively charged electrons of your skin, nails or hair. Touch is always indirect; it runs athwart to bodies offering no contact, only repulsion.

As touch is always indirect it becomes open; touch can stick around, be deferred and touch elsewhere other than the initial haptic contact. Nancy considers the inherent indirectness of touch when he makes apparent the bodies that touch upon the pages of his book: his hands writing and our hands holding. This touch is infinitely indirect, deferred by machines, eyes, other hands, and yet, touch continues 'as a slight resistant, fine texture, the infinitesimal dust of a contact, everywhere interrupted and pursued' (Nancy 2008: 51). In the space between touch are the residues, infinitesimal dust and weights of a myriad of others. Touch not only circulates the sensations of entities and forces in immediate proximity, but the residual lingers of past encounters. Rebecca Schneider, writing on the circulation of materials, hand to hand, object to object, hand to object, suggests that the touch of a body, its sweat and perhaps even its gestures and sounds, remain upon the device, 'in the ongoing after life of contact' (2019: 56). Taking up Bienia's instruction to reconsider how matter role-plays, I suggest that these residual spills of matter and gesture should be recognized in the circulating currents of role-play, to be touched, sensed and felt. The miniature gaming model tells us of these affective lingers, and while it does not sweat, it does role-play, and the material and gestures residues of such contact remains to be enlivened once again at the close of touch.

Barad proposes that matter and meaning are not separate elements, '[t]hey are inextricably fused together, and no event, no matter how energetic, can tear them asunder' (2007: 3). This is not a return to essentialism, matter does not delimit itself to being settled, rather it is a claim for matter's radical entanglement with meaning. According to Barad, matter is always touching and sensing, it is a 'condensation of responsibility' (2012: 215). It is an enfolding and dynamic overlaying of iterative reconfigurations; in response matter materializes. On matter's (re)iterative materialization with role-play, Chloé Germaine Buckley tells of the emergent and generative capacity of props in live action role-play (LARP). LARP props, for Germaine Buckley, 'prescribe specific imaginings, trigger emotions, and generate the fictional world of the game' (2020: 364–5). The humans besides the props figure this as well, as they dress up and perform to generate those very same imaginings, emotions and worlds. Together, object and human each add to, as Bienia writes, the game's material network.

Considering the miniature gaming model in this – an Ironbreaker designed for the miniature wargame *Warhammer Age of Sigmar* (Games Workshop 2015–) – like me it must always role-play when appearing within the fantasy worlds of *Dungeons & Dragons*. Akin to crossover fiction when multiple worlds grind together, the model is insistent in igniting connections and bringing with it the residues of another game with each recurrent encounter. It is specifically its out-of-place/in-placeness when role-playing that touches upon the slip and slide of matter and meaning that is reconstituted with each iteration of play. When this model and I role-play, we become partners in errantry. As it stands upon the role-playing mat, I extend a hand to move us into the fray. Schneider (2019) tells us that there is an ongoing afterlife of contact, and so, these touches, feelings and movements are a recurrence, another congealing of gesture, sweat and affect. It stands besides more models, each of them textured bodies, dragging with them more residual material affects into this sensuous gyre. To extend a hand, and move this miniature model, is to feel this heft despite its slight weight.

It becomes apparent that touch is not principally a material affair; it is highly affective. Barad states that '[t]ouch moves and affects what it effects' (2012: 208). Following Barad, it should also be recognized that affect moves and touches with it effects. In *Touching Feeling* (2002), Eve Kosofsky Sedgwick proposes that thought has materiality, that it has texture, erogenous zones, weight and temperature with which meaning can be vibratory and amorphous. She holds that there is an intimacy between textures and emotions, signified by the epithet 'touchy-feely', and its implications of contact besides affect, affect beside contact. Parallels can be drawn here to the works of Elizabeth Grosz who suggests that ideality and materiality are not two substances but two modes across which the real is distributed. Ideality, for Grosz, 'enables materiality to be in touch with itself, to be autoaffective, which is the condition which materiality can complexify itself' (2017: 251). This understanding of touch enables the potentiality to be touched, moved and affected by the amorphous, the sentimental, the theoretical

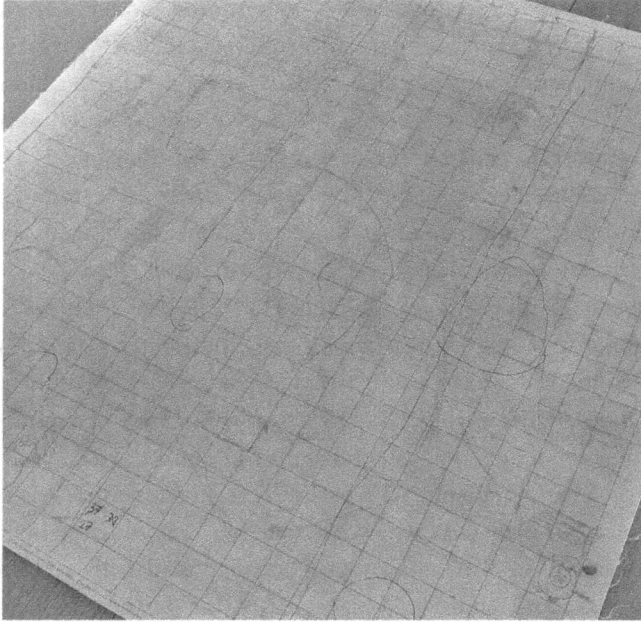

Figure 4.2. Role-playing mat. Photograph taken by the author.

and the mediatic. In the recurrent intimacy of role-play, the affective, imaginary and mediatic circulate sensuality as much as hands and objects touch too.

In the intimacy with this miniature gaming model the dynamic conflux that is touching, feeling, matter and meaning are aroused. As skin feels the dull and smooth textured figure of the model, it too enlivens the sensuous forces that the object drags with it. Matter and meaning cannot be separate but they can shift, accruing or losing matter and meaning as residues congeal or are ground away. Role-play will always feel this effect as matter and meaning from various media becomes relational through objects. This effect is not only spiralled inwards, but the residues of role-play also reach out into other media, where they can then be absorbed once again, along with whatever is accrued or lost in the process. This position is illustrated in the next section, with the help of a role-playing mat, where the residues of affects and matter can be understood as sticky (Figure 4.2).

Leaking/sticking

Baked into the surface of this role-playing mat are many stains. These are the remains of marker pen that have seeped deep into the body of the mat and can no longer be removed. On the mat are crooked lines, misshapen circles, squiggles, numbers, names and a mirky tinge composed of ink that was erased yet still clings tightly as an amorphous blur. At one time, those crooked lines might have been the wooden walls of a tavern, the dingy sides of a cave, or the sheer drop of a rocky cliff. The misshapen circles were maybe stones and rocks, a pillar or a swampy pool. The squiggles were perhaps a tree, a broken cart or a campfire. The numbers have all but lost their meaning, and the names have almost been forgotten. These stains are the residues of six years of role-play. They are the material affective remains of beloved characters, intricate campaigns, bloody conflicts, raucous laughter, tender moments, heart-wrenching deaths and arduous scrambles across worlds. For six years, this mat has gathered role-play, the people, materials, media, imaginations and affects of it all. In the ongoing afterlife of contact, the residues of role-play have all bled into each other, persistent traces of the fantastical.

The weight of matter touching – whatever the form of each might be – is a grinding articulation of sensuality. This intimate embrace of borders and boundaries, specifically the caress of the limen of the nonhuman, is posited to *melt away* discrete distinctions between those touching (Giffney and Hird 2008; Jones 2002). However, as Jane Bennett notes, 'members of an open whole never melt into a collective body' (2010: 35). A conceptual shift is required to understand the intimacy of borders, not as a melting away of categories but rather as a generative grinding. Dana Luciano and Mel Y. Chen (2015) hold that with in/human intimacies, boundaries grind on and against each other, generating friction and leakage. This grinding and leakage is highly sensuous, provoking the exchange of sensation through touch in a highly generative manner. Alysse Kushinski (2019) understands leaks as signifiers and material occurrences; that which leaks is a substance which seeps through while, as the adjective: 'leaky,' is defined as something without the ability to contain. Role-play is leaky; it cannot contain its contents, and so, it leaks, spilling affective and mediatic gestures and residues into other networks. Friction and leakage guide this section; they are the aftereffects of the grinding of bodies, forms and figures in play.

Considering the role-playing mat in this discussion of leaking, I elaborate upon it as an overlaying of matter and meaning. The inky residues of each layer are entangled, sometimes these remains are readily apparent, elsewhere they are nought but infinitesimal dust caught up in the blur. Jussi Parikka (2015), in a discussion of the mineral and chemical elements of media, traces its geologic matter to prehistory, found within the deep places of the Earth. Six years is but a moment on the way back to prehistory, yet the inky remains of role-play can, likewise, be unearthed from this mat. Those remains can be understood as leaks generated by the bumps and grinds of role-play that have stuck around. Those residues are stuck fast and have been congealing since the very first session of play. In this dialogue of touch, 'stickiness' becomes apparent. As Schneider writes, '"sticky" residue and resonant aftereffects of manufacture extend a media object off of itself into the broader scene of its hand-lings and mark said object as participant in rituals, habits, and encounters' (2019: 56). The leaks generated from the friction of play have substance, they are sticky and as matter and meaning are inseparable, meaning can be sticky too.

By proposing that meaning, comprised of sensations, theories, and affect, has substance, it can be treated similarly to other sticky matters, and sticky things can stick to other sticky things or things that are not themselves sticky, and that which is sticky can get stuck. Sara Ahmed ([2004] 2014) imagines affects as movement, they can circulate and pick-up further affects because affect is sticky. Objects, such as the role-play mat, can become sticky, saturated and sites of tension. Affects, through their stickiness, come to signify the fleshy and physical, you may be 'touched' or 'moved' by affect, which is to feel their stickiness and leakiness congeal on you. According to Ahmed, affects stick to entities, objects and even other affects. As they circulate, they might get stickier or less sticky depending on the directions of movement, and whether affects slide or stick. Emotions cannot be untangled from bodily sensation, and nor can they be untangled from objects. As Ahmed notes '[e]motions are both about objects, which they hence shape, and are also shaped by contact with objects' (2014: 7). She clarifies that objects are not repositions of feelings and emotions, likened to Ann Cvetkovich's (2003) 'archive of feelings', but rather affects circulate objects, they can generate feelings and affects. To borrow Julietta Singh's (2018) sensuous notion of *leaning* into queerness, objects, matter and meaning in leaning into queerness become insistently sticky. Objects are not empty but embodied through the unlimited intimacy of entanglements. Consider, for example, the role-playing mat, its body is a composite of the sticky afterlives of matter, affect and gesture that have stuck to it, that it has stuck to. So, when it impresses upon a player, a miniature gaming model, or a character sheet, it circulates, impressing those physical and emotion remains in response to contact.

To be affected by something is to get stuck in, and by getting stuck in is to become sticky, accumulating affect with each sticky touch. To get stuck into role-play is stick to all the surfaces of its myriad forms. The role-playing mat is not a repository of affect, though affects do co-constitute it. Rather, it has gotten stuck into role-play in the same way that a player does. The physical residues of stained pen ink mark the object as participant in ritual, habit and encounter. Through this material substance, role-play can be seen as leaky, it is unable to be contained, and these residues are only one example of leaking but demonstrative of role-play on a larger scale. Media content is another effect that overflows from the friction of role-play. Image boards, websites, media sharing apps and forums – such as Reddit, 4chan, TikTok, and DeviantArt – are brimming with fantasy art, memes, stories, ideas, models, music, maps, characters, cartoon strips, pornography and cosplay. Objects, such as dice, model scenery, props and table set-ups feature as heavily as digital art and ideas.

Each thread of content is like a bit of ink stained on the role-playing mat. Upon close inspection, the residues can be traced where meaning will emerge, like a line that was once a tavern wall, a squiggle that was a tree. Then, upon a larger scale, the whole circulatory gyre of mediatic affects becomes evident. Schneider (2019), on media and devices, notes that the biobody is not usually considered a means of material extension; it is limited compared to technology. She writes that such assumptions eschew the co-constituting entanglement of human biology with other matter. Instead, the biobody should be seen as mediatic, it can extend and broker experience, just as matter does. Role-play makes this evident, as objects, bodies, characters, affects, medias and imaginations all circulate without distinction as to where one ends and the other starts. Each can extend each other in the intimacy of play and its afterlife.

Self/touch

Where the ongoing afterlives of role-playing games extend the sensuality of the game itself across media into digital spaces, the physical artefact discloses even more intimate moments of the self and touch. Figure 4.3 is a paper character sheet. These sheets are a record of a player's character and will include details, notes, game statistics and background information that the player will need for each session of play. A character sheet will likely include the attributes of a character's name and class, such as Warlock, Ranger, Fighter or Bard. It will also include values such as a character's vitality (known as hit points), statistics that represent a character's strength, wisdom, charisma, a list of spells and items in their inventory. This particular character sheet is also covered in doodles, each a little critter sparked into existence upon the paper. Some of the doodles are familiar: a mace, a sword, a staff, a scroll and a lightbulb. Other doodles are more abstract: spirals, meandering lines, dots, nebulous shapes.

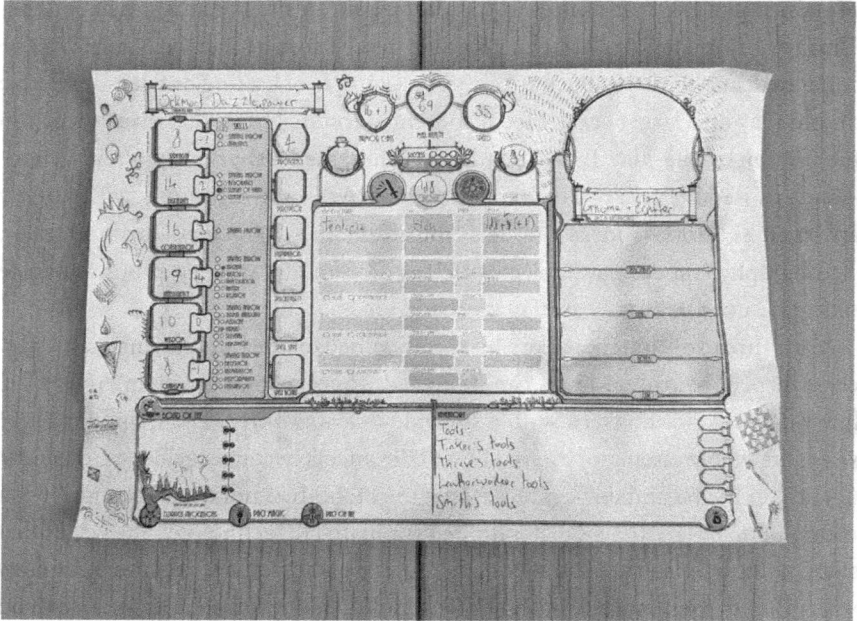

Figure 4.3. Paper character sheet. Photograph taken by the author.

Doodling is drawing when your attention is elsewhere, somewhere other. Jane Bennett (2020) remarks that doodling helps people to process ideas, concepts, tones and figures of speech. To doodle, according to Bennett, is to draw from the virtual, see critters as they emerge and roam across a page. She writes, '[t]he doodle brings obscure news of a netherworld in which I partake; it is somehow subjective without being the expression of an interiority all my own' (2020: x). Doodling partakes in a process of influx and efflux, an evocative process that describes the tendency 'for outsides to come in, muddy the waters, and exit to partake in new (lively/deathly) waves of encounter' (Bennett 2020: x). The doodle is a shape that beholds both virtual powers and a self-evident body. This seemingly automatic becoming signifies an 'I' for Bennett that is a porous and susceptible shape riding waves of influx and efflux. Like role-playing, doodling embodies a process of brimming potentials, where the spiralling of materiality and imagination arouse the actual and virtual. In dialogue with Bennett, this provocative 'I' prompts questions of touch and the self during role-play. These include questions of what shape of the self is touching and what shape of the self is touched in play. Or, to put it another way, in this sticky encounter of the self that is automatic and virtual, can the self-touch itself?

The notion of a self-touch has been the subject of work by Jean-Luc Nancy, Jacques Derrida and Karen Barad, where they recognize that the openness of touch can be aroused in the self. Leaning into its masturbatory allusions, a self-touch is autoaffective, sensuous and stimulating. Nancy (2008) writes that the body delights in being extended by touch, an extension that can be aroused by the self. In their essay, 'On Touching – The Inhuman That Therefore I am', Barad suggests that when two hands touch there is an exchange of sensuousness, warmth, pressure, presence and proximity that brings otherness close to the self. Then, should the touch be between two hands of the same person, it might 'enliven an uncanny sense of the otherness of the self, a literal holding oneself at a distance in the sensation of contact, the greeting of the stranger within' (2012: 206). Such enfolding explains the co-constitution of matter and meaning, virtual and actual, where no matter how idiosyncratic, entities, agencies, ideas, textures and sensations always touch. Like Bennett's doodles, this section discloses a self in role-play that is, at once, a muddying influx and efflux of the virtual and the self-evident, and a self always touching itself. In being promiscuous with promiscuity, an unfettered intimacy with the self emerges in this muddying self-touch, a promiscuity that arouses all of role-play's unlimited folds.

In this chapter I have suggested that media, affects and imaginations are as much the 'meat' of role-play as the miniature model, role-playing mat, character sheet and player. Like Donna Haraway's cyborg, to role-play is to be a 'condensed image of both imagination and materiality' (2016b: 7). As Cohen argues, '[t]he body is not human (or at least, it is not only human) nor [. . .] is it inhabited by an identity or sexuality that is unique to or even contained fully within its flesh' (2003: 41). In the grinding and leaking gyre of role-play, sensations can feel disruptive, and it can at times feel as if each component becomes each other, the gestures of each collaborator act without distinction to where one ends, and another begins. So, if each collaborator seems to become each other, role-play is an involution; role-play is already always touching itself. Role-play's self-touch grinds at the exteriority of meaning and matter, arousing, as Barad suggests, an infinity of other beings, spaces and times.

Self-touch is understood by Barad through the foundational, yet perplexing, ideas of quantum field theory, and holds that queerness is inherent at the subatomic level of touch. Barad advocates a move away from classical physics and its understanding of ontology, specifically that physical particles are separate from the void. In quantum field theory, the void is a 'living breathing indeterminacy of non/being'; it is a vacuum, a 'jubilant exploration of virtuality, where virtual particles – whose identifying characteristic is not rapidity, but rather, indeterminacy' (2012: 210). Barad continues, explaining that there are virtual particles in the void that do not exist in space and time. Instead they are 'ghostly non/existences that teeter on the edge of the infinitely fine blade between being and non/being' (2012: 210). The electron, a physical particle, encounters and precipitates through the void; it is fundamentally inseparable from it. As the electron figures the outer orbit of an atom, to touch and be touched is to feel the negatively charged repulsion of electrons.

According to quantum physics, the electron is a point particle, meaning that it has no substructure, unlike composite particles (such as protons) that have an internal substructure. The electron has 'self-energy', which represents the interaction of the electron with the surrounding electromagnetic field that it, and its fellow electrons, creates. This self-energy, Barad explains, 'takes the form of an electron exchanging a virtual photon with itself' (2012: 212). As the virtual photon that the electron exchanges with itself exists in the void, it is an exploration of virtuality, and so each electron of every entity is the coalescence of physical particles and the jubilant indeterminacies of the void. This understanding of matter is crucial as something beyond analogy (though analogy remains pertinent). For Barad, queer identity and embodiment *do* quantum field theory. Barad remarks upon how troubling this is by citing physicist Richard Feynman for whom the electron-photon exchange is a perverse moral dilemma. Feynman states, '[i]nstead of going directly from one point to another, the electron goes along for a while and suddenly emits a photon; (horrors!) it absorbs its own photon. Perhaps there's something "immoral" about that, but the electron does it!' (Feynman, quoted in Barad, 2012: 212). Touch is radically intimate, a promiscuous exploration of the otherness and potentiality of the void. As we *do* theory, this perversity is always in effect, and so to promiscuously touch and feel your way through worlds, as role-play does, is to dwell in this perversity.

Touch, as exposed by this account of quantum physics, is a paradigm of electromagnetic interaction. So, when role-playing, touching and being touched by the miniature gaming model, the role-playing mat, the table, the character sheet and other hands, is a matter of electromagnetic repulsion. Negatively charged electrons dance in a communicative push. Another layer of involution and convolution become apparent too, as the promiscuous electron not only exchanges a virtual photon with itself, within the void there is the possibility to interact with an infinite set of virtual particles. As Barad remarks, '*there is a virtual exploration of every possibility*' (2012: 212). Since touch, as we feel it, is the touch of electrons touching, touching themselves, then all touch is perverse, an infinitely perverse exploration of every possibility. When two parts that belong to the same entity self-touch, there emerges an encounter with the infinite otherness of the self. 'Polymorphous perversity raised to an infinite power' declares Barad, who then notes 'talk about a queer intimacy!' (2012: 213). Like a doodle, the electron can bring news from the obscure void from within which its being is so entangled. Touch is radically intimate, a promiscuous exploration of the otherness and potentiality of the void, the meeting point of two realities.

The self-touch of role-play will arouse the void in the same way, existing as Barad's superposition of uncertainty. A self-touch is radically open, yet queerly intimate. It can enliven the strangeness within, a myriad of others, and the indeterminacy and potentiality of all these touching forces becomes mutually arousing, an omnidirectional grinding. So, in this gyre, role-play works to extend the effects of the virtual and the material as much as it is composed by them. This gyre of self-touch is circulatory; it both transmits and extends. As impressions of the immanent virtual are expressed in the actualities of digital role-play, role-play will impress upon the virtual felt as, to recall McGlotten (2012), feelings of connection and sensuality. The context of scale becomes evident, role-play, scaled down to the subatomic level, mirrors the electrons that compose it, an exploration of matter and indeterminacies of the virtual. In circulation, role-play promiscuously arouses to (re)iterate the potential machinations of fantasy, gesture, media and affects. Like the electron, role-play goes along for a while and emits its own energy, which it then, at once, reabsorbs.

As energy pushes and pulls, emits and reabsorbs and is transformed, touch can be imagined as a performance, a dance that ebbs and flows. Carla Hustak and Natasha Myers write that it is momentum that 'helps us to get a feel for the affective push and pull among bodies, including the affinities, ruptures, enmeshments, and repulsions among organisms constantly inventing new ways to live with and alongside one another' (2012: 97). They understand momentum less through the lens of Newtonian physics and more through what dancers feel as they lean into, and follow, movement. These movements are affective and physical responses to energy, through momentum dancers respond to the energy of music, emotions, senses and other dancers; dance is always relational. Barad, in dialogue with Derrida, proposes that individuals 'are infinitely indebted to all others, where indebtedness is about not a debt that follows or results from a transaction but, rather, a debt that is the condition of possibility of giving/receiving' (2012: 214). Each debt mounts the relational indebtedness of all agencies and entities that is made apparent at the site of touch. Role-players may only dance with the feelings, sentiments and sensations of fictional worlds in relation to other entities. Each player in role-play is indebted to the other actors;

to give and receive is to fuel the dance. It is only through this circulation of touch that role-play can be a passionate and sincere figuring of queerly intimate play.

The momentum of performance carries substance. José Esteban Muñoz (2009) understands performance, namely queer dance, as a vast material weight that can be performed as much as performers draw sustenance from it. Like energy, queer dance never disappears or dematerializes, it only transforms and rematerializes (Muñoz 2009). Sebastian Deterding and José P. Zagal write that when we go to the theatre, read a book or watch a movie, 'bits of their fictional world may linger with us' and reemerge in role-play (2018: 1). Performance reveals the capacity for lingerings like these, alongside a myriad of other ephemeral gestures, touches and remains, to upswell and expand into material weight. To quote Muñoz once more: it 'matters to get lost in dance or to use dance to get lost: lost in the evidentiary logic of heterosexuality' (2009: 81). Role-play, dance and self-touch are all forms of momentum; they transmit energy which ricochets and transforms with gesture and movement. Between the material, the digital, the quantum, the mediatic and the affective, role-play is an energetic entanglement to get lost in, lost in the arousal, the sensations, the momentum and the promiscuity of it all.

Notes

1 Barebacking in this context is always consensual and should not be confused with non-consensual bareback sex or 'stealthing', which is the non-consensual removal of a condom, both of which are forms of sexual violence.
2 'Gyre', in this context, is a word I borrow from Rebecca Schneider. See Schneider (2019).

References

Ahmed, S. (2014), *The Cultural Politics of Emotion*, Edinburgh: Edinburgh University Press.

Barad, K. (2007), *Meeting the Universe Halfway: Quantum Physics and the Entanglement of Matter and Meaning*, Durham, NC: Duke University Press.

Barad, K. (2012), 'On Touching – The Inhuman That Therefore I Am', *Differences: A Journal of Feminist Cultural Studies*, 23 (5): 206–23.

Bennett, J. (2010), *Vibrant Matter: A Political Ecology of Things*, Durham, NC: Duke University Press.

Bennett, J. (2020), *Influx & Efflux: Writing Up with Walt Whitman*, Durham, NC: Duke University Press.

Bienia, R. (2016), *Role-Playing Materials*, Berlin: Zauberfeder Verlag.

Biswas, S. (2010), 'Possibilities for Queer Community-Building Through LARP', *First Person Scholar*, 27 March. Available online: http://www.firstpersonscholar.com/queer-larp-community/ (accessed 18 October 2021).

Chen, M. Y. (2012), *Animacies: Biopolitics, Racial Mattering, and Queer Affect*, Durham, NC: Duke University Press.

Cohen, J. J. (2003), *Medieval Identity Machines*, London: University of Minnesota Press.

Cohen, J. J. (2015), *Stone: An Ecology of Inhuman*, London: University of Minnesota Press.

Cox, J. (2018), 'Documenting Larp as an Art of Experience', *International Journal of Role-Playing*, 9: 24–30.

Cvetkovich, A. (2003), *An Archive of Feelings: Trauma, Sexuality, and Lesbian Public Cultures*, Durham, NC: Duke University Press.

Dean, T. (2009), *Unlimited Intimacy: Reflections on the Subculture of Barebacking*, London: The University of Chicago Press.

Derrida, J. (2005), *On Touching – Jean-Luc Nancy*, trans. C. Irizarry, Stanford, CA: Stanford University Press.

Deterding, S. and J. P. Zagal (2018), 'The Many Faces of Role-Playing Game Studies', in S. Deterding and J. P. Zagal (eds.), *Role-Playing Game Studies: Transmedia Foundations*, 1–16, London: Routledge.

Germaine Buckley, C. (2020), 'Encountering Weird Objects: Lovecraft, LARP, and Speculative Philosophy', in M. Rosen (ed.), *Diseases of the Head: Essays on the Horrors of Speculative Philosophy*, 361–94, Santa Barbara, CA: Punctum Books.

Giffney, N. and M. J. Hird (2008), 'Introduction: Queering the Non/Human', in Noreen Giffney and Myra J. Hird (eds), *Queering the Non/Human*, 1–16. Aldershot: Ashgate Publishing.

Grosz, E. (2017), *The Incorporeal: Ontology, Ethics, and the Limits of Materialism*, New York: Columbia University Press.

Haraway, D. J. (2016a), *Staying with the Trouble: Making Kin in the Chthulucene*, Durham, NC: Duke University Press.

Haraway, D. J. (2016b), *Manifestly Haraway*, London: University of Minnesota Press.

Hustak, C. and N. Myers (2012), 'Involuntary Momentum: Affective Ecologies and the Science of Plant/Insect Encounters', *Differences: A Journal of Feminist Cultural Studies*, 23 (3): 74–118.

Jones, A. (2002), 'Performing the Other as Self: Cindy Sherman and Laura Aguilar Pose the Subject', in S. Smith and J. Warson (eds), *Interfaces: Women, Autobiography, Image, Performance*, 69–102, Ann Arbor, MI: University of Michigan Press.

Kushinski, A. V. (2019), 'The Potential of Leaks: Mediation, Materiality, and Incontinent Domains', PhD diss., York University, York.

Luciano, D. and M. Y. Chen. (2015), 'Has the Queer Ever Been Human?', *GLQ*, 21 (2/3): 183–207.

Marks, L. (2002), *Touch: Sensuous Theory and Multisensory Media*, London: University of Minnesota Press.

McGlotten, S. (2014), *Virtual Intimacies: Media, Affect, and Queer Sociality*, New York: SUNY Press.

Muñoz, J. E. (2009), *Cruising Utopia: The Then and There of Queer Futurity*, London: New York University Press.

Nancy, J.-L. (2008), *Corpus*, trans. R. A. Rand, New York: Fordham University Press.

Parikka, J. (2015), *A Geology of Media*, London: University of Minnesota Press.

Ruberg, B. (2019), *Video Games Have Always Been Queer*, New York: New York University Press.

Schneider, R. (2019), 'Slough Remains', in I. B. Jucan, J. Parikka and R. Schneider (eds.), *Remain: In Search of Media*, 49–107, Minneapolis, MN: University of Minnesota Press.

Sihvonen, T. and J. Stenros (2019), 'On the Importance of Queer Romances – Role-play as Exploration and Performance of Sexuality', *Widerscreens*, 7 November. Available online: http://widerscreen.fi/numerot/2019-1-2/on-the-importance-of-queer-romances-role-play-as-exploration-and-performance-of-sexuality/ (accessed 18 October 2021).

Singh, J. (2018), *No Archive Will Restore You*, Santa Barbara, CA: Punctum Books.

Stenros, J. and T. Sihvonen (2015), 'Out of the Dungeons: Representations of Queer Sexuality in RPG Source Books', *Analog Game Studies*, 2 (5). Available online: https://analoggamestudies.org/2015/07/out-of-the-dungeons-representations-of-queer-sexuality-in-rpg-source-books/ (accessed 18 October 2021).

Stokes, M. (2017), 'Access to the Page: Queer and Disabled Characters in *Dungeons & Dragons*', *Analog Game Studies*, 4 (3). Available online: https://analoggamestudies.org/2017/05/access-to-the-page-queer-and-disabled-characters-in-dungeons-dragons/ (accessed 18 October 2021).

Vist, E. (2018), 'Dungeons and Queers: Reparative Play in *Dungeons & Dragons*', *First Person Scholar*, 30 May. Available online: http://www.firstpersonscholar.com/dungeons-and-queers/ (accessed 18 October 2021).

Wake, P. (2019), 'Token Gestures: A Theory of Immersion in Analog Games', *Analog Game Studies*, 6 (3). Available online: https://analoggamestudies.org/2019/09/token-gestures-towards-a-theory-of-immersion-in-analog-games/ (accessed 18 October 2021).

5

Lead fantasies

The making, meaning and materiality of miniatures

Mikko Meriläinen, Katriina Heljakka and Jaakko Stenros

Introduction

In this chapter, we discuss the pastime of what we call *miniaturing*, or engaging with miniature figures (see Meriläinen, Stenros and Heljakka 2020). It is formed around a dual core or organized activities around crafting (e.g. painting and modifying miniatures) and gaming, although storytelling, collecting, socializing and appreciating also feature. Miniaturing is not just gaming with miniatures but instead encompasses the wide range of activities in the pastime, including gaming. As implied by the name of the pastime, it pivots around the material miniature figurine. However, miniaturists have different orientations towards miniatures, which both overlap and conflict with each other.

In the context of this chapter, we define miniatures as scaled-down metal or plastic representations of historical and fictional characters, creatures and objects, typically used for gaming and display purposes. They are usually either single-part or otherwise non-poseable after construction. Miniatures come in different sizes, also referred to as scales, usually using the height of a typical humanoid character in millimetres for reference. Common sizes for gaming are 10 mm, 15 mm and especially the loosely defined 28–32 mm bracket, while larger sizes such as 54 mm and 75 mm typically find more use as display pieces.

Miniaturing is a particularly material pastime. Enthusiasts collect miniatures and their components, construct and paint them and use them for building dioramas. Miniatures are used as tokens in fantasy and historical gaming, displayed in glass cabinets and shared online as pictures, and stored – sometimes in purpose-built cases, sometimes in generic storage boxes. The unpainted miniatures are raw material, a valued treasure, but sometimes also a 'pile of shame' of excessive consumption and stalled projects (Meriläinen, Stenros and Heljakka 2022).

The pastime features a constant interplay of the material and the immaterial: the miniature serves as a focus for activities, and the activities contextualize the miniature. Stories about games are told and written, miniatures are customized to correspond to narratives, and specific miniatures inspire creation of fiction. Other hobbyists' miniatures, photographs, dioramas and stories are appreciated, and many enthusiasts engage with a broader transmedia landscape (see Keidl 2018), for example playing digital games or reading books that expand the universe of their miniatures.

In this chapter, we explore miniaturing, paying particular attention to the tangible miniature and the activities, material implements and spaces surrounding it. We ground our chapter in a thematic analysis of open-ended questionnaire responses by adult Finnish miniaturists, which we further discuss in the light of Heljakka's (2020) framework that explores the physical, functional, fictional and affective dimensions of object play.

Background

Although the roots of modern-day miniaturing can be traced back to the eighteenth-century *Kriegsspiel* tradition and the incorporation of tin soldiers in wargames during the nineteenth century, a more relevant anchoring point for the respondents in this study is the emergence of fantasy role-playing games from historical miniature wargames in the 1970s, leading to the release of the miniature gaming ruleset *Warhammer: The Mass Combat Fantasy Role-playing Game*, designed by Bryan Ansell, Richard Halliwell and Rick Priestley in 1983 (Meriläinen, Stenros and Heljakka 2020; see also Hyde 2013; Livingstone 1983). Since then, miniaturing has grown massively both in variety and commercially, and there are now hundreds of manufacturers and rulesets available.

Miniaturing has received limited research attention, with studies primarily focusing on the gaming aspect instead of the pastime more broadly (see Meriläinen, Stenros and Heljakka 2020). However, because of the overlapping and interlinked activities (e.g. Carter, Gibbs and Harrop 2014), including gaming, inherent in miniaturing, these previous studies also provide us with important insight into the pastime more generally.

A unifying thread in the existing research is the blending and weaving together of a variety of activities and approaches, happening on both the broader level of the pastime and inside individual aspects, such as gaming (Carter, Gibbs and Harrop 2014). Another blending together is that of different media, for example digital adaptations of miniature games (Kankainen 2016), the sharing of miniature photos online (Meriläinen, Stenros and Heljakka 2020) and linking miniatures to broader transmedial wholes (Booth 2015; Keidl 2018). Miniaturing is a diverse pastime, and people engage in it for many different reasons (Körner and Schütz 2021; Körner, Kammerhoff and Schütz 2021).

Materiality is central to miniaturing, as the pastime revolves around the physical miniatures and their different uses, from crafting to gaming and from doll play to storytelling. These partially overlapping activities are culturally framed in ways that create tension. While framings of miniaturing, for example, gaming, play or crafting, can render parts of the pastime legible, they are not fully shared between participants. The competing framings have different cultural valuation attached to them. For example, seeing miniaturing as toy play is particularly contested.

Revolving around physical miniatures, specialized tools and gaming rulesets, miniaturing is highly commercial. Games Workshop, currently the dominant force in miniaturing owning the global *Warhammer* brand (see Cova, Pace and Park 2007), is a publicly listed company with a revenue of £353.2 million in 2021 (Games Workshop Group 2021), while Reaper Miniatures' hugely successful Kickstarter campaigns for their Bones line of plastic miniatures have each drawn millions of US dollars in crowdfunding (e.g. Kickstarter 2021). Although miniatures can be bought second-hand and modern manufacturing processes allow for a cheaper product, miniaturing can be an expensive hobby, its cost limiting participation (Carter, Gibbs and Harrop 2014).

Miniatures are brought to life not only by industry producers but also by productive enthusiasts – hobbyists, gamers and players. Traditional tools, such as paint brushes, knives and files are used to paint and customize miniatures, while modern technologies allow digital sculpting and 3D printing of new miniatures. The emergence of so-called maker cultures connects miniaturing to the broader whole of material-digital toy cultures. Just like adult toy enthusiasts are interested in dolls and action figures, players of all ages express an interest in crafting and tinkering with miniatures, customizing industrially produced toys, then employing them as part of visual, photographed displays and finally sharing the photography online. In this way, users become makers whose activities manifest through material creativity and related skill-building practices and link to online communities (Heljakka 2015; Heljakka and Harviainen 2019). This aesthetic dimension of miniatures relates to perceptions of them not only as playthings suitable for game play but also as (art)works demanding investments of time, space and dedication from their users. Miniatures are valued because of their materiality and visuality, both contributing to their functionality: their playability and their use as decorative items.

Method and data

This chapter explores miniaturing through data collected in 2019 using a qualitative Finnish language online questionnaire with seven open questions and six demographic questions. The questionnaire was distributed on social media (Facebook groups, hobby forums, Twitter), resulting in a total of 127 answers.

Previous studies (Körner and Schütz 2021; Singleton 2021) have suggested that most people engaging in miniaturing are men. This is echoed in our data, as only 7.9 per cent ($N = 10$) of the respondents identified as women, while 91.3 per cent ($N = 116$) identified as men and one participant (0.8 per cent) did not disclose the information. The minimum age for participation was 18, and respondent age ranged from 18 to 56, with a mean of 35.7 and a median of 35. Respondents reported a broad range of starting years for miniaturing, from 1970 to 2018. The median year was 1998, suggesting a sample with plenty of experience of the pastime, even taking into account the long breaks that many respondents reported. This expert knowledge contributed to a rich data set with long and detailed answers from many of the respondents.

The data were explored using thematic analysis, a flexible method to systematically identify and organize qualitative data into patterns of meaning or themes (Braun and Clarke 2006). We conducted our analysis primarily on the semantic level, focusing on what the respondents explicitly wrote, instead of exploring the underlying assumptions and ideologies informing their responses. We had performed a thematic analysis on the data previously (Meriläinen, Stenros and Heljakka 2020) but supplemented it with a new analysis; whereas the initial analysis, and the related publication, explored the miniaturing pastime in general, our new analysis focused specifically on the materiality of miniaturing. While this chapter and our previous publication draw from the same data and share parts of the analysis, they are two distinct, original studies with a different focus.

The results of the questionnaire were coded using the Atlas.ti 8 software. Our codes and themes are derived from the data (see Braun and Clarke 2006) rather than from a pre-existing theoretical frame. We placed extra focus on responses that addressed the physical, material dimensions of miniaturing. This process resulted in fifty-six individual codes, which were then combined into five themes, each highlighting a different dimension miniatures: *Miniatures as objects, Material for crafting and self-expression, Toys* or *gaming pieces?, Display objects and works of art* and *Vessels and prompts for dreams and imagination.*

Results

In the following sections, we discuss the five themes constructed. Each theme has been illustrated with quotes from the data, translated from Finnish by the authors. Minor changes, such as punctuation and capitalization, have been made as part of the translation process, but we have sought to retain the original tone and wording as closely as possible. Respondent IDs have been reported after the quotes.

Miniatures as objects

As defined in this chapter, a miniature is first and foremost a physical, material object occupying a space in the world. While all the other aspects identified in our analysis are optional, this ubiquitous dimension of the miniature cannot be ignored. Here, we focus primarily on the space and money required for miniaturing, while the physical manipulation of miniatures is discussed under the theme of *Material for crafting and self-expression.*

Although marginally discussed in our data, the miniature life cycle starts before they reach consumers: they are sculpted physically or digitally, moulded, cast or printed, stored, packaged and shipped. Construction material also plays a part. Originally, miniatures had a high lead content, needing extra care when handling. After the mid-1990s move to reduce lead, miniatures have been increasingly produced in lead-free alloys and different plastics. Even so, 'lead' is still a common word to refer to miniatures among enthusiasts. While affecting the tactile qualities of miniatures such as weight, the material component also introduces potential hazards, from operating with molten metal to inhaling resin dust to contact with a variety of glues, resins, putties and solvents.

The miniature itself is material, and it also prompts a variety of other activities which introduce new requirements. Miniaturing activities require space and time, and bring with them the need for tools, paints, rulebooks and storage solutions; acquiring miniatures and materials is often a major part of the pastime (Meriläinen, Stenros and Heljakka 2022). Most of this material costs money, and many of our respondents reflected on their shopping behaviour, sometimes referring even to hoarding.

> The greatest part [of the pastime] is thinking up new projects and finishing them. The most horrifying part is the realization that there are dozens of projects stalled half-way lying about in the cupboard. In general hoarding instead of the actual hobby is a little sick. (ID27)

> I buy minis and miniature games and painting-related products a little too much. Kickstarter [crowdfunding platform] has been in heavy use and there's a shameful amount of backlog. Buying is not financially problematic but rather that I tend to acquire too much material compared to what I could ever realistically use. (ID71)

The collected miniatures need storage space, and once they are put together and painted, the space requirements increase. As delicate objects, the finished figures are prone to breaking, bending and paint chipping. While unpainted miniatures can be stored more carelessly, after construction, and especially painting, they need purpose-built storage and possibly display solutions that take up more room. As the pastime takes up space, it can create tensions with other family members.

> My partner doesn't quite understand my hobby and feels that I own too much stuff related to it. It annoys them that I have many boxes full of miniatures, but nevertheless they support me in my hobby, they just wish there wasn't so much stuff. It is because of this that I keep my minis hidden in the basement and advertise it when I finish something or sell it off (meaning there is less stuff). (ID130)

> I've found that the best solution for someone with children is that I paint in the living room at the dinner table, so I'm at the centre of family activities and in principle present. This means that all the stuff has to be put together and taken apart before and after the session. Every evening. I live in a detached house so there's more than enough space, but isolating myself from the family and kids causes so much grumbling, it's better to just settle for a temporary solution. (ID5)

> I have my own room for crafts and working. This was an important criterion back when I was choosing a home, modern places don't really tend to have space for any sort of handicrafts. I have time for crafting on weeknights and weekends. I spend maybe 700-800 hours painting on a good year. The living room glass cabinet has some minis on display, but most are stored away. My collection consists of a little over 6000 painted minis. (ID32)

Finding ways to weave the pastime into quotidian family life may require skill, planning, financial means and material solutions. Some informants had put together their miniaturing and crafting material in a modular way for easy moving and storing, while others had a dedicated space, with special tools and equipment.

Material for crafting and self-expression

The crafting side of miniaturing is essentially material: it revolves around not only the physical model itself but also the materials and tools used to modify and paint it. We have previously identified crafting as the most important core component of miniaturing (Meriläinen, Stenros and Heljakka 2020), and it features prominently in our data.

Crafting is not just painting: after the removal of mould lines and other casting artefacts, a miniature often requires construction – gluing pieces together, sometimes reinforcing joints with metal wire and using putties to smooth over gaps and minor defects. It is common to combine pieces from different sources to create a single, unique miniature, and there is an entire sub-industry creating individual components, such as heads or weapons, for *converting* (customizing) miniatures.

Miniatures receive multiple layers of paint using different paints and inks deployed with brushes, sponges, spray cans and air brushes. Additional material, such as sand and synthetic grass, can be added to the miniature's base, the plastic or metal stand the miniature is attached to, to create texture and visual interest. Crafting is also present in the building and modification of scenery, such as hills, forests and buildings. These are used for both gaming and displaying purposes. Dioramas, narrative vignettes of figures in a setting, are also created.

An important and often reported aspect of crafting is the meditative state the long sessions of intense but relaxing concentration induce. Informants referred to painting as almost a meditative practice or something inducing a state of 'flow' (Nakamura and Csikszentmihalyi 2002) in which everyday concerns are forgotten and sense of time is lost. Some considered painting and modifying miniatures as their primary avenue of creative self-expression and enjoyed developing their painting and modelling skills.

> The best moment is probably when I've noticed that I actually can paint and the moments in which you realize you've been painting for several hours without any outside thoughts or anxiety over work. (ID18)

[There is] a certain trance that comes from perfectly focusing on the miniature being painted. (ID5)

Crafting served as an important and necessary bridge between an imagined idea, such as a character concept, and a finished piece. One respondent, discussing their engagement with *The Lord of the Rings* miniature game (Games Workshop 2001) described this process of transformation:

Mostly it's working with your hands; a piece of metal and the contents of paint pots turn into a knight of Dol Amroth, or balsa wood and fake fur into a Rohan house. (ID119)

Crafting is a concrete and creative activity that requires significant time investment and concentration that can become meditative. In addition to being enjoyable in itself, painting and other crafting also tied to many of the other aspects: after painting, miniatures often find use in games or as display pieces.

Toys or gaming pieces?

The physicality of the objects relating to miniaturing is undeniable and the core of crafting is pervasively recognized by our informants, yet the *use* of the miniatures and how this use frames miniaturing are contested questions. For some of our informants miniatures were toys that one plays with, whereas for others the miniatures were implements for games and gaming. As Dan Fleming (1996) observes, a (plastic) plaything is a complex object and recognizing it as a toy is an act of recognition dependent on settings, prior experience and culturally derived associations.

Miniaturing features plenty of play and playful behaviour, in line with what Roger Caillois has termed *paidia*, characterized by 'free improvisation' and 'carefree gaiety' (2001: 13). It is relevant to note that in Finnish, the language of the questionnaire, there is a clear linguistic difference between 'play that one plays' and 'games that one games', similar to Caillois's distinction between *paidia* and *ludus*. A simplification sufficient for the purposes of this chapter is that in Finnish, 'play' is something done with toys, and it is culturally connected to children's play, whereas 'gaming' is associated with games, which is regarded as more of an adolescent and adult pursuit. Numerous informants specifically discussed 'playing' instead of 'gaming' in their responses. Playing took different forms, from imagining back stories to the characters to making shooting noises while gaming and playing with miniatures with one's children. In children's play with toy soldiers and figures, a great deal of time is spent arranging and looking at them (Hellendoorn and Harinck 1999), an activity also reported by our adult respondents.

> Miniatures and miniature games are toys, like console or board games and their components. Gaming with miniatures is playing. And when I think about it, converting and painting them is also play. For me at least. (ID104)

> I mainly try to play games with my minis, but on the other hand it gives me great satisfaction arranging my hundreds of little people in parade and drill formations on the table. (ID118)

> I play with miniatures with the child (5 years old) occasionally, and they have shown great interest towards them. They've helped me basecoat several miniatures. The problem is that most of the miniatures in my collection are metal and thus suffer from paint easily coming loose when playing. When this happens the child gets frustrated easily and is embarrassed by the damage caused. I believe, however, that they'll remain interested in miniaturing and that as they grow up they'll find a suitably gentle touch to playing and later gaming with them. (ID22)

Aspects of miniaturing can be seen as toy play (Meriläinen, Stenros and Heljakka 2020), and some respondents explicitly referred to their miniatures as toys, echoing the term 'man dollies' used by some of the wargamers interviewed by Mitchell Harrop, Martin Gibbs and Marcus Carter (2013). The innate 'toyness' of miniatures relates to their materiality in multiple ways: although miniatures are seldom articulated and have limited poseability and resulting play value (Keidl 2018), the use-value of miniatures also derives from their aesthetic dimension.

The other approach to miniatures was rooted in the denial of freeform, frolicsome, childish play, and instead connected to what Caillois calls *ludus*. These informants saw playing with miniatures more as gaming or game playing with miniatures, that is structured, rule-constrained play. Some respondents viewed miniatures mainly as gaming pieces, sometimes referring to them as 'tokens'. This approach frames miniatures through their functional, utilitarian value as carefully constructed, custom made game pieces. However, aesthetics and function are not disconnected in miniaturing, as in some miniature wargaming tournaments contestants receive points for the outlook of their army (Carter, Gibbs and Harrop 2014). In addition to playing miniature games, a typical approach was using miniatures as part of role-playing games. Here, the miniatures were in a more peripheral role, while the core of the game was in the discussion and role-playing:

> I game with minis. I don't really put together or paint anything that I don't need for a future game/campaign/tournament. . . . Building, converting, painting [of miniatures], and building scenery come with it, but without gaming I wouldn't do them either. (ID11)

> The RPG is social, but in that the mini could just as well be a coin for all I care (although the mini does help with character immersion). . . . Painting is occasionally fun and a mini is a good token. That's all. (ID112)

The tension between more playful and game-like framings for miniatures is clearly a known and acknowledged source of tension and discussion in miniaturing cultures. Some respondents who foreground game-related aspects of miniaturing actively reject the more playful framings and self-expressive activities. Some respondents explicitly mentioned not being invested in the 'fluff', or background narrative. Instead, models were bought mainly for gaming use and stored in boxes that allowed for easy transportation and unpacking for gaming, after which they went back into storage (see also Kankainen 2016).

However, while there is a tension between these two approaches, most informants had no trouble combining the free play and fantasy with rule-governed game playing. Some explicitly challenged the distinction between gaming and playing. This echoes previous findings (Carter, Gibbs and Harrop 2014; Singleton 2021), showing plenty of play and playful behaviour also in the context of tournament miniature gaming, arguably the epitome of rule-governed game play with miniatures.

> I like to describe my gaming in a 'I play with little figurines' style. I'm even a little serious about it. Of course there need to be rules, but this is play after all. (ID21)

> In a way I both play and don't play with minis. If I have magnetized a part of a mini [attaching a part such as an arm with a magnet], I may move it around for fun. In a game I turn the turrets of tanks to point at the enemy, and may yell out 'boom' and roll dice. Maybe this is play? (ID114)

From the point of view of materiality this distinction between the miniature as a toy for playing and a token for gaming has relevance, as the most central aspect of games is usually seen as being the rules (Stenros 2017). A game piece in and of itself is something seen as insignificant; the so-called *rules of irrelevance* state that it does not matter if a chess piece is a beautiful piece carved from ivory or if it is a stone you found in your shoe (Goffman 1961). On the other hand, with toys the materiality of the toy is important, as are the physical affordances that the piece provides (Gibson 1986). The gaming piece is, from the point of formalism, defined by its affordance within the rules of the game. In actual practice this division is obviously not this strict, as our data shows. Also, many miniature games and tournaments advocate for miniatures to be accurate representations of characters in terms of equipment, obstacles and line of sight can matter in game play, and so on. The miniature, as a crafted game token, does carry communication from the player who has created and is using it (Wasserman 2020). Even so, the materiality of an object tends to be, in comparison, deprioritized when it is framed as a game token instead of a toy.

Display objects and works of art

Miniatures provide tactile and sensuous pleasure – they can be tiny, yet have weight, they have shapes and textures offering haptic interest, and they may have a scent depending on their raw material or paint. Miniatures materialize simultaneously as both products of industry design and machinery and personal handicrafts.

Because of the centrality of crafting and aesthetics in miniaturing, it is unsurprising that respondents often discussed their miniatures as something visually pleasing and as objects to be displayed. It was common to display models in glass cabinets, sometimes prominently in the home, and to share pictures of painted miniatures online. Respondents who enjoyed the crafting aspect of the pastime commonly bought miniatures without intention of playing or gaming with them. Instead, miniatures were bought to be painted and displayed.

> We are like visual artists hiding in ateliers: we do our creative work largely in solitude and as if in secret from the rest of the world. However, in the end the final products are always displayed to the public. The finished artworks are placed in a visible spot in the glass cabinet of the bookcase (suitably close to J. R. R. Tolkien's works), the rest in storage boxes and cases at the bottom of the cupboard or in the storeroom. (ID111)

Some respondents likened their miniatures to art pieces. Single figurines and dioramas are certainly objects that are created to be looked at, and there are artists working in fine art whose works have a clear aesthetic connection to miniaturing. For example, the snowglobe works of Walter Martin and Paloma Muñoz (see Lethem, Martin and Muñoz 2008) and Jake and Dinos Chapman's works such as *Old Kent Road* (2014) and *Ship of Fools* (2009) feature intricately crafted fantastical miniature dioramas reminiscent of those created by miniaturists. However, the idea of the miniature as an art piece links miniatures more closely with designer toys, which to many adults are only 'playable' in terms of dis-*playing* them. As one respondent writes:

> I think of my minis mostly as collectable art pieces. They don't really have any practical function after they're 'done'. And there are thousands both painted and unpainted. While I do have a webpage with photos of finished minis, even those have been photographed immediately after painting in a fairly static environment and then 'archived' on the shelf. (ID15)

Here, the respondent's comment echoes Phoenix's (2006: 27) observation that designer toys are usually made to be displayed instead of played with. While miniatures signal invitations to the many forms of object play discussed in this chapter, such as imaginative scenarios and *photoplay*, narrative and artistic photography with a storytelling capacity (Heljakka 2012), they are often static in their form. Because of this they may not be considered to have similar dynamic potential as action figures and dolls would due to their articulation and poseability.

While there is limited research on displaying miniatures, many activities in miniaturing parallel those of *dolling*, or pastimes of adult doll players. Dolls such as *Barbie*, *Pullip* and *Blythes* are first personalized, then displayed and even *photoplayed* (Heljakka 2012) by their players.

> Having the miniatures on display in the living room glass cabinets and sometimes on a play table set for kids is an important part of miniaturing. The minis on display spark discussions with both familiar miniaturists and those less knowledgeable about the hobby. (ID27)

> Photographing games and sharing pictures with friends is also an exciting part of the hobby. . . . I appreciate crafting skills, great painting and stylish set pieces. Finished armies with created backstories. Thus I don't think minis can be called toys, although of course you can take great photos of toy setups like *Star Wars* plastic figures or *Lego*. (ID28)

The miniature as a displayed item in domestic space allows communication that occurs between the miniature and the player, but when the photography is shared, the activity becomes reciprocal – a dialogue between the displayer or enthusiast and their peers. Displaying and photographing miniatures can also be seen as a way of preserving and documenting miniaturing culture.

Vessels and prompts for dreams and imagination

Miniatures are designed to spark the imagination. Models are sculpted with facial expressions and often in dramatic action poses: swinging swords, reloading guns and casting spells. Even without further context, through their posing and features such as gear, expression and other details, a 30 mm tall miniature can in itself tell a story.

While it is conceivable that ready-made physical miniatures, pre-existing narratives and a set canon could constrain imagination and creativity, our data suggests the opposite. While some historical miniature enthusiasts strove for historical accuracy and exact representation, they also came up with dramatic narratives for gaming scenarios grounded in actual historical events. For many of our respondents, it was the considerable role of imagination that made miniaturing special. Physical miniatures and photographs of them served as a spark for the imagination. Imagining took place both when planning a new project and while crafting the models. Miniatures and entire armies were sometimes imbued with backstories, also reflected in their painting and other crafting, tying into the toy aspects discussed earlier. This melding of the crafting and imagining aspects echoes Brian Sutton-Smith's (1986) claims that creativity and flexibility are derivatives of the imagination and that imaginative play is a celebration of our personal originality (Sutton-Smith 2008).

> Without the fiction related to miniaturing I think miniaturing would lose something that separates it from 'regular' board games and toys. Minis are after all just toys and gaming tokens. (ID80)

> Narrative strongly connects to it. I rarely write down stories, but they always develop in my mind as I paint and craft. Maybe the most important aspect is giving imagined things concrete form. (ID34)

Aspects of dreaming and imagining were not limited to individual miniatures or the gaming or crafting session. Respondents consumed media connected to their miniature projects, turning their miniaturing into a transmedia (Booth 2015; Keidl 2018) experience. Although fiction connected to the *Warhammer* franchise and published by Games Workshop's Black Library was most commonly mentioned, the same phenomenon was present with historical miniature gamers grounding their projects in non-fiction detailing their period of choice. Here, the miniature becomes a physical focus for a much greater whole: while a piece of plastic or metal, it is also a character occupying a space in a much larger imagined story.

The world of [*Warhammer 40,000* miniature game] in its harshness instantly sucked me in and I'm staying . . . I've gotten tattoos related to WH40k, I read Black Library books, I may write stories etc. Then there's of course assembly and modelling, painting etc. The 'solid core' lies in the story of the world of Warhammer 40k, the lore. [It's a v]ery complex and interesting world. For me everything else supports this. (ID66)

Discussing wargames, James Dunnigan (1997) explains how it can be enough for a player of wargames to just read the rules, examine the pieces and perhaps place them on a map, which enables experiencing the dynamic potential of the game without actually playing it. A similar sentiment was expressed by one of the respondents regarding miniature projects:

I follow gaming communities quite a lot and my actual hobbying includes a research part, during which I read fiction, rules, army lists, and tactics, before I start a new project. Sometimes I do this, even though I have no intention of starting said collection, instead I play with the thought. (ID52)

Especially in the case of imagining background stories and personalities for miniatures, there is a close connection to and overlap with play, as discussed earlier. As Peter Gray (2015) states, whenever adults imagine and create, they are to some degree playing. We could reverse this thinking and argue that whenever adults play with material entities, such as miniatures, they are to some extent imagining.

It doesn't matter if an elf's sword snaps in the middle of a campaign – it's battle damage and a reminder, and I don't usually even fix them, but let the wear and tear of use show in the minis. (ID7)

The fiction and the physical miniature exist in symbiosis: the figurine can be an expression of the fiction, crafting it both a physical and an imaginative act. Reciprocally, what happens to the miniature in crafting and in play feed back into the fiction. The miniature thus acts as a *prop* (Bateman 2011; Walton 1990) for imagining; it prescribes imaginings. What happens to the prop also happens within the fiction, according to some translation rules.

Physical, functional, fictional and affective

Our study describes the plural uses of miniatures. To theorize the dimensions of miniatures as objects with affordances allowing and inviting many kinds of actions, we use the framework interested in the experiential dimensions of object play. This framework (Heljakka 2020) comprehends the physical, functional, fictional and affective dimensions of experiences with artefacts associated with playful manipulation, such as toys (see Figure 5.1). As understandings of what miniatures are extend beyond toys and toy-like game pieces, we acknowledge the multiple uses of figurines, both in terms of physical manipulation as well as their capacity to set the imagination in motion, and to inspire personal reflections and social dialogues due to their nature as playthings, conversational objects and contemplative artworks.

Our analysis demonstrates how many of the uses of miniatures are grounded in the *physicality* of miniatures. However, before they become playable, they manifest mentally as objects of desire: miniatures are dreamt of, yearned for and designed in the mind's eye before they materialize by their manufacturers and makers. Imagination plays a significant role in this process, and it is only the limits of adult imagination that constrain what is to be done with the miniatures once they have taken their form.

The *functionality* of miniatures depends on the aspiration of their users, as demonstrated by our informants' diverse descriptions of their miniaturing. Besides being crafted items, miniatures may be collected, used for open-ended, paidic play, employing them as toys for imaginative use or for playing games in the sense of ludic play, making them functional in the context of game play. Our results show that both players and gamers tend to appreciate miniatures as displayable items with aesthetic value to which space and logistic considerations

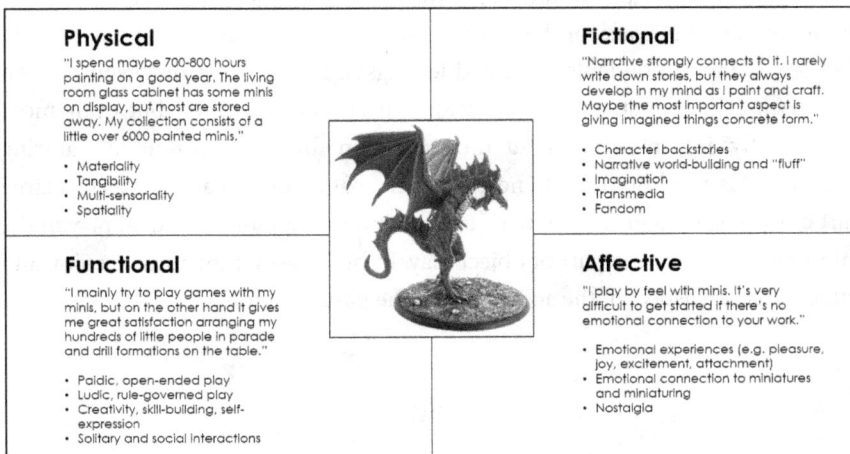

Physical

"I spend maybe 700-800 hours painting on a good year. The living room glass cabinet has some minis on display, but most are stored away. My collection consists of a little over 6000 painted minis."

• Materiality
• Tangibility
• Multi-sensoriality
• Spatiality

Fictional

"Narrative strongly connects to it. I rarely write down stories, but they always develop in my mind as I paint and craft. Maybe the most important aspect is giving imagined things concrete form."

• Character backstories
• Narrative world-building and "fluff"
• Imagination
• Transmedia
• Fandom

Functional

"I mainly try to play games with my minis, but on the other hand it gives me great satisfaction arranging my hundreds of little people in parade and drill formations on the table."

• Paidic, open-ended play
• Ludic, rule-governed play
• Creativity, skill-building, self-expression
• Solitary and social interactions

Affective

"I play by feel with minis. It's very difficult to get started if there's no emotional connection to your work."

• Emotional experiences (e.g. pleasure, joy, excitement, attachment)
• Emotional connection to miniatures and miniaturing
• Nostalgia

Figure 5.1 The experiential dimensions of object play. Photograph by Mikko Meriläinen.

are provided. Miniaturists find clever solutions to display, store and move their miniatures around in and between spaces of use, both domestic and public. Miniatures find their way to photographed archives of collections, demonstrative and tutorial images of paint jobs and photoplay. In this way, miniatures afford creative activities built around skill-building and artistry in the present, as well as play value with completed miniature characters, meaning their employment as part of static displays or dioramas (see, for example, Heljakka and Harviainen 2019), or the more dynamic contexts of gaming arenas.

The *fictionality* of miniatures has significance to many. Miniatures have relationships to narratives: they usually represent characters that come with a certain physiognomy and attire related to either human history or fantastic storyworlds. Thanks to the creativity, skills and artistry of miniaturists, industry-made backstories for miniatures are continued, contested and contrasted with enthusiasts' own ideas about what kind of characters best serve them in terms of appearance. In addition to choosing paint schemes, many miniaturists are eager to make conversions to produce unique characters assembled from pieces of other miniatures and purpose-produced conversion parts. The fictionality of miniatures also stems from 'fluff' created by gaming companies to support and expand their gameworlds and written by miniaturists themselves as a form of fan-fic.

Finally, the *affectivity* associated with both miniatures and miniaturing relates to the miniaturists' emotional relationships to their beloved artefacts, and the communities that make them functional in various ways. As Kankainen (2016) has pointed out, miniatures can offer an anchor for emotional attachment. It is in the context of this experiential dimension that caring for and cultivating collections of miniatures takes place, or the appreciation of special, individual pieces come to the fore. Many respondents described feelings of nostalgia for their youth when reminiscing their firsthand encounters with specific figurines, but even more prominently, informed us about their affection for their current miniaturing activities. It is also important to note the social nature of miniaturing, as to a large part of the respondents the miniature is either a prompt for individual play of the mind or a prop used as part of object play. In both cases, miniaturists enjoy and value the social aspect of the activities that the pastime affords.

Coda

Miniaturing is a pastime that has a dual core of crafting and gaming activities, yet both activities pivot around the physical, material miniature. Miniatures are crafted to fit specific fictional worlds and different genres. They can be bought and sold, downloaded and printed, collected and hoarded, re-sold and re-imagined, stored and treasured, and fantasized about and imagined with for years and decades before being constructed. Unique pieces are created by combining parts of figurines, crafted with care with knives, glue, brushes and paints. The sites of miniature construction, storage, display and play shape the living space, influence the purchase of homes and create tensions in families. The finished pieces are displayed in cabinets and online, toyed and imagined with and used as gaming pieces. The physical figurines have numerous functions that are practical, fictional and deeply affective.

References

Bateman, C. (2011), *Imaginary Games*, Winchester: Zero Books.

Booth, P. (2015), *Game Play: Paratextuality in Contemporary Board Games*, New York and London: Bloomsbury Academic.

Braun, V. and V. Clarke (2006), 'Using Thematic Analysis in Psychology', *Qualitative Research in Psychology*, 3 (2): 77–101.

Caillois, R. (2001 [1958]), *Man, Play and Games*, trans. M. Barash, Champaign: University of Illinois Press.

Carter, M., M. Gibbs and M. Harrop (2014), 'Drafting an Army: The Playful Pastime of *Warhammer 40,000*', *Games and Culture*, 9 (2): 122–47.

Cova, B., S. Pace and D. J. Park (2007), 'Global Brand Communities across Borders: The Warhammer Case', *International Marketing Review*, 24 (3): 313–29.

Dunnigan, J. F. (1997), *The Complete Wargames Handbook*, 3rd edn. Available online: http://www.professionalwargaming.co.uk/Complete-Wargames-Handbook -Dunnigan.pdf (accessed 7 October 2021).

Fleming, D. (1996), *Powerplay. Toys as Popular Culture*, Manchester: Manchester University Press.

Games Workshop Group (2021), 'Annual Report 2021'. Available online: https://investor .games-workshop.com/wp-content/uploads/2021/07/2020-21-accounts-full-report -cover.pdf (accessed 7 October 2021).

Gibson, J. J. (1986), *The Ecological Approach to Visual Perception*, New York: Psychology Press.

Goffman, E. (1961), *Encounters: Two Studies in the Sociology of Interaction*, Indianapolis, IN: Bobbs-Merrill.

Gray, P. (2015). 'Studying Play Without Calling It That', in J. Johnson, S. G. Eberle, T. S. Henricks and D. Kuschner (eds), *The Handbook of the Study of Play*, 121–38, Lanham, MD: Rowman & Littlefield.

Harrop, M., M. Gibbs and M. Carter (2013), 'Everyone's a Winner at Warhammer 40K (or, at Least not a Loser)', *DiGRA 2013 - Proceedings of the 2013 DiGRA International Conference: DeFragging GameStudies*. Available online: http://www.digra.org/wp-content/uploads/digital-library/paper_169.pdf (accessed 7 October 2021).

Heljakka, K. (2012), 'Aren't You a Doll! Toying with Avatars in Digital Playgrounds', *Journal of Gaming & Virtual Worlds*, 4 (2): 153–70.

Heljakka, K. (2015), 'Toys as Tools for Skill-building and Creativity in Adult Life', *Seminar.Net*, 11 (2). https://doi.org/10.7577/seminar.2356.

Heljakka, K. (2020), 'Pandemic Toy Play Against Social Distancing: Teddy Bears, Window-Screens and Playing for the Common Good in Times of Self-isolation', *WiderScreen*. Available online: http://widerscreen.fi/numerot/ajankohtaista/pandemic-toy-play-against-social-distancing-teddy-bears-window-screens-and-playing-for-the-common-good-in-times-of-self-isolation/ (accessed 7 October 2021).

Heljakka, K. and J. T. Harviainen (2019), 'From Displays and Dioramas to Doll Dramas: Adult World Building and World Playing with Toys', *American Journal of Play*, 11 (3): 351–78.

Hellendoorn, J. and F. J. H. Harinck (1999), 'War Toy Play as Reflection of Family Culture', in L.-E. Berg, A. Nelson and K. Svensson (eds), *Toys in Educational and Socio-Cultural Context. Selection of papers presented at the International Toy Research Conference, Halmstad University, Sweden June, 1996*, 245–61, Stockholm: Kungliga Tekniska Högskolan.

Hyde, H. (2013), *The Wargaming Compendium*, Barnsley: Pen & Sword.

Kankainen, V. (2016), 'The Interplay of Two Worlds in *Blood Bowl*: Implications for Hybrid Board Game Design', 13th International Conference on Advances in Computer Entertainment Technology, Article No. 8. ACM. Available online: https://trepo.tuni.fi/handle/10024/117127 (accessed 7 October 2021).

Keidl, P. D. (2018), 'Between Textuality and Materiality: Fandom and the Mediation of Action Figures', *Film Criticism*, 42 (2).

Kickstarter (2021), 'Reaper Miniatures Bones 5: Escape from Pizza Dungeon'. Available online: https://www.kickstarter.com/projects/reaperbones5/reaper-miniatures-bones-5-escape-from-pizza-dungeon (accessed 7 October 2021).

Körner, R., J. Kammerhoff and A. Schütz (2021), 'Who Commands the Little Soldiers?: A Comparison of the Personality Traits of Miniature Wargame Players with Other Gamers and Non-Gamers', *Journal of Individual Differences*, 42 (1): 19–29.

Körner, R. and A. Schütz (2021), 'It is Not All for the Same Reason! Predicting Motives in Miniature Wargaming on the Basis of Personality Traits', *Personality and Individual Differences*, 173.

Lethem, J., W. Martin and P. Muñoz (2008), *Travelers*, New York: Aperture.

Livingstone, I. (1983), *Dicing with Dragons. An Introduction to Role-Playing Games*, New York: Plume.

Meriläinen, M., J. Stenros and K. Heljakka (2020), 'More Than Wargaming: Exploring the Miniaturing Pastime', *Simulation and Gaming*.

Meriläinen, M., J. Stenros and K. Heljakka (2022), 'The Pile of Shame: The Personal and Social Sustainability of Collecting and Hoarding Miniatures', in S. S. Muthu (ed.), *Toys and Sustainability*, 57–77, Singapore: Springer.

Nakamura, J. and M. Csikszentmihalyi (2002), 'The Concept of Flow', in C. R. Snyder and S. J. Lopez (eds), *Handbook of Positive Psychology*, 89–105, New York: Oxford University Press.

Phoenix, W. (2006), *Plastic Culture. How Japanese Toys Conquered the World*, Tokyo: Kodansha International.

Singleton, B. E. (2021), '"We Offer Nuffle a Sausage Sacrifice on Game Day." Blood Bowl Players' World-building Rituals through the Lens of Theory of Sociocultural Viability', *Journal of Contemporary Ethnography*, 50 (2): 176–201.

Stenros, J. (2017), 'The Game Definition Game: A Review', *Games and Culture*, 12 (6): 499–520.

Sutton-Smith, B. (1986), *Toys as Culture*, New York: Gardner Press.

Sutton-Smith, B. (2008),'Beyond Ambiguity', in F. Brown and C. Taylor (eds), *Foundations of Playwork*, 139–42, Maidenhead: Open University Press.

Walton, K. L. (1990), *Mimesis and Make-Believe. On the Foundations of the Representational Arts*, Cambridge, MA: Harvard University Press.

Wasserman, J. A. (2020), 'Materially Mediated. Boardgames as Interactive Media and Mediated Communication', in D. Brown and E. MacCallum-Stewart (eds), *Rerolling Boardgames. Essays on Themes, Systems, Experiences and Ideologies*, 71–87, Jefferson, NC: McFarland & Co.

III

Ideologies

6

'Men should try playing the woman's part to see what it feels like. Remember ~ it's only a game . . .'

The representation of gendered experience in chance-based board games

Holly Nielsen

In the context of a book on material games, this chapter considers the ways in which games themselves come to embody a politics that are themselves embodied. Specifically, my concern is with gender politics of twentieth-century Britain. As material objects these games are complex, the boundaries of what they are and represent are fluid and can be changed depending on how they are engaged with. All of these games ask the player to engage and embody a role with the intention of representing an experience centred on gender. These games allow us to see different feminisms and activism at distinct historical moments that have been produced by different forms of class and race identity.

To 'play the game' is synonymous with thinking strategically, outwitting your opponents and winning through your cunning and skill. However, there is a popular genre of board game that does not reflect this idiom. Instead, these games are purely chance based. Roll-and-move board games have been a mainstay of popular board gaming for years. The ubiquity of roll-and-move in many simplistic children's games (such as Snakes and Ladders) means 'it has the reputation as an anti-pattern' (Engelstein and Shalev 2020: 355). These games are often mechanically simple. Typically, the goal is to reach the end point of a path featuring a number of spaces on the board. The chance element is brought in by players taking turns to generate a random number (usually by throwing dice), which then indicates how many spaces a player should move their counter along. These spaces can then feature further directions that either help or hinder the player on their progress. For example, moving forward a certain amount of space, going back to a space or missing a turn.

Chance plays a part in many games. It can add excitement, level the playing field for players or add the vagaries of concepts of fate to a play scenario. Roger Caillois's classification of games refers to games involving competition, in which the player utilizes skill to win, as agôn. Chess would be an example of this agôn category. In contrast to agôn, Caillois refers to games that rely solely on chance as alea. This means 'all games that are based on a decision independent of the player, an outcome over which he has no control, and in which winning is the result of fate rather than triumphing over adversary' (2001: 17). In other words, games in which 'destiny is the sole artisan of victory' (Caillois 2001: 17). Most games feature a combination of both agôn and alea, skill and chance. However, the three main examples that will be explored in this chapter all rest firmly within Caillois's categorization of alea games in which all players' movements are dictated by where chance places them; the players make no decisions of their own.

This chapter analyses how these purely chance-based board games were designed with gendered issues in mind and thus explore the gendered value systems of the people who designed them in the past. Chance-based board games are sometimes dismissed in games analysis because of their apparent simplicity and the lack of skill it takes to play and experience them. But it is this very lack of skill that has made them such powerful tools with which to explore and provide a commentary on gendered experience. By trapping the player with a mechanic that affords them no power over the outcome, the designers of these games explored their own experience of gender constructs. Through these games we can see how women used a purely chance-based mechanic to explore such ideas as inevitability, lack of control and unfairness. Historically, these games were sites of protest, satire, celebration and education about lived and social experiences of gender. This chapter will focus on the games as material explorations of the gendered experience of their designers and how they challenged the gendered conventions of their time, it will not look at the potential play that could have happened with the material. From the material games we can see designer intention, but we cannot presume that the play that happened with them followed this intention, it is for this reason this chapter will focus on the designers rather than the players.

These ideas will be explored through three case studies: *Pank-a-Squith* made by the suffragettes in 1909; *The Ladder of Academic Success*, a game drawn in 1951 by Muriel Bradbrook, who in 1961 became the first female professor of

English at the University of Cambridge; and *Womanopoly* made by Black women's activist Stella Dadzie in the late 1970s. The three games all hail from Britain and were designed throughout the twentieth century in response to particular experiences of gender in particular contexts. The British culture of play, humour and satire can therefore be analysed as part of the cultural context in which these games were created.

As my analysis of the case studies show, each game asks the player to engage with the experience of these women in different cultural and social situations. There is no winning through cunning or strategy; you are left at the whim of chance, fighting to progress in a setting you currently have no power in altering. This gameplay of course relies on the idea that the player does not have control or input, but we should not assume that what to modern board game players seems totally chance based was viewed as such by those playing. However, because of the time frame and location of these three games, the chance-based elements of the games would have been viewed as how we currently perceive chance: as something not within our control. When talking about historical board games it is important to acknowledge that mechanics may not be perceived or understood as we understand them today. However, because all of these games are from the twentieth century, we can be safe in our reading of chance being perceived as it is currently. Chance in these games is not just the primary mechanic; it is a symbol, a statement and a metaphor.

Pank-a-Squith

The women's suffrage movement was a fertile topic for game designers. A number of publishers and newspapers released games themed around the movement in the early twentieth century. The Women's Social and Political Union (WSPU) developed at least one board game which was distributed and sold through a network of high street shops run by the organization and at indoor meetings in order to raise funds. Pank-a-Squith (an amalgamation name of Pankhurst and Asquith) was published in 1909 and sold for the reasonable price of 1s. 6d. Through New Journalism, newspapers increasingly became sites for advertisements and profit-making. New Journalism is the rise in a type of popular journalism that developed in the 1880s that had an emphasis on the personal and the 'sensational', a lightness in tone and a reliance on gimmicks (which could include board games) to sell newspapers in high-stakes circulation wars (see Hampton 2004: 36–9). The suffragettes utilized the possibilities of the new advertising culture created by New Journalism to develop commercial relationships with suffrage supporters (see Atkinson 1992; Miller 1998; Brown 1999; Finnegan 1999; DiCenzo 2003; Mercer 2004; Green, 2008). This board game was part of a commercialized material culture that promoted the cause of suffrage through play.

The game depicts the suffragettes' struggle with Prime Minister Herbert Asquith and the Liberal government. The player's goal is to move the suffragette from her home, where she is depicted sitting alone watching a baby, to the Houses of Parliament through dice rolls. The game's progression condenses the idealized narrative of a suffragette transforming from a lone domestic inhabitant to a public political being. The square before parliament illustrates the figure of justice, draped in the suffragette colours of purple, white and green – symbolizing that by the action of the suffragette reaching parliament, justice has been done. *Pank-a-Squith* offers no player agency in terms of choice; the player is pre-destined to end at parliament, and the only variable is how long this journey will take. Within this game the path and the obstacles are clearly represented on the board and through the play intended by the designer.

Pank-a-Squith was first advertised in the suffragette newspaper *Votes for Women* on 22 October 1909. The advert features a picture of space number forty-two from the board: a suffragette sitting in a blank prison cell with the caption in quotations 'are we down-hearted? *No!*' [emphasis in original] (Votes for Women 1909: 60). The advert then continues, '"Down-hearted?" Never – while there's the New, Fascinating, Suffragette Game, *Pank-a-Squith*'. The advert emphasizes that the game's purpose was to alleviate the emotional burdens of being a suffragette by keeping spirits and morale high. The image of the suffragette in a prison cell and the large print 'down-hearted?' in bold found on the advert highlight *Pank-a-Squith* as an object of amusement with its 'attractively designed' board and 'witty rules'. This aim of providing enjoyment and being a cure for down-heartedness is particularly pertinent as on page fifty-two of the same *Votes for Women* issue, only eight pages before the advert, a whole page was dedicated to incarceration and 'a new form of assault' – the brutal force-feedings of suffragettes on hunger strike (*Votes for Women* 1909: 52). This idea of keeping up morale is also explicitly depicted on space number twenty-two of the game, which features a group of suffragettes shouting 'cheer up' into Holloway prison. *Pank-a-Squith* aimed to boost the morale of a movement that was very quickly slipping into a dark period. *Pank-a-Squith* even portrays some of the more testing and unpleasant aspects of being part of a militant suffrage movement. For example, on space thirty-three, a suffragette is shown in prison refusing food.

Yet, these setbacks are only temporary; the procedures of the game only allow the player to march forward to a pre-destined outcome. This linearity eases the unpleasantness with a sense of progress and purpose; the rules mean that there is a simple, predetermined destination. The rhetoric provided by the mechanics of the game is one of linear progression, with victory as the only outcome. Though chance may slow down the progress, or quicken it, ultimately the goal will always be reached by at least one player. The only role of the player is to follow the instructions given to them, reflecting the WSPU's own organizational goals.

The game allows for no other outcome than the achievement of parliamentary suffrage, and it portrays trials that many of its members were currently facing and makes many references to recent events. Space number thirteen depicts Inspector Jarvis. Thirteen could be a reference to the date Inspector Jarvis arrested Flora Drummond, Christabel Pankhurst and Emmeline Pankhurst on 13 October 1908 after the WSPU urged Londoners to rush the House of Commons. The direction for players landing on space thirteen of *Pank-a-Squith* is 'if two "suffragettes" occupy this square together the inspector feels obstructed and sends them both back to square ten'. The requirement of two players being present on the space, referencing the multiple arrests enacted by Inspector Jarvis, show how the rules were adapted to represent recent events. The police are consistently portrayed in *Pank-a-Squith* as an enemy that should be avoided at all cost, demonstrating that as well as being a performative and fun distraction, the game was also informative, aiming to shape attitudes and strategies. Space twenty-six features a policeman saying, 'how brave I am fighting women', adding a touch of political humour, and space twenty-three is a warning to all suffragettes playing the game as it shows a policeman with the words 'Suffragettes beware of me'.

This game offers a different way of consuming and engaging with the suffrage cause. It also potentially brings political ideology into the domestic setting where board games were most commonly played. Games rarely allow for total passivity. Even in totally chance-based games such as *Pank-a-Squith*, a player has to throw the dice and move a piece. The player ideally adheres to the rules. *Pank-a-Squith* necessitates consistent and direct input from the players and asks for the players' involvement with the subject matter. This game allows us to perceive an engagement with contemporary political topics within domestic life; they were items bought to become part of a home, and to play them required interaction with the suffrage cause.

Games were also part of an impressive WSPU marketing strategy that included not only board games but also card games, postcards, rosettes, magazines and even soap (for further information on other materials, see Atkinson 1992; Finnegan 1999; Mercer 2004). Because these games were sold in the WSPU network of shops and at meetings, it seems improbable that they were designed to openly convert people to the cause. *Pank-a-Squith* features a playing space that states 'any player landing on this space must send a penny to the suffragette funds', which is unlikely to have appealed to those against or undecided about the group. By taking part and playing the game, the game makes the players complicit in agreeing suffrage would be the end result.

Suffragettes in and out of prison

Unfortunately, the copies of the material game do not tell us exactly how it was played or experienced. While there is currently no way to know exactly who owned or engaged with *Pank-a-Squith*, we do have more detail in this regarding another chance-based and suffragette-themed board game. The London based daily newspaper *The Morning Leader* (1892–1912) also published a race game entitled *Suffragettes In and Out of Prison* in 1908. The newspaper was sympathetic to the women's suffrage cause. For example, when reporting on the release of Mrs. Pethick Lawrence, the treasurer for the WSPU, from Holloway prison in 1906, the newspaper commented that it was due to her being 'seriously ill as the result of hardships she has endured' (*Morning Leader* 1906). The aim of the game is to find your way out of Holloway goal, trying to avoid the 'wardress' and 'policeman' spaces that impede your escape. The game, which allows the player to embody a suffragette, was compatible with the newspaper's sympathetic reporting on suffragette news. The game encouraged the player to not only play as a suffragette but to defy authority and escape from prison. The game proved so popular and profitable to *The Morning Leader* that a number of versions were issued.

The Morning Leader released a more decorative version (1908b) of the game printed in colour chromolithography on a sheet of paper pasted onto a board. This version was originally owned by Maria Louisa Newman who was born in Camberwell, London, on 5 March 1886. She was the youngest of five children from a working-class family. Despite an offer from the headmistress to stay on at the school and be trained as a teacher, Maria left school to find work to help contribute to the family's income. She found work as an apprentice bookbinder. It was while running errands during this apprenticeship that Maria first encountered suffragettes campaigning on the street. Although she sympathized with the suffragettes' cause, Maria felt she could not join the campaign due to her work and family commitments. She managed a grocery with a post office attached while bringing up her son and daughter. Maria lovingly kept *Suffragettes In and Out of Prison* as a memento of her support of the movement and passed the game to her daughter Margaret on her death in 1970. Margaret then donated the game, along with a description of its significance to her mother, to the Museum of London in 2016 at the age of 102.[1]

This information about Maria and why she purchased and kept the game is important for several reasons. First, it shows us that the game was purchased and kept in support for the suffragettes. Second, despite it not being published by the WSPU, Maria saw this game as a material aspect of the suffrage movement to which she did not have time to dedicate herself. Thus, the game functioned as a site of continued remembrance (for more information on suffragette collections and continued remembrance, see Kean 2005). This game illustrates how women often cherished their participation in and support for the suffrage movement through commercial objects not directly linked to the organization. Third, this game was so important to Maria that she kept it safe throughout her life and then left it to her daughter – it was not its monetary value or quality as a game that made it significant, but rather its connection to the suffrage movement and its significance to its first owner. Board games as material objects can be many things beyond a game, as demonstrated here they can be material sites of remembrance or solidarity.

The Ladder of Academic Success

Page eighteen of the *Girton College Annual Review*, published in 1951, features a black-and-white roll-and-move board game titled *The Ladder of Academic Success*. The game consists of a stylized ladder within which there are fifty spaces. Around the ladder are small illustrations relevant to the spaces and theme of academia, such as a woman in a graduation gown, a young girl and an inkpot.

The Ladder of Academic Success was created by literary scholar Muriel Bradbrook who at the time of the game's publication was a fellow of Girton College and a lecturer at the University of Cambridge, and who would later become the first female professor of English at Cambridge and mistress of Girton College. Girton College was founded in 1869 and was the UK's first residential institution offering university-level education for women. However, the University of Cambridge did not grant women degrees until 1948 – the last of the big institutions in the UK to do so. When Bradbrook created the game for the review it had only been three years since women could be granted a degree from Cambridge, and as the game highlights, women still faced many hurdles in university life. Despite Cambridge granting women degrees, the number of women students remained low. In 1964–5, over a decade after *The Ladder of Academic Success* was printed, only 9.65 per cent of undergraduates were women, the lowest percentage of any university in the country (Weiss 2016: 494).

The *Annual Review*, within which the game was printed, featured articles and features relating to college life and updates from the college. Within this space Bradbrook used the game to humorously highlight the experience of women within the institution. While the inclusion of women at universities like Cambridge is often told as 'a battle won', Bradbrook's game shows us that these narratives are perhaps too simplistic for the lived reality of the gendered experience. It could be viewed as an early feminist reading of the perception of the challenges that women faced in the world of work, the idea of both progress and impediments.

The game features no explicit rules and so it is assumed that from the layout, and the ubiquity of the roll-and-move board game at the time, that by looking at the layout and 'board' the reader and/or player would understand what it is they are looking at. Of course, as with all the games looked at in this chapter, we cannot know from the games themselves, who played these games, how they played them or if they played them at all. *The Ladder of Academic Success* is particularly notable as it does not particularly seem to encourage the reader of the *Girton College Annual Review* to play the game; no rules are given, and the only thing on the page is the title, board and accompanying illustrations. Rather it seems that the game is a metaphor that would have been recognizable to the audience of the college review. The game does not need to be played to be understood, particularly as the game was created to reflect the experiences and potential experiences of the intended audience. It is a comedic and poignant reflection on the difficulties facing women in academia during the time. Chance-based board games themselves were occasionally used as a metaphor for unfairness and progress impeded by obstacles and the role of luck in life. Nineteenth-century moralist Christian games which then became the basis for popular family games in the twentieth century, such as the *Game of Life*, reflect this. It is a reminder that not all material games are played and that their messages and rhetoric can be understood by different methods of consumption.

The Ladder of Academic Success does not just show the stepping stones of an academic career but the emotional repercussions of university attendance and a life in academia as a woman. Space eleven is labelled 'research subject unprofitable – nervous collapse' and requires the player to go back to space five. Space thirty-five is also labelled 'nervous collapse' and requires the player to go back five spaces. Nervous collapse seems to be represented as a likely outcome for both early career academics and those who are more established.

The relationships that can both progress and impede a woman during her time on the ladder of academic success feature in the game. Space three has the caption 'meets Trinity freshman in train', which then leads the player to space eight which features 'kissed under archway'. Space fourteen is 'marries supervisor', which then leads to space twenty 'dines with vice chancellor' which also allows the player to take one extra throw. Space seventeen, 'snubs professor by mistake', requires the player to go back to space twelve. These spaces are an acknowledgement that 'academic success' and career progression were not just a case of working hard. Instead, the success was aided by interpersonal relationships and having access to people in positions of power.

The goal of the game is not just the attainment of the general concept of 'academic success', it is also to change the structures that impact female students. It is, therefore, partly an aspirational depiction of academia, one showing not only the current difficulties facing women who wish to pursue a career but also the potential for change. The last four spaces on the game show this aspirational progression. Space forty-seven is labelled 'elected chancellor' and from that point on the game depicts structural change. Space forty-eight states 'reverses decision of Septem Viri', which is the disciplinary court for senior members of the university and/or college. The space represents the growing power of the female player/academic to change university structures. This depiction of power continues on space forty-nine, which states 'suspends vice-chancellor', and ends with space fifty, the end and goal of the game, labelled 'revises statutes by decree', thus changing the constitutional framework of the university.

Although it speaks to the more general experiences of women trying to work and progress in academia, the game also explores a very particular gendered experience. One with assumptions of class and privilege. There are a number of phrases and references that only those familiar with higher education, more specifically the experience of attending or teaching at Cambridge, would understand at first glance. Like *Pank-a-Squith* the game is for those with a very particular gendered experience. Unlike *Pank-a-Squith*, it does not seem concerned with speaking to those outside of that gendered experience. This would make sense considering that the game was published in the Annual Review of a women's college. It functions more as satire and a joke for those who would understand the specific references. Andy Medhurst has noted that the consumption of comedy is not passive, that the engagement demanded by stand-ups and the re-circulation of mannerisms and dialogue by fans of popular TV and film comedy 'calls into serious question any idea that their consumption is "passive"' (Medhurst 2007: 68). These games also rely on their players to engage and understand their references for the humour to be found, as well as for the games themselves to progress. The difficulties facing women before getting into academia, or outside of academia, are not acknowledged. There is no socioeconomic reflection on who can even get to the point of being on a university college waiting list.

The message of *The Ladder of Academic Success* is still within the bounds of Bradbrook's own views on the matter of women's education and coeducation. This view was not one that included an egalitarian opening of an elite institution. During and after the Second World War there was an increase in pressure for universities to make more provisions for women who wanted to study. In 1946 Cambridge amended its University Ordinances to allow the proportion of women to rise to one-fifth of the total of men (University of Cambridge 1950: n.p.). However, the subject of increasing the number of women students at Cambridge and introducing a third women's college was not without contention. Bradbrook was one of a number of women academics who wrote to the vice-chancellor in 1952 suggesting that it would be a 'disservice' to bring more women 'of modest general ability' into Cambridge, this attitude was fuelled by both wanting to retain a monopoly over women candidates and 'a conservative – or defensive – elitism on the part of some in the women's college, which persisted well into the second half of the century' (Dyhouse 2006: 86).

The separate histories of men's and women's colleges within Cambridge led to deep differences in their culture and organization. Male student culture often focused on drinking and rowdiness. Ritualized, and largely contained, challenges to authority were accepted as part of the construction of masculinity. In contrast, women's colleges 'had a history of keeping a low profile, of trying to earn respectability through good behaviour and avoiding any head-on challenges to social convention' (Dyhouse 2006: 177). In the game, then, the transgressions that place the player further from their goal reflect this cultural difference in the gendered experience of student and academic life. Space twenty-five, for example, informs the player that 'tactless reviewing' has led to their lectureship lapsing, thus requiring the player to go back to space eighteen. Space thirty-seven is labelled with the ominously vague words, 'commits strategic error', which then requires the player to go back to space thirty-five. These spaces reflect the disastrous consequences that could occur when not keeping a tactically low profile.

Even though the game depicts a woman changing the constitution of the university and reversing decisions put forward by the Septem Viri, because of its presence in the annual review it is not only safe (in the sense that the audience would largely comprise students and academics who were part of that all women's college) but also potentially transgressive as it was still published and not in secret. *The Ladder of Academic Success* is a humorous metaphor for the experience of women students and academics at the time; it also features an optimistic end to the game, one that is potentially aspirational to its intended audience.

Womanopoly

Womanopoly is a game created by Stella Dadzie in the late 1970s and is housed in the Black Cultural Archives in London. Dadzie was born in London in 1952 to a white mother and Ghanian father. In the early 1970s she took a degree in German at King's College London and became involved in radical Black politics. She was a founding member of the Organisation for Women of Asian and African Descent (OWAAD) – perhaps the most well-known British Black women's groups and, as Ranu Samantrai has written, 'the most suggestively iconic' (Samantrai 2002: 10) – and co-author of *The Heart of the Race: Black Women's Lives in Britain* (1985).

Womanopoly is a roll-and-move board game for two players, 'a game for woman v. man', with each player taking the role of a woman or man. The game features fifty-one numbered spaces as well as a starting space and finishing space labelled 'you win'. The goal of the game is to be the first player to reach the last space. However, the game is heavily weighted against whoever is playing the role of the woman player. In contrast to the other games, not all players are equal in their chance of winning.

The repurposing of mechanics is common in board game development and Dadzie freely admits that it was probably based on 'something I saw somewhere' (Black Cultural Archives n.d.: n.p.). A simple roll-and-move board game would have been almost universally known and understood by the British public. It was a recognizable item and one that could be understood quickly. As seen with the other games discussed in this chapter, roll-and-move games that addressed current issues or were satirical in nature were not unheard of. Roll-and-move board games as a metaphor for life or stages of life were also a common occurrence. Board games have a long history of being used as educational tools, and moralistic board games dominated from the late-eighteenth to mid-nineteenth centuries (Shefrin 1999: 251–75). *The New Game of Emulation* (1827–30) and *The New Game of Human Life* (1790) are typical didactic games from this period. These types of games persisted into the twentieth century, though heavily didactic games seemed to fall out of fashion. However, the idea of learning through play and chance representing what we cannot control in life was not new. While generalized notions of 'fate' and time were the uncontrollable aspects in these earlier board games, all three of these examples show the uncontrollable aspect that is represented by chance as being of human origin; a systemic oppression and restriction that limits and dictates women's outcomes. While *Pank-a-Squith* communicates a sense of the inevitability of progress aiding the idea that their tactics would lead to positive outcome and success, *Womanopoly* is a demonstration of how society oppressed women and propelled men. Thus, it is closer to a kind of interactive and playable protest placard. However, even if they are intended as being closer to a playable protest placard, or even if play is not necessary to engage with the message, I would argue they are still games. A game is still recognizable as a game as an object, even if it is not being actively played. *Womanopoly* was neither sold to fundraise like *Pank-a-Squith* nor part of a publication like *The Ladder of Academic Success*, but it is no less a game because of this.

Rather than being a commercial game-like *Pank-a-Squith* or published in the context of a paper or magazine like *The Ladder of Academic Success*, *Womanopoly* is a hand-drawn game, a unique object. This provides us with an interesting mirror to changing approaches to feminist and activist objects. While the suffragettes whole-heartedly embraced politicized consumption, the British women's liberation movement of the 1970s was less keen. This is unsurprising considering the anti-capitalist and socialist roots of a lot of the activism. Lucy Delap has argued that 'there was nothing like the early-twentieth-century explosion of colour-themed mass retail, but instead a turn to "world-making" and protest objects' (Delap 2020: 155). This change is mirrored by *Pank-a-Squith* and *Womanopoly*.

Womanopoly is intended as a satirical attack on a woman's experience of society and the hurdles they face throughout their lives. The game features this descriptor on it: 'a game for woman v. man in a society where the cards are stacked against women.' It then goes on to suggest, 'Men should try playing the woman's part to see what it feels like. Remember ~ it's only a game . . .'

As mentioned earlier, in contrast to the two games examined previously in this chapter, there are two parts for the players to play in this roll-and-move chance-based board game. One of 'man' and the other 'woman'. As the introduction suggested, men are encouraged to play the role of women, 'to see what it feels like'. The game is not only humorous but a potential teaching moment, a chance for men playing to feel the frustration lived by women. The inequality between the two roles is apparent from the very beginning as to start the game, while men need to throw one six to start the game, women need to throw two sixes. It is fundamentally harder for the player taking the role of the woman to win. This game takes the well-known metaphor of a roll-and-move board game being a metaphor for life and the unknown forces that dictate our outcomes and makes those forces plainly clear. While both the man and woman roles may have bad and good throws of the dice, the man will find himself propelled forward while the woman struggles to progress. While chance dictates both players on their journey across the board, it is not an equalizer because the game itself is rigged.

As well as the assigning of roles and suggesting that men should try playing the woman's part in order to encourage reflection outside of the game, *Womanopoly* also encourages players to step away and discuss what they are being faced with. Space forty-four tells the player, 'WOMAN – you bring your daughter up to "saver herself" for marriage. MAN – you encourage your son to sew his wild oats. Both miss a turn and talk about it.' The classic roll-and-move device of 'miss a turn' is here used to provoke a conversation when confronted with the double standards.

There is also a particular focus on women's success being based on physical appearance rather than skills or talent. Space twenty-eight tells the players, 'WOMAN you are hired for your looks not your talents. Back 5. MAN – you aren't.' Space thirty-eight has a similar message, 'WOMAN Bonus for looking pretty forward 1. MAN – bonus for working hard. Forward 2.' Even the bonuses given to the player who has taken the role of the woman are marred by double standards.

As well as displaying the accumulating impact of exclusion and inequality via the medium of a chance-based board game, *Womanopoly* also includes occasional facts. Space forty-eight informs the players, 'The average wage for women is 40% less than the median wage for men doing the same work. WOMAN. Go back 2.' Space twenty-three states, 'MAN. You are elected an MP. You are one of many, but well done anyway. WOMAN. You become one of 23 female MP's for forward 4.' It is an effective juxtaposition between the colourful board games and its serious subject matter and sobering figures.

Unlike *Pank-a-Squith*, this game was not drawn for the purpose of being a commercial product; it is an item of protest and a tool to express ongoing inequalities. While *Pank-a-Squith*'s roll-and-move formula has chance leading the player to the inevitable of women's suffrage with setbacks only delaying this outcome. The end of *Womanopoly* does not have a goal or purpose: both male and female players end with the same 'you win' space. However, the entire point is in the journey and centres on how, although both players are at the whim of chance, the cards are stacked against the player taking the role of 'woman'. In this way, the game displays clear inequalities between the two players' roles of a 'man' and 'woman'.

Despite Dadzie being a leading Black activist and being highly involved in Black liberation politics, the game does not directly address racial inequalities. The roles of the 'man' and the 'woman' seem to be universal with the intersections of race not explicitly mentioned. The main focus in the game is the difference in the gendered experience of career progression, opportunities and wage-earning. For example, space fourteen informs and instructs the player, 'WOMAN – You are in line for a promotion – but will men work under you? Miss a turn and worry about it. MAN – No doubt about you – take an extra turn.' Space forty-seven states, 'MAN – You are creative & become an artist, designer etc. Take an extra turn. WOMAN – So are you. Become a teacher – or a creative man's wife.'

This game was created within the context of heightened labour struggles within Britain during the late 1970s which may have contributed to the particular focus. However, it could also be due to Dadzie's own background in socialist feminism. Natalie Thomlinson has highlighted the difference between Black American and the Black British women's movement: this difference 'underlines the rootedness of Black British women's activism in Black socialist thought, and the autonomy and unique nature of its praxis' (2016: 102). Thomlinson's analysis of Dadzie's papers and attendance of socialist-feminist discussions show the role socialist feminism had in providing a potential discursive space that could be shared by both Black-and-white feminists. This does not mean that white socialist-feminists were by default anti-racist, but rather, she argues, that the socialism shared by Black-and-white feminists was 'inherently antithetical to simplistic racial essentialism, providing a stronger theoretical base for working together' (Thomlinson 2016: 167). This base still had to address racism and racial inequalities, but a key starting point was the belief that all women could only end their oppression when capitalism as a world system was destroyed.

'Feminism' can be a complex term to use and apply. All three of the games examined in this chapter are 'feminist' in the sense that they recognize women are treated differently to men in a way that is detrimental to women. They also intimate that this treatment is unjust and is not just individual but is systematically grounded in social structures. *Pank-a-Squith* and *The Ladder of Academic Success* show a very particular type of feminism, one that is white and middle class. That is not to say that the issues being addressed in both those games only affected white middle-class women, but that was primarily their intended audience for the games. While *Womanopoly* is a 'feminist' object in the sense that it acknowledges this unjust and systematic detrimental treatment of women. It is also important to be aware that these labels are complex and could be rejected. This is particularly true in the case of the context that *Womanopoly* was created. We must acknowledge that 'feminism' or 'feminist' is a term refused by some Black women who, while they align with the belief stated earlier, reject the term on the grounds that it denoted a middle-class white movement that oppressed, rather than liberated, Black women. Therefore, we must be cognizant of this and of the context within which these items were created. Rather than these three objects showing a linear history of women's activism that has utilized chance-based board games, they instead show different feminisms or activism that have all found a way of using chance-based board games.

Conclusion

Scholars Alison Bartlett and Margaret Henderson have written about feminist material culture and activist objects. They divided their approach to 'things' into categories that include corporeal things such as clothing, wearable items and intimate objects; world-making things such as books, films and art; knowledge and communicative things like newsletters and briefing documents; and protest things, which includes badges, banners and posters (Bartlett and Henderson 2016: 163). When considering these three games as feminist and activist objects we could argue that using this categorization they are all world-building things as they bring into being a feminist (or woman's activist) world. All three games enable the person engaging to experience a 'world' that highlights women's struggles in different contexts within a temporal and controlled framework. *Pank-a-Squith* and *The Ladder of Academic Success* offer the player an aspirational ending, while *Womanopoly* shows the cumulative struggle. These three board games are part of a history of material activist objects that promote and explore their viewpoints while also being world-making. They are not only board games, but they are also part of the material culture of protest, satire and sites of activism, whether or not they were intended to be played or understood as a metaphor.

These games are not unique in terms of their game design. All three are simple roll-and-move board games, with only *Womanopoly* expanding on this by adding unequal player experiences. However, activism has a history of repurposing objects for a cause. Lucy Delap in her book, *Feminisms: A Global History* (2020), has pointed out how the 'creative feminist reuse of "things" has been widespread' (Delap 2020: 145). Some may look at roll-and-move chance-based board games as being derivative, an easy base upon which to quickly layer a new theme, the mechanics of the game not reflecting the rhetoric or message. While this may be true of some roll-and-move chance-based board games, it would be overly dismissive not to acknowledge in these three case studies that this type of game was picked for a reason. They are a metaphor for the gendered experience itself, a way to produce inevitability of outcome and exploring agency (or lack of). These games are not interesting and valuable despite being purely chance based; they are worthy of analysis because of it.

Note

1 This information was provided by the archive of the Museum of London where the game is held. Upon its donation the donor was asked about how the game came to be in their possession.

References

Atkinson, D. (1992), *Suffragettes in the Purple, White and Green*, London: Museum of London.

Bartlett, A. (2016), 'Feminist Material Culture and the Making of the Activist Object', *Journal of Australian Studies*, 40 (2): 156–71.

Bartlett, A. and M. Henderson (2016), 'What Is a Feminist Object? Feminist Material Black Cultural Archives (n.d)', *Womanopoly: A Board Game that is Anything But Boring. . . If You're a Man' Google Arts & Culture*. Available online: https://artsandculture.google.com/story/OAUxXI933cCqFw (accessed 22 November 2021).

Brown, B. (1999), 'The Secret Life of Things (Virginia Woolf and the Matter of Modernism)', *Modernism/Modernity*, 6 (2): 1–28.

Caillois, R. (2001), *Man, Play and Games*, trans. M. Barash, Urbana and Chicago: University of Illinois Press.

Delap, L. (2020), *Feminisms: A Global History*, London: Pelican Books.

DiCenzo, M. (2003), 'Gutter Politics: Women Newsies and the Suffrage Press', *Women's History Review*, 12 (1): 15–33.

Dyhouse, C. (2006), *Students: A Gendered History*, London: Routledge.

Engelstein, G. and I. Shalev (2020), *Building Blocks of Tabletop Game Design: An Encyclopedia of Mechanisms*, Boca Raton, FL: CRC Press.

Finnegan, M. (1999), *Selling Suffrage: Consumer Culture and Votes for Women*, New York: Columbia University Press.

Green, B. (2008), 'Feminist Things', in A. Ardis and P. Collier (eds), *Transatlantic Print Culture, 1880–1940*, 66–79, London: Palgrave.

Hampton, M. (2004), *Visions of the Press in Britain, 1850–1950*, Urbana and Chicago: University of Illinois Press.

Kean, H. (2005), 'Public History and Popular Memory: Issues in the Commemoration of the British Militant Suffrage Campaign', *Women's History Review*, 14 (3–4): 581–602.

The Ladder of Academic Success (1951), [Board game], Designer: Muriel Bradbrook, *The Girton Review*: 18–19. GCPP 2/1/4 pt.

Medhurst, A. (2007), *A National Joke: Popular Comedy and English Cultural Identities*, London and New York: Routledge.

Mercer, J. (2004), 'Commercial Places, Public Spaces: Suffragette Shops and the Public Sphere', *University of Sussex Journal of Contemporary History*, 7: 1–10.

Miller, D. (ed.) (1998), *Material Cultures: Why Some Things Matter*, Chicago, IL: University of Chicago Press.

The Morning Leader (1906), British Library- General Reference Collection 1906 Microform. MFM.M41264–67. 29 October.

The New Game of Emulation or the Road to Knowledge (1827–1830), [Board game], UK David Nunes Carvalho. [V&A Museum of Childhood, London, Museum No. E.1777-1954].

The New Game of Human Life (1790), [Board game], UK: John Wallis and Elizabeth Newberry. [V&A Museum of Childhood, London, Museum No., E.217-1944].

Pank-a-Squith (1909), [Board game], UK: Women's Social and Political Union. [Museum of London, London, ID No. 50.82/1511].

Samantrai, R. (2002), *AlterNatives: Black Feminism in the Postimperial Nation*, Stanford, CA: University of Stanford Press.

Shefrin, J. (1999), '"Make It a Pleasure and Not a Task": Educational Games for Children in Georgian England', *The Princeton University Library*, 60 (2): 251–75.

Suffragettes In and Out of Prison (1908a), [Board game], UK: Morning Leader. [Museum of London, London, ID No. 80.525/256].

Suffragettes In and Out of Prison (1908b), [Board game], UK: Morning Leader. [The Museum of London, London, ref: 2016.18].

Thomlinson, N. (2016), *Race, Ethnicity and the Women's Movement in England, 1968–1993*, London: Palgrave.

University of Cambridge (1950), 'Students: A Gendered History', *University Committee on Women Students, 1949–1971*, Cambridge: Cambridge University Library. [UA R 1795 A-E].

Votes for Women (1909), October 22.

Weiss Malkiel, N. (2016), *'Keep the Damned Women Out': The Struggle for Coeducation*, Princeton, NJ: Princeton University Press.

Womanopoly (c. 1970), [Board Game], Designer; Stella Dadzie. Cultural Archives, BCA Catalogue Reference Number: DADZIE/1/1/29.

7

Deterritorializing game boards

Mapping imperialism in *RISK* and modern board games

Jonathan Rey Lee

'Imperialism and mapmaking intersect in the most basic manner', writes geographer Matthew Edney. 'Both are fundamentally concerned with territory and knowledge' (1997: 1). In a similar vein, play historian Johan Huizinga writes, 'Ever since words existed for fighting and playing men have been wont to call war a game' (1950: 89). Empire and map, war and game – these four intertwined cultural histories are linked by a territorial vision that pictures worlds as divisible, contestable, conquerable spaces. This chapter traces these interrelated ideologies of empire, map, war and game as they play out in the war-themed 'troops-on-a-map' territory game *RISK* and other comparable games to explore the critical possibilities for *deterritorializing*[1] game boards – that is, deconstructing and disrupting how they materially and visually manifest territorial world views.

The games explored in this chapter are distinct from a wargaming tradition that has its own ideological entanglements with the 'military-entertainment complex' (Dyer-Witheford and de Peuter 2009; Halter 2006; Stahl 2010). Board wargaming typically plays out the *practice* of war through complex simulations of military strategy (Costikyan 2011), which has historically depended on mapping contested landscapes (Black 2016). Military maps and simulationist wargames pursue fidelity: the better these media represent the particularities of terrain, the more effectively they simulate combat. *RISK*, however, eschews fidelity by using too-simplified battle mechanics and taking a too-global perspective to effectively represent military tactics. Yet, by sacrificing accuracy, *RISK*-style wargames can effectively represent the visual imaginary that rationalizes imperialism. These games explore how mapmaking advances empire 'not just as a highly effective informational weapon wielded strategically and tactically by directors, governors, military commanders, and field officials, but also as a significant component of the "structures of feeling" which legitimated, justified, and defined that imperialism' (Edney 1997: 340). Whereas simulationist wargames play out the former, *RISK*-style wargames play out the latter – an imperialist picturing of a world to be divided that links visual media to power. As such resonances between virtual gameplay and real-world ideologies collapse the 'magic circle' of board games, these ideological games exemplify the paradoxical blending of materiality and virtuality that defines material play.

This chapter begins by broadly theorizing how game board aesthetics, data visualizations and operational environments construct playable worlds and world views. Then, drawing on the theories of Martin Heidegger, Benedict Anderson and Megan Norcia, it deconstructs how the *RISK*'s game board and gameplay stage the conquest of the world picture, a territorial vision that perceives the world as divisible and conquerable. This chapter then explores how two Area Control games – Ananda Gupta and Jason Matthews's *Twilight Struggle* and Andrew Parks's *Ideology: The War of Ideas 2nd Edition* – nuance this territorial vision according to Rey Chow's theory of the world target and how two cooperative games – Matt Leacock's *Pandemic* and Brian Mayer's *Freedom: The Underground Railroad* – reject a territorial vision in favour of a humanitarian logistics. Together, these divergent case studies reveal a spectrum of territorializing and deterritorializing visions, a wide possibility space for how game boards can construct ideological world views.

Theorizing game boards

Unlike most storytelling media, board games construct actual, navigable *worlds* within which agents can (inter)act. These worlds are simultaneously material and virtual in that material game environments constitute navigable spaces unto themselves while simultaneously picturing a collectively imagined world into which players project their agency. Players make moves in both spheres at once, materially manipulating components across a physical game environment (often a game board) in ways that project action into the virtual game world. As structuring environments, game boards constitute navigable worlds while literally constructing *world views*, visual microcosms of the structuring logics of virtual game worlds. To deterritorialize board games, it is therefore necessary to develop methods for deconstructing how the material and visual design of game boards constructs ideologically inflected and often territorial world views.

Despite literally giving 'board games' their name, game boards have been surprisingly undertheorized. Within the emerging canon of board game studies, game boards are typically included as either supplementary details in individual game analyses or one of many elements within general theories, as when Aki Järvinen (2007) situates game boards within his broad schematization of game elements and Paul Booth (2021) includes game boards as one of many elements in ludo-textual analysis. Scholarship that links game boards to geography tends to be disciplinarily rooted in cultural or historical research, most notably Megan Norcia's *Gaming Empire* (2019), a postcolonial exploration of how nineteenth-century geographical board games brought imperialist ideologies into children's culture. Although valuable insights can be gleaned from these examples, game boards constitute a sufficiently unique media form to merit more substantive media-specific theories and analytical methods. While not every hobbyist 'board' game features a central board and game boards are too diverse to be universally theorized, this section explores several common ways game boards materially mediate the player experience of virtual game worlds.

Even before game boards materially construct virtual game worlds, they physically structure the communal space of multiplayer board gaming. So, a brief media-specific aside is in order. While film – a medium in which the spectator is oriented perpendicularly to the screen – is theorized according to the *gaze*,[2] board games – a medium in which players are arranged around a shared tabletop – must be theorized according to the *glance* (Figure 7.1). Board gaming is structured by the doubled intersubjective experience of alternately glancing up towards other human players and glancing down towards a shared game environment. These two glances are inseparable – to glance up at the players is to observe the material humanity behind virtual play and to glance down at the board is to observe the virtual agency of real players materially projected onto the game board.

This doubled vision is possible only because board game designs construct a visible parallelism between material and virtual board game states. As board games are designed to materially mediate player agency in this way, deconstructive analysis – a method that spans the *ludo-textual analysis* and *ludic discourse analysis* described by Booth – can reveal how the material design of game boards ideologically constructs virtual game boards. Consequently, the remainder of this section outlines *artistry*, *data visualization* and *operational environments* as three central components of a deconstructive analysis.

Artistry – Game boards are aesthetic objects, whether they adopt the minimalist abstraction of *Go* or the richly detailed landscapes of a Michael Menzel design.

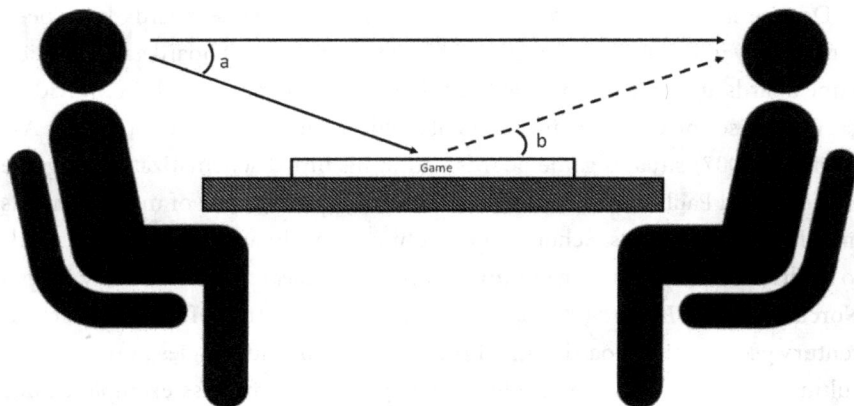

Figure 7.1 Diagramming the glance. Angle 'a' depicts *glancing at* as the alternation between gazing at the game (both board and world) and at the other player(s). Angle 'b' depicts the gaze metaphorically *glancing off* the board as the player sees other players' agency in the virtual game world projected onto the material game environment. As Angle 'b' is metaphorical, this glance may 'reflect' the presence of other agents refracted in the board state even without the physical presence of another human player (as when a solo mode 'reflects' the agency of a virtual opponent).

Yet, despite some similarities to other two-dimensional art forms, game boards are not primarily designed for silent aesthetic contemplation. Instead, board games weave an aesthetic experience in and around gameplay, often to interject theme into gameplay. As wargaming artist Mark Mahaffey puts it, whereas many modern maps 'favor scientific precision', game maps 'do not merely communicate data but also speak to our humanity, inviting introspection, empathy, and curiosity' (2016: 63). While thematic board games offer strategic decisions that could be theoretically reduced to abstract optimization puzzles, thematic artistry invites players to imagine that their decisions as having specific meaning (waging war, trading in the Mediterranean, etc.). In other words, artistry invites players to immerse themselves in the fiction of the virtual world within which they are making moves.

While players may certainly gaze at game art, artistry immanently inflects how the roving glance absorbs the background atmosphere of the game world while pursuing other goals. Consequently, deconstructing game board artistry requires more than interpreting a visual rhetoric; it also requires exploring how artistry ideologically inflects a *procedural rhetoric*, Ian Bogost's (2007) term for how games structure and create meaning by inviting players to make decisions and perform actions. Rather than standing apart as an object of pure aesthetic contemplation, game artistry infuses and inflects the data visualizations and operational environments that make up a material game system.

Data visualization – Although Mahaffey argues that board game artistry resists the data-fication of play, most board games require tracking some manner of data that lend significance to player agency. Indeed, the core strategic decisions in a board game typically involve maximizing or optimizing data like victory points, money or health. While numerical values can be tracked in multiple mathematically interchangeable ways such as tracks, cards, tokens, scorepads or companion apps, different data visualization strategies significantly alter how players access and perceive relevant information. For instance, using a victory point track along the outside of a game board makes the relative positions of players easily visible, promoting a more race-like feel than games with different approaches like endgame tabulation or hidden victory point tokens. In other words, data visualization strategies constitute different world *views* through which virtual game worlds are experienced.

In this way, even game boards that do not resemble traditional maps are fundamentally map-like in how they meaningfully pictorialize information to construct ideologically laden world views that in turn organize how players navigate game worlds. Although board games are sometimes called 'analogue games', the only gaming subgenres that consistently adopt an analogue representational paradigm are some miniatures and dexterity games. These games resemble topographic maps in using an analogue representational logic in which physical distance between pieces matters. In contrast, most modern hobby game boards more closely resemble territorial maps in organizing information through digital spatial layouts that divide the board into discrete areas. The dominant data visualization paradigms for board games, that is, intrinsically resonate with a territorial vision dependent on the digital division of space. While this resonance is explicit for territorial games like *RISK* that use spatial maps to represent contested physical spaces, the digital informational space of game boards relies on visually bounded spatial divisions being used to represent just about anything. For instance, when *The Game of Life* uses space to represent temporal life narratives and *Monopoly* uses space to represent abstract economic opportunity, they both data-fy progress in similar ways. Through all these variations, spatiality functions as the media-specific lens through which a wide variety of thematic significances can be visualized.

Operational environments and the operational glance – Board games invite players to make moves within *operational environments*, navigable possibility spaces in which players can act both in and on these environments by tangibly altering material game states. Although artistry and data visualization are important ways games construct world views, they cannot construct full-fledged game worlds by themselves – indeed, many non-play media combine artistry and data visualization without facilitating the playful performances that Booth (2021) argues define the board game medium. Thus, it is operational environments and the *operational glances* they elicit that make games what they are – simultaneously navigable worlds and world views.

A game's operational environment is its rule-governed system for paralleling material and virtual moves – that is, how physically manipulating the material game state symbolically alters the virtual game state. The operational environments constructed by game boards and inhabited in gameplay are *int(e) ractable* in that their affordances and constraints sustain each other. Games are interactable only because their material representations and rulesets are to some extent intractable. To play a game is to make moves that are only possible within the rule-governed constraints of the game. While the physical movement of pawns across a chessboard is governed only by the laws of physics, to actually make a move in *Chess* requires following player-enforced rules that lend special significance to this material activity. Operational environments are at once maps of what players can do and the sites where these moves take place.

As gameplay requires socially reinforced adherence to these virtual rules, moving in a virtual game world is less like moving in a natural environment and more like moving in a socially constructed environment governed by explicit and implicit rules. Whereas gladiatorial 'games' directly play out brute analogue violence, wargames only indirectly represent combat. Instead, wargames play out the violent construction of geopolitical entities on paper through maps and treaties. Board games are not ideological only when they portray real-world themes – the very nature of the medium is an exercise in social-constructedness. Thus, while thematic games use 'player interactions and player/environment conflicts' (Condis 2014: 86) to explicitly lend narrative significance to gameplay, even abstract games constitute virtual worlds within which players can move and act.

In addition to providing material systems for tracking in-game agency, board games script this agency by providing clear goals or winning conditions. This teleology radically recontextualizes the visual rhetoric of the game by lending purposiveness to the glance. This *operational glance* flits across the board to assess strategic opportunities rather than contemplate a visual aesthetic, much in the same way a military tactician might survey a map while formulating a strategy. As game environments are simultaneously world views and worlds unto themselves, this operational glance somewhat contradictorily invites players to oscillate between projecting themselves into the world as goal-directed agents and distancing themselves from the world to take a tactical view of the operational environment as map.

In summary, artistry and data visualization constitute *world views* by visually inflecting how players conceive the virtual game world, while operational environments constitute actual *worlds*. Thus, when players glance down at the game, they not only glance off the game to see player agency reflected in the material game state but also glance *through* the game to see the virtual world immanent in the material environment. As players waver between these glances, they enter into the simultaneously immersive and non-immersive space of interacting with and within a board game medium that necessarily oscillates between world and world view.

Territorializing game boards: *RISK* and the world picture

The rulebook for the first English edition of *RISK* opens with an unusual invitation: 'Before starting the actual play of the game, players should study the board which represents a map of the world' (Parker Brothers 1959: 2). Designed by French filmmaker Albert Lamorisse as *La Conquête du Monde*, *RISK* presented itself as a new style of mass-market wargame for a post-war culture processing the horrors of the war while simultaneously reinvesting in leisure culture. A game of *RISK* begins with players' armies spread across its central territorial map, after which players use simple dice-driven combat to vie for territory until one player conquers the entire globe. The world of *RISK* is therefore a world of divided territories whose only purpose is to be conquered. And, as the opening invitation indicates, the map-centric world of *RISK* is also a *world view* that invites players to play out the conquest of the map itself.

This world view is constructed primarily through the territorial map that constitutes the *RISK* game board (Figure 7.2), which draws on a historical aesthetic that Mahaffey describes as characteristic of wargames:

> Through most of history, the mapmaker's task was relating spatial and ideological information rather than pure geographical precision. As mapping has become more and more utility-oriented and now even computer-based, this artistic aspect has often suffered. Given that major goals of map wargames are to evoke an historical period and to immerse the player in an experience, they provide a

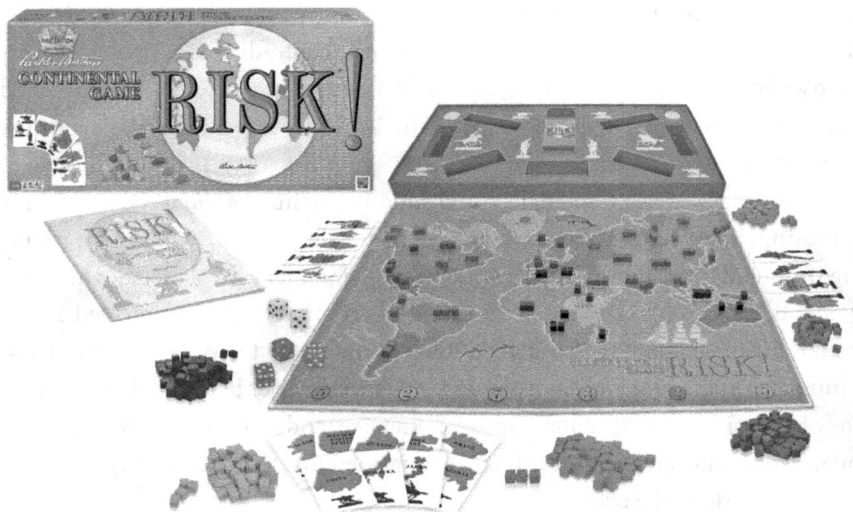

Figure 7.2 A reproduction of the 1959 first edition of *RISK* staged to replicate the downward glance of a player seated over the game board. This glance centres the perspective of the red player, who is depicted as having the most armies, most controlled territories and most cards. This is also a solipsistic glance as the inhuman precision of the other player hands alongside the haphazard arrangement of the other player cubes around the periphery of the game (but not on the opposing side) blurs the sense of opponents' presence. Thus, this image partially invites players into the world view of a plausible in-game state while also foregrounding the components in ways that evoke nostalgia for this 'classic reproduction', as the box cover proclaims. Overall, the design extends its territorial world view beyond the board with a recurring motif of the globe on the cover, rulebook, and insert and with the bold map-as-logo design of the player cards. Image courtesy of Winning Moves Games.

> useful opportunity to address the basic aesthetic of a given place and time – and thus represent one of the few remaining commercial avenues where this broader tradition of mapmaking can survive and thrive. (2016: 70)

Rather than precise analogues of real-world geography, game maps are aestheticized environments designed to elicit particular experiences. As a colour-coded territorial map with gratuitous aesthetic features like sea creatures and sailing ships, *RISK* evokes the tradition of historical imperial maps to situate its expansionist fantasy within real-world geopolitics. At the same time, with its streamlined, brightly coloured aesthetic, *RISK* attempts to make the game of global domination thematically compelling without feeling too heavy or serious, a delicate balance necessary to make a lighter wargame accessible in the mass market. Similarly, *RISK* divides some countries and combines others to streamline its operational environment. As the rulebook states, the 'sizes and boundaries of the territories are not accurate, but have been set to facilitate the play of the game' (Parker Brothers 1959: 2). Rather than accurately simulating historical expansion, *RISK* distils the expansionist impulse into a singular, accessible, playable world view.

This world view not only facilitates strategic war play but also construes the world as inherently organizable, divisible and controllable – a territorial vision that exemplifies the modern phenomenon that philosopher Martin Heidegger names the *world picture*:

> The fundamental event of the modern age is the conquest of the world as picture. The word 'picture' [*Bild*] now means the structured image [*Gebild*] that is the creature of man's producing which represents and sets before. In such producing, man contends for the position in which he can be that particular being who gives the measure and draws up the guidelines for everything that is. (1977: 134)[3]

In describing this picturing *as* conquest, Heidegger portrays an entire cultural ideology as a game of global domination, a world view predicated on objectifying the world into controllable territories or exploitable resource reserves. Conversely, by playing out the conquest a territorial map – the world as picture – *RISK* invites players to enter into a data visualization that maps the world entirely in terms of control. More than representing imperial maps, the rule-governed operational environment of *RISK* itself plays out the totalizing representational sway of the world picture constructing the world in its own image.

One particularly important example of this is how *RISK* not only represents but also operationalizes the nationalist icon of the map-as-logo, 'the practice of the imperial states of coloring their colonies on maps with an imperial dye' such that '[a]s this "jigsaw" effect became normal, each "piece" could be wholly detached from its geographic context' (Anderson 2000: 175). In this way, by isolating its territories on discrete cards, *RISK* reinforces an anthropocentric and nationalist picture of a fragmented world defined more by geopolitical boundaries than geographic ones. After all, *RISK* territories are merely bordered outlines with no geographic or historical specificity outside adjacency relationships that determine movement and part-whole relationships that determine continental groupings.

This method of visualizing a nationalist imaginary further connects *RISK* to a historical tradition of using a map-as-logo aesthetic to promote imperial ideology. As Megan Norcia relates, the historical tradition of colonial puzzles wove an imperialist territorial vision into children's play:

> The puzzle was born in the same workshops as its more formal sibling, the imperial map. Yet both were serious documents reflecting the process of consolidating a national imaginary; the imperial map presented the world in its mapped state, and the puzzle allowed users to continually rehearse the project of mapping the world by piecing together its parts. (2009: 5)

Like puzzles, *RISK*-style wargames borrow from the cultural history of imperial maps to create performative spaces for players to 'continually rehearse' territorial visions. Yet these games transcend the performativity of the puzzle by not only rehearsing imperial map logic but also playing out imperial expansion. Consequently, the aesthetics and data visualizations in *RISK* invoke a territorial vision to construct a distinctive gaming experience that utilizes its map board for playing out the literal conquest of the world picture – the conquering of the map board itself.

To play out the conquest of the world picture, *RISK* players must navigate an operational environment that organizes both the means (gameplay) and ends (win conditions) that define the game. Agency in *RISK* primarily means placing and moving armies, triggering combat and potentially conquering territories. As there is not much strategy to the dice-driven combat itself, the primary strategic considerations are where and when to attack, how to pursue necessary expansion without overextending and creating vulnerabilities for counterattacks (hence the English title 'Risk'). Thus, as the operational glance searches for strategic opportunities to breach an opponent's line of defence or to shore up its own, it perceives landmasses only in terms of contested borders. This world of shifting borders but no capitols, dwellings, nor other territorial features is an operational environment whose only agential possibilities are entirely in service of imperialist expansion.

Within this operational environment, players place and move abstract, colour-coded wooden cubes that ostensibly represent armies but more pointedly represent the imperial dye that marks affiliations on territorial maps. At the start of their turn, players receive armies based on the number of territories and continents (groups of territories) they control. Ideologically, this links the expansion of territorial borders to the accumulation of *biopower*, as Michel Foucault would call national populations treated as human resources. This presents war as a self-sustaining feedback loop – the spoils of war are more resources for waging war. As territories generate biopower automatically without any sense of assimilation or resistance from the conquered populations, *RISK* simulates less actual warfare and more the distilled territorial ideal of the imperial map.

While territorial control in *RISK* is a zero-sum game – the same forty-two territories keep changing hands – the accumulation of militarized biopower is not. The world of *RISK* is a world in which control automatically generates more means of control (armies), a militarized version of Althusser's description of ideology as how 'the ultimate condition of production is therefore the reproduction of the conditions of production' (1971: 127). This is a world designed to be conquered not dwelt in. More than a commentary *on* the world picture, *RISK is* the world picture materialized in a navigable game world. Its artistry, data visualization and operational environment play out a distilled historical fantasy of absolute imperialist control as the game invites players 'to occupy every territory on the board and in so doing, eliminate all other players' (Parker Brothers 1959: 1). Notably, this rhetoric gives primacy to the conquest of the world picture, only secondarily noting that it entails eliminating the other human players. Once again, this all-encompassing territorial vision presents an idealized historical fantasy whose emotionally distanced world view performs the very ideology of detachment that justifies actual war.

The operational glance invites player agency, but only in a world as picture, a world of pure information, objective and absolute. And yet, 'how that abstraction is applied to a given historical situation can have great effect on the experience of gameplay and the perception of the game's topic' (Mahaffey 2016: 63). In the case of *RISK*, abstraction characterizes an operational glance that situates players above the fray even as they project agency into it. As armies and territories are possessed (both owned and animated) by players who remain aloof and literally above the action, players are invited to play out the fantasy of controlling the globe from a clinically detached war room.

While author and wargamer H. G. Wells (1913) optimistically argued that critical distance helps 'little wars' critique 'great wars', this abstraction of war into a game has an ambivalent ethical character. It would be naïve to assume that uncritically playing out a territorial vision that has historically rationalized imperialism is inconsequential or benign. At the same time, it is not entirely clear that this post-war wargame advocates the ideologies it plays out. While the framing rhetoric of the game is largely uncritical, it is possible to create critical potential within how *RISK* neatly pictures the world picture. As a playful and even carnivalesque performance, *RISK* translates an ideological world view so pervasive that it is largely invisible into a material world view and navigable world, offering a uniquely playful and performative perspective on what makes the world picture a picture.

Reterritorializing game boards: Area control and the world target

Although *RISK*'s almost perfect microcosm of the world picture has certainly influenced the more recent revolution in modern hobby board game design, most *RISK*-style troops-on-a-map war games permute or nuance this singular vision. Consequently, this section performs a comparative analysis of how two Area Control games – *Twilight Struggle* and *Ideology: The War of Ideas 2nd Edition* – offer alternate territorial visions that reimagine the world picture for the age of the world target.

Modern board gaming offers countless variations on the troops-on-a-map formula, but while a few genuinely subvert imperialist ideologies, many simply permute or soften its core territorial vision. Most contemporary games replace *RISK*'s draconian win condition with something less totalizing, like accumulating victory points (*Kemet, Blood Rage, Small World*) or achieving a set of in-game goals (*Lords of Hellas, Inis*). Similarly, these games use fantasy (or historical fantasy) settings to create distance from the theme of real-world conquest. Some of these games (along with many wargames designed as realistic military simulations) employ a smaller map scope that presents a differently and less global territorial world view that instrumentalizes terrain (instead of territory) to provide topographical nuance to a dynamic battlefield. Even within the *RISK* franchise, Rob Daviau's *RISK Legacy* adds topographical nuance by showing how warfare can inscribe permanent changes (the defining feature of the Legacy system) on the land itself. Although in all these ways these games present world views that are less totalizing than the world picture, they all maintain a distinctly territorial vision that underlies the world picture.

One significant variation on *RISK*-style war games is Area Control, sometimes also called Area Majority or Area Influence. Instead of expanding and contracting territorial borders, Area Control games like *El Grande* and *Mission: Red Planet* allow players to influence any territory in the right circumstances, even such that multiple players may have presence in a territory at the same time. This simple change significantly reimagines territorial affiliation. Whereas the *RISK* world picture fixates on contested borders because it assumes absolute control *over* territories, Area Control games depict struggles for influence or control *within* territories. One consequence of this shift is that these games are more conducive to portraying 'soft power' like cultural influence. For the purposes of this chapter, the more significant consequence is that these games present all territories as perpetually and simultaneously contestable, a change that redirects the operational glance away from contested borders and towards a plurality of targets.

Contrasting Heidegger's theory of the world picture, Rey Chow calls this paradigm the *world target*, a tactical vision layered atop the world picture and defined by the optics of aerial warfare:

> While battles formerly tended to be fought with a clear demarcation of battlefronts versus civilian spaces, the aerial bomb . . . destroyed once and for all those classic visual boundaries that used to define battle. Second, with the transformation of the skies into war zones from which to attack, war was no longer a matter simply of armament or of competing projectile weaponry; rather, it became redefined as a matter of the logistics of perception, with seeing as its foremost function. (2006: 32)

While most maps adopt a bird's-eye view, territorial maps visually *ground* warfare by presenting military expansion as the horizontal transgression of borders, 'those classic visual boundaries that used to define battle'. In this map logic, space is both battleground and prize – with each successful battle, the empire expands to encompass the former battlefield. In contrast, the optics of the world target scans the totality of a landscape for available targets, pressure points that can be attacked or threatened as non-territorial leveraging of power.

Area Control games like the acclaimed *Twilight Struggle* and the lesser-known *Ideology: The War of Ideas 2nd Edition* (Figure 7.3) retain elements of territorial maps while changing the primary visual paradigm. *Twilight Struggle* reinscribes the territorial map by drawing a network of interconnected regions atop a *RISK*-like map that displays border lines although they are completely irrelevant to the gameplay. While the network of lines specifies adjacency for certain in-game functions, the large rectangular nodes provide independent spaces of contestation where players place influence markers. Although, like in *RISK*, players gain benefits from controlling continents, this board visualizes the world not as a site of expanding territories but as a network of interconnected targets to be perpetually and simultaneously contested. Taking this visual shift even further, the second edition of *Ideology* dispenses with the territorial map altogether, instead deconstructing and fragmenting the territorial map across a set of map-as-logo tiles that can each be contested independently.

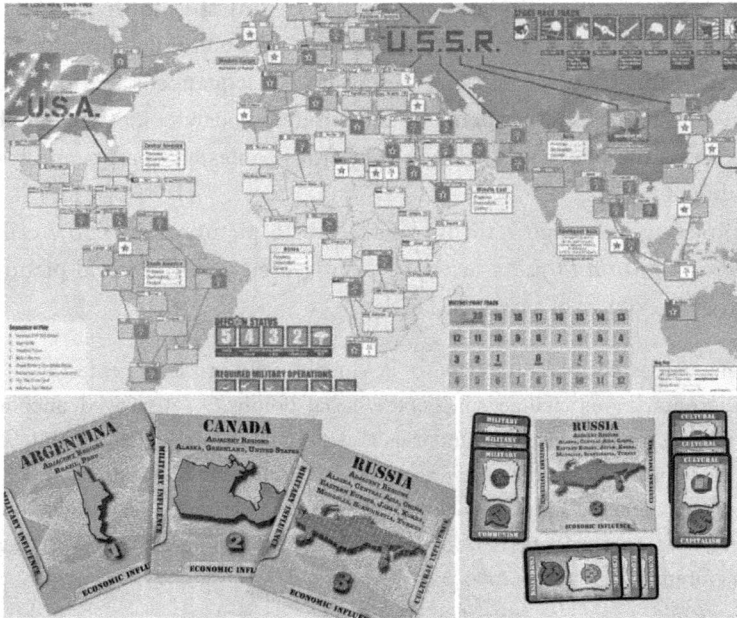

Figure 7.3 Images from the *Twilight Struggle* rulebook (top) and *Ideology* game (bottom), showing how the games map territorial control. Ironically, while the *Twilight Struggle* board includes a complete world map, its visual field is dominated by abstract territorial influence boxes while global parameters like DEFCON status and Victory Points are tracked in empty ocean areas. Conversely, while *Ideology* tiles (shown in the three Region sizes on the bottom left) dispense with the world map and instead list adjacencies as text, the centrality of the map-as-logo reinforces a territorial aesthetic. In both games, the territories are designed to display a struggle for influence within territories – *Twilight Struggle* providing boxes where influence tokens can represent a territory's seesawing affiliation and *Ideology* providing three areas where multiple players' influence cards can be displayed (as shown on the bottom right). Image of *Twilight Struggle* rulebook courtesy of GMT Games.

The culmination of the world target is the deterring presence of the atomic bomb, which revolutionized geopolitical conflict and facilitated the shift from the age of the world picture to that of the world target. For Chow, the atomic bomb represents the virtualization of war in which the act of targeting itself can change the balance of geopolitical power. A reimagining of the Cold War, *Twilight Struggle* depicts the virtual power of the atomic bomb through a highly unusual system – players can perform powerful actions that increase nuclear tensions (visualized by a DEFCON track), but a player forced to initiate nuclear war immediately loses the game. Less drastically, *Ideology* also attributes symbolic value to its 'Weapon of Mass Destruction' in that possessing an unused WMD yields a Global Influence point. Thus, the targetable but not usable atomic bomb exemplifies an ideology of virtual war, as Chow describes, 'Warring in virtuality meant competing with the enemy for the stockpiling, rather than actual use, of preclusively horrifying weaponry. To terrorize the other, one specializes in representation, in the means of display and exhibition' (2006: 33).

In a world where weapons are signifiers and signifiers are weapons, warfare is waged in both reality and possibility across geographic terrain and delocalized information networks. Game scholars Nick Dyer-Witheford and Greig de Peuter describe this state as 'the emergence of a new planetary regime in which economic, administrative, military, and communicative components combine to create a system of power "with no outside"' (2009: xix). Consequently, while this ideology disrupts the territorial vision of total militaristic world conquest, it maintains a totalizing vision of power that has a kind of post-geographic territorialism that plays out in the war of ideas. In some ways more ambitious than military expansionism, the age of the world target positions all aspects of society – including playing at war – as simultaneously contested spaces for the war of ideas, producing a state of *perpetual war*, a game that can never be won.

Replacing *RISK*'s war to end all wars with perpetual war significantly complicates what it means to 'win' in a particular game world. While *RISK* distils the totalizing fantasy of the world picture into an unrealistically hyper-nationalist fantasy (Anderson 2000: 7), Area Control games better simulate the actual power dynamics of competing for national or ideological affiliations by awarding relative rather than absolute victories (accumulating the most points over a given period, controlling the most territories at a particular moment, etc.). Such games allow players to play out the paradoxical fantasy of winning an unwinnable, perpetual war. Again, while this is another unrealistic fantasy, this fantasy motivates and sustains actual perpetual war. Precisely because such a war cannot be won once and for all, contestants are motivated to struggle to be on top at every possible moment. Consequently, Area Control games offer relative, provisional victories that reflect the murky, symbolic advances that characterize virtual, perpetual wars.

Board games are particularly well suited to materializing virtual wars, as the medium is entirely concerned with the strategic play of signifiers. As game representations play out war, they neatly model how war becomes an act of representation. Thus, I suggest that the notion of the world target is broadly applicable to board games, which invite players to adopt a targeting glance within contested virtual worlds. Most board games physically position the operational glance such that strategic decisions of any thematic significance are visualized through aerial targeting. Most board games are perpetual insofar as they offer conflicts designed to be reset and replayed. And most board games are predicated on some form of contestation that often relies on a territorial vision of contested space.

Indeed, these tendencies are common even outside war-themed games, as when worker placement games offer an eerily familiar optics of targeting fragmented spaces or when *Monopoly* construes capitalist accumulation according to an eerily familiar territorial vision predicated on contesting divided land until all properties are controlled by a single player. So, it should not be surprising that so many board games imagine land less as a fully open topography and more as artificially divided, discrete areas parcelled out through territorial borders or capitalist ownership. Deterritorializing game boards, therefore, requires more than asking board games to embody anti-war or anti-imperialist sentiments. Instead, it requires deconstructing the territorializing visions that permeate the board gaming experience itself.

Deterritorializing game boards: Humanitarian logistics and cooperative play

Since territorializing visions can transcend theme, there is no game genre inherently immune to imperialist world views – even some cooperative anti-war, anti-imperialist games like *Spirit Island* and *Dawn of Peacemakers* maintain a territorial vision and promote an ideology of redemptive violence that justifies war to end war. Conversely, there is no game genre inherently incapable of critically interrogating its own world view, as when *Spirit Island*'s lands come alive, animating their guardian spirits to resist colonization and its environmental blight. Yet, some types of games do tend to disrupt conventional gaming in particular ways. Dexterity games often disrupt virtuality by bringing play immanently back into the material, legacy games often disrupt perpetual gameplay by permanently altering material components, and cooperative games often disrupt (or at least reimagine) longstanding cultural alignments of play and contestation that incline people to 'call war a game' (Huizinga 1950: 89). To offer a brief counternarrative to territorial visions, this section looks to this latter category to discover how two cooperative humanitarian logistics games – *Pandemic* and *Freedom: The Underground Railroad* – offer deterritorializing world views based on population flows.

Both game boards maintain familiar map elements, with *Pandemic* being more topographical and *Freedom* (Figure 7.4) more territorial. Atop these familiar maps, both games add a network of paths that at first glance resemble

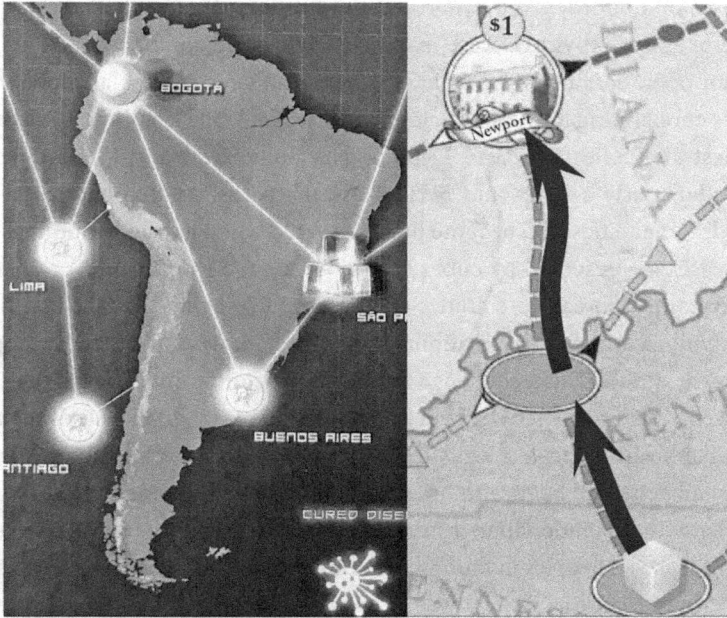

Figure 7.4 A comparison of the networked maps on the *Pandemic* (left) and *Freedom* (right) boards, both of which train the player to direct their operational glance towards lines of flow rather than territories. The *Pandemic* example shows how the interconnected lines between population centres enable movement of both player characters (see the player pawn in Bogotá) and disease cubes (should a fourth yellow cube need to be added to São Paolo, cubes would instead be added to the four connected cities). Note how the board shows no territorial boundaries and instead uses a geometric grid and topographic shading to aestheticize the scientific viewpoint. The *Freedom* example from the rulebook shows how players may move enslaved peoples along a network of routes representing the Underground Railroad inscribed atop a territorial map of the United States. Here, the lines drawn atop the historicized map illustrate the transgressive movement of the Underground Railroad. Image of *Freedom* rulebook courtesy of Academy Games.

the interconnected nodes in *Twilight Struggle*. Yet, whereas the nodes in *Twilight Struggle* represent controllable nations with spaces for influence and a national flag in the corner, the networks in *Pandemic* and *Freedom* are road maps whose lines of flow visually present the world as a network of interconnected population centres. This also contrasts with the territorial *RISK* map, which is functionally equivalent in terms of representing adjacencies for movement (two adjacent bordered regions and two nodes with a connecting line provide the exact same gameplay possibilities). Yet, this alternate data visualization strategy deterritorializes the operational glance by drawing the eye not towards the transgression of borders but towards the utilization of transportation networks. Instead of a world divided, these maps picture a world connected.

As an operational environment, *Pandemic* situates players as global health workers cooperating to win by curing four diseases while keeping the diseases in check lest they collectively lose. Depicting its globalized transportation network as simultaneously a boon and peril, the same pathways that allow players to access different cities also become lines of spread when a disease outbreaks. It is the diseases (represented by cubes that resemble the *RISK* armies) rather than the players that spread to colonize the board. Leveraging the fact that disease targets biological rather than national humanity, *Pandemic* plays out the logistics of global health work as a challenge for the global community, depicting medical teams as having unrestricted access to the world. This world view uses the theme of a global health crisis to idealistically imagine a world of – to appropriate the name of an actual global health organization – doctors without borders.

Similarly, the operational environment in *Freedom* depicts the logistical challenge of aiding enslaved peoples in finding freedom in Canada. This map more explicitly transgresses a territorial vision by depicting the networked lines that represent the Underground Railroad literally transgressing the drawn borders of the territorial map. Here, visual separation of the United States from Canada recontextualizes the nationalist aesthetic of imperial dyes to emphasize an underlying tragedy of slavery, namely that native non-citizens can find freedom only in expatriation. In these ways, these deterritorializing games thematize humanitarianism by redirecting how the operational glance views the territorial map.

Coda

The ethics of play is complex, especially since board games often materialize ideologies without taking a clear rhetorical stance for or against them. Since board games typically lean less on traditional rhetoric and more on procedural rhetoric, their primary ethical consideration is how they invite players to act within worlds governed by implicitly ideological world views. The very operational glance that allows players to project agency into game worlds simultaneously immerses players in totalizing world views. While some games adopt the cultural ideologies theorized as the *world picture* and *world target*, all games picture their worlds in ways designed to elicit and organize targeted visions.

It should be concerning that – in the profound cultural intertwining of empire and map, war and game – territorial visions have thoroughly inflected board game history. Even while *Pandemic* and *Freedom* deterritorialize their game boards, they construct different yet equally monolithic world views that retain aspects of territorial or targeted visions. As the glance materially positions players as glancing down on the game world from above, board games tend to situate players as master-tacticians holding power over the world and map alike. Like the implied maleness of the cinematic gaze, the operational glance may be disposed to a kind of paternalism that celebrates the linkage of power and knowledge. Is humanitarian play just another power fantasy of individual saviours rescuing otherwise helpless populations? It is certainly not implausible, especially since *Pandemic* and *Freedom* both translate humanitarianism into winnable logistics puzzles. Yet, perhaps it is better to say that the operational glance is fundamentally contested – the ethically charged yet ethically ambivalent glance flits across contested spaces in ways that can both play with and play out territorial vision.

To deterritorialize board games is to disrupt these territorial visions through critical play and critical game design. And, because these visions are inherently embodied and performed, to deterritorialize board games is also to deterritorialize ourselves.

Notes

1   Deleuze and Guattari proposed this critical term as a radical reimagining of psychoanalytic thinking in *Anti-Oedipus: Capitalism and Schizophrenia*. My use of the term loosely fits into their paradigm but is used much more narrowly to specifically target modern hobby board gaming.

2   Two notable examples include *Cinema 1: The Movement Image* by Gilles Deleuze and *Visual Pleasure and Narrative Cinema* by Laura Mulvey. Deleuze's analysis of the affective impact of the close-up relies on a sustained gaze that the movement of the glance disrupts. Mulvey's ideological critique of the supposed objectivity of the film camera should raise questions about whether games construct the imagined player's viewpoint according to a privileged, patriarchal subject position. Although games vary in this respect, the imperialist world view explored in this chapter certainly has patriarchal and paternalist dimensions.

3   It is important to note that Heidegger has been justly criticized for his involvement with the Nazi Party and his philosophy should be read and applied only with an appropriate suspicion. In this case, I believe citing Heidegger is useful for articulating the nuances of the world picture precisely so we can ethically interrogate this world view, which has become problematically entwined with the territorial vision of this post-war wargame.

References

Althusser, L. (1971), *Lenin and Philosophy and Other Essays*, trans. B. Brewster, New York: Monthly Review Press.

Anderson, B. (2000), *Imagined Communities: Reflections on the Origin and Spread of Nationalism*, New York: Verso.

Black, J. (2016), *Geopolitics and the Quest for Dominance*, Bloomington: Indiana University Press.

Bogost, I. (2007), *Persuasive Games: The Expressive Power of Videogames*, Cambridge, MA: The MIT Press.

Booth, P. (2021), *Board Games as Media*, New York: Bloomsbury Academic.

Chow, R. (2006), *The Age of the World Target: Self-Referentiality in War, Theory, and Comparative Work*, Durham, NC: Duke University Press.

Condis, M. (2014), 'Adaptation and Space: Thematic and Atmospheric Considerations for Board Game Environment Construction', *Intensities*, 7: 84–90.

Costikyan, G. (2011), 'Boardgame Aesthetics', in G. Costikyan and D. Davidson (eds), *Tabletop: Analog Game Design*, 179–84, Pittsburgh, PA: ETC Press.

Dyer-Witheford, N. and G. de Peuter. (2009), *Games of Empire: Global Capitalism and Video Games*, Minneapolis: University of Minnesota Press.

Edney, M. H. (1997), *Mapping an Empire: The Geographical Construction of British India, 1765–1843*, Chicago: University of Chicago Press.

Halter, E. (2006), *From Sun Tzu to Xbox: War and Video Games*, New York: Thunder's Mouth Press.

Heidegger, M. (1977), 'The Age of the World Picture', in *The Question Concerning Technology and Other Essays*, trans. W. Lovitt, 115–54, New York: Harper Torchbooks.

Huizinga, J. (1950), *Homo Ludens: A Study in the Play-Element of Culture*, Boston, MA: Beacon Press.

Järvinen, A. (2007), 'Games without Frontiers: Theories and Methods for Game Studies and Design', PhD Thesis, University of Tampere, Tampere.

Mahaffey, M. (2016), 'Historical Aesthetics in Mapmaking', in P. Harrigan and M. G. Kirschenbaum (eds), *Zones of Control: Perspectives on Wargaming*, 63–70, Cambridge, MA: The MIT Press.

Norcia, M. A. (2009), 'Puzzling Empire: Early Puzzles and Dissected Maps as Imperial Heuristics', *Children's Literature*, 37: 1–32.

Norcia, M. A. (2019), *Gaming Empire in Children's British Board Games 1836–1860*, New York: Routledge.

Parker Brothers (1959), *RISK!*, Rulebook, Salem: Parker Brothers.

Stahl, R. (2010), *Militainment, Inc.: War, Media, and Popular Culture*, New York: Routledge.

Wells, H. G. (1913), *Little Wars*, London: Frank Palmer.

8

'Nature' games in a time of climate crisis[1]

Chloé Germaine

Introduction: Climate change and nature games

Climate educator Bill McKibben (2015) argues that the science on climate change has been clear for over twenty years: environmentalists have already won the argument. Moreover, as poll after poll demonstrates, citizens across the globe would like their governments to take action on the climate (UNDP 2021). Climate action has not stalled, then, because of a lack of awareness and because people are not educated in the facts. Rather, there has been a widespread political and imaginative failure to confront the crisis. Philosophers suggest that this failure is in part due to the way in which we conceptualize 'nature' (Haraway 2016; Latour 2017; Morton 2016; Vetlesen 2019). The social, scientific and moral paradigms that dominate current environmental and economic thinking make it difficult to build solidarity between humans and the more-than-human world. In this context, this chapter considers the role of board games in a time of climate crisis and identifies the conceptual problem of 'nature' as a call for imaginative as well as practical and political responses.

In game studies scholars and designers are exploring the potential for games to intervene in all these domains (the practical, the political and the imaginative) and to think about the affordances of games in the context of the climate crisis. Alenda Chang, for example, argues that 'games are intermediary objects through which swirl both imaginative fantasy and real activity and places, with real, if not directly predictable effects' (2019: 4). In this chapter I consider Chang's proposal that games are (inter)mediations of ecological problems, concepts and ethics, focusing on the recent trend for 'nature' board games that purport to either simulate, or engage players with, nonhuman organisms and life processes. I evaluate the problems and possibilities that inhere in the systems (or rules), mechanics (what players do during the game), and the aesthetics of 'nature' board games. This taxonomy draws on concepts developed by Miguel Sicart (2008) and Robin Hunicke, Marc LeBlanc and Robert Zubek (2004) for game analysis. Following their work, I am interested in the rules of 'nature' games as a 'possibility state' (Sicart 2008) and as a pre-coded system freighted with ethical and ideological implications about the ontological and relational status of the 'natural' objects and beings represented in the game. I distinguish between rules and mechanics, considering the latter as the 'methods invoked by agents' in their interaction with the game system (Sicart 2008: n.p.). This distinction separates player actions from the pre-coded system of the rules and, so, allows me to extrapolate the different possibilities of gameplay. Finally, my designation of the 'aesthetic' dimension of board games incorporates the classical meaning of the word as to do with 'sensuous perception' and, more broadly, visual appearance and effect (Baumgarten 1750; Williams 2015: 1–2), as well as the meaning deployed in the MDA framework, which specifies the emotional responses of the player prompted by the game (Hunicke, LeBlanc and Zubek 2004). Typically, game studies has, through such analytic terminology, discussed play as the province of the human subject, a way of 'being in the world, through objects, towards others' (Sicart 2014: 39). This chapter pushes at the boundaries of this humanist assumption about play to consider the ways in which 'nature' games might connect human players with other (both imagined and real) actors with whom we are interconnected and with whom we share the consequences of climate change. My approach here builds on a trend for developing frameworks that seek to evaluate games in a time of climate crisis, such as those developed by Hans-Joachim Backe (2017) and Aysem Mert and Sandra van der Hel (2016), both of which pertain to video games. Where these critics are interested in how video games construct social meanings of climate change, the accuracy of their representations and the ways they engage human players in thinking about ecological issues, I consider how board games construct non-anthropocentric 'natural' agents within the broadly anthropocentric medium of play.

There has been a proliferation of climate-themed board games in the past two decades that explicitly address the issue through the lens of sustainability. The board game *Keep Cool* (2004), designed by climate scientists Klause Eisenack and Gerhard Petschel-Held, and *Daybreak*, which – at the time of writing – is being developed by Matt Leacock and Matteo Menapace, engage players with the global politics of climate change. *Tiny Footprint* (2019), designed by Marcus Jargarden, asks players to consider their personal responsibilities, inculcating carbon literacy at the level of domestic consumption. *Carbon City Zero* (2020), designed by Sam Illingworth and Paul Wake, and *Tipping Point* (2020), designed by Ryan Smith, both engage players with thinking about sustainability and responsibility for the accumulation of emissions at the scale of the city community. Eisenack (2013), Kwok (2019) and Fjaellingsdal and Klöckner (2020) argue that such games can be used as tools for communicating the science of climate change and for engaging players in discussions about social responsibility with a view to transforming attitudes and behaviour. However, understanding how games might intervene in the contemporary climate crisis involves more than assessing them as tools for science communication or for teaching sustainability. Considering games as an intervention implies that they challenge or disrupt dominant scientific, moral and educational paradigms that constrain thinking about the environment. This includes sustainability. As Christopher Groves suggests, the concept of sustainability remains 'within the limitations of modernist ways of thinking, in which the future is imagined solely in terms of the continuation of present projects, which are then projected into the future in a way that colonizes future possibilities' (2019: 915). Tim Morton goes further, calling 'sustainability' a 'vacuous' term that is good news for neither human, coral and kiwi bird nor lichen, since what is being sustained is the 'capitalist world-economic structure' (2017: 88). Sustainability will not build solidarity because it is reliant on humans remaining outside of nature, albeit as custodians.

Following this call for an intervention that challenges the limitations of current thinking about human interrelationships with the environment, I want to suggest that the ecological possibilities of 'nature' games are not dependent on their scientific accuracy, although my analysis will consider the ways in which the systems and mechanics of board games both erase and evoke the lively entanglements that are being uncovered by scientists working in biology, botany and ecology. That is, scientific concepts are valuable in my analysis but do not function as the arbiter of the validity of games because, as a praxis developed in the Minority World, science has itself contributed to the de-animation of the earth and to a concept of nature as pure externality (see, e.g., Ingold 2000; Latour 2017; Vetlesen 2019). I use the term 'Minority World' here instead of the usual term, the West, following Shahidul Alam's (2008) expression of 'the majority world' as a challenge to the dominance of Western perspectives. One such perspective is perpetuated by scientific discourse. As Tim Ingold suggests, science is shot through with a paradox that asserts humans as biological organisms, on the one hand, while the scientific account 'rests on a separation of humanity from organic nature' on the other (2000: 11). Science alone is not good for building solidarity between the inhabitants of the earth, then. Moreover, as Myanna Lahsen and

Esther Turnhout (2021) have suggested, there persist power structures and interests within the institutions of climate science that obstruct reform and that are preventing a shift from the modelling of biogeochemical conditions to efforts to understand the socio-political obstacles to action. Scientific institutions and environmental education do not possess all the answers. Thus, my analysis engages with eco-philosophical and ethical principles, as opposed to assessing scientific accuracy, as I investigate how 'nature' games both perpetuate and challenge the conceptual and imaginative failures of the climate crisis.

Against 'nature': Solidarity and situatedness

Throughout this chapter I adhere to a line of thought in the humanities in which 'nature' signifies a problematic designation with 'unsustainable intellectual foundations' (Cronon 1996: 50). As Bruno Latour insists, one of the challenges of the climate crisis is that it has so thoroughly exposed a naïve construction of 'nature' as something from which humans are apart: the very notion of 'nature' once invoked to stabilize and reassure 'has made the world uninhabitable' precisely because this separation is what has fuelled the crisis (Latour 2017: 35, 36). To an extent, 'nature' games are an uneasy compatriot in negotiating climate change, since many perpetuate a naïve fantasy of 'nature' as an edenic domain separate from human 'culture'. The award-winning *Wingspan* (2019), designed by Elizabeth Hargrave, for example, asks players to produce a pristine 'wildlife preserve' that will be a haven for birds. In *Renature*, designed by Michael Kiesling and Wolfgang Kramer, players compete with dominoes to 'restore a polluted valley with plants and animals' (2020). The art in these games favours eco-mimesis with respect to depictions of animals and birds, and human actions take place in the abstract domain of the rules, rather than being represented aesthetically within the game. Yet, however removed the human might be in such games however 'edenic' the aesthetic representation, the rules and mechanics of board games nonetheless entangle human 'culture' with 'nature', producing uneasy 'naturecultures' that recognize the inseparability of these mutually dependent terms (Haraway 2003). Put simply, I will argue that the ludic affordances of 'nature' board games contain possibilities for tackling the conceptual problems of the climate crisis even where the games seem to uphold an edenic conception of 'nature' as a separate domain.

My intervention in game studies advocates for a reorientation to what Latour names the 'terrestrial' as an antidote to the idealism of 'nature'. The terrestrial names a new political actor, which is the earth itself, but in so doing also recognizes the multitude of agents that comprise it (Latour 2018: 40–1). The terrestrial defines the unstable territory of earth in a time of climate crisis, which is no longer the stable ground of 'nature' nor the environment as mere background of human activity. Furthermore, the terrestrial refuses the old modes of distancing and separation that have defined modernity and science in the Minority World. While many nature games imply such a distance through rules that describe how players ought to manage a natural habitat or ecosystem and literally objectify the more-than-human worlds in the form of tokens, dominoes, and pieces on a board, the game mechanics (what players do) necessarily engage players with entangled naturecultures, resituating them within a terrestrial domain from which they never were separate. This is precisely what the climate crisis has revealed, of course, that the separation of humans from nature is a catastrophic fantasy.

To locate what Latour calls the terrestrial, I trace the contradictory directions in contemporary 'nature' gameplay that encourage different modes of knowledge about ecology. On the one hand, I follow an ascendant trajectory that seeks to tackle the scalar problem of the climate crisis by directing players' attention to large-scale systemic thinking. On the other hand, I consider the need for what Morton calls 'subscendence' (2016: 245, 2017: 102–3), which names a descendent trajectory to counteract both a transcendent gaze that would encapsulate 'nature' as holistic and an objectifying scientific view from nowhere. The ascendant trajectory aims for what James Lovelock (1972) and Lynn Margulis (1973) call Gaia, the earth as a synergistic, self-regulating complex system that supports life. This biospheric view of the earth as an organism is quite different to a view of the earth as a planet, a Galilean object seen from a remote and virtual vantage point somewhere in the universe (Latour 2018: 67). The problem with Gaia, however, particularly in a time of climate crisis characterized by unexpected disruptions, tipping points and feedback loops, is its fiendish complexity and vast scale, both of which are difficult to comprehend. As Timothy Clark argues, the climate crisis is a challenge to human conceptions of scale, requiring us to think 'counter-intuitive relations' across multiple scales at once because the normal 'human scale' for negotiating problems is misleading (2015: 13, 30). Biospheric thinking, then, is a difficult but necessary counter to thinking at the human scale even if it is always in danger of collapsing into an objectifying view from above or outside the system.

To counteract the objectifying tendency of the ascendant view, I consider the descendent trajectories in gameplay, which mire players within the terrestrial as soily beings enmeshed in entangled ecosystems. As Latour suggests, the climate crisis requires that we 'try to descend from "nature" down toward the multiplicity of the world' because Gaia is not a whole that is somehow more than the sum of its parts' (2017: 36). Moreover, within the terrestrial there is no possibility of detachment, no view from without (Latour 2018: 72). The anthropologist Tim Ingold uses the same directional metaphor in his exhortation to 'descend from the imaginary heights of abstract reason and resituate ourselves in an active and ongoing engagement with our environments', which involves replacing the 'stale dichotomy of nature and culture with the dynamic synergy of organism and environment' (2000: 16). In Tim Morton's 'dark ecology' this descendent trajectory is bound up with *subscendence*, a conceptual inverse of transcendence, and a movement that connects us with a multitude of things that are more than their sum (2016: 245, 249). Indeed, *subscendence* refuses to countenance that the multiple agencies, objects and beings within a system are mere components transcended by the whole. The ways in which board game mechanics engage players with just such subscendent thinking is a unique affordance of the hobby. That is, our engagement with individual pieces, tokens, counters and cards, which in 'nature' games might be seeds, saplings, wolves or rivers, and their interrelated functions within the game go some way to counteracting the holism of 'Gaian' thinking and generates the possibility for solidarity between lifeforms, even if these are only abstractly represented in a game.

Tracing these opposing directions in ecological thought, then, I suggest that board game play contains possibilities for systems thinking at scale (biospheric thought) and for subscendence (terrestrial entanglements), which are complementary models for ethical and ecological situatedness. Certainly, the games I consider encourage human interaction with different kinds of agencies and relationships at different scales. While many 'nature' games may evoke problematic concepts of the natural or the ecological, they also represent possibilities for play and design that might resituate human players within the terrestrial.

From ethics to mechanics: A framework for evaluating 'nature' games

The concept of 'nature', discourses of sustainability that tend to dominate in environmental education, and the ethics of science in its present modernist incarnation do not provide the best foundation for developing solidarity between lifeforms. To make, and understand, games that might be able to forge such a solidarity requires scoping new conceptual ground. In what follows, I set out an evaluative framework that draws on ideas extant in eco-philosophy, environmental ethics and ecology. This framework provides a way of thinking about how games might make an intervention in engaging players with the climate crisis beyond their use as tools for communicating existing paradigms in environmental education. I recognize that some of the ideas on which the framework draws are not necessarily a good fit with established board game mechanics. There is a challenge here for game designers, then, to interrogate this mismatch and so better develop the potentials that inhere in board games for engagement with ecology. My framework is in sympathy with the eco-ethical framework for analysis of video games set out by Hans-Joachim Backe (2017: 47–9), which asks a range of questions about how games engage players with ecological concerns. Their fifth question, which asks about the degree to which game mechanics and semantics are anthropocentric, is the dominant concern here. I drill down into the ethical specificities of how games might challenge their tendency to anthropocentric representations and mechanics.

Turning away from existing frameworks constructed in game studies and science communication, my evaluation of 'nature' games takes inspiration from different elaborations of biocentric and ecocentric ethics. Broadly construed, these are ethics that extend moral considerability to more-than-human beings, including ecosystems, and that contest the idea that value is determined by a human agent. An ethical nature game would be one that did not elide the different conditions and needs of organisms within an ecosystem but that recognized the value and moral standing of the ecosystem itself. Such an ethics would complement the trajectories of ecological understanding discussed earlier, especially the need for *subscendence* and solidarity. There are also valuable ethical concepts emerging from the work of thinkers who identify as 'new materialists' and 'animists'. Stacy Alaimo and Susan Hekman's material feminism, for example, engages in 'developing theories in which nature is more than a passive social construction but is, rather, an agentic force that interacts with and changes the other elements in the mix, including the human' (2007: 7). Such theories do not divide the natural and the political but reconfigure the political to 'imagine ongoing democratic conversations in which nonhuman nature can participate in nondiscursive ways' (Alaimo and Hekman 2007: 7). However, a democracy inclusive of the more-than-human world relies on radically different notions of agency and sociality, such as those found in animist ontologies across the Majority World. Drawing on a concept of animism that extends sociality to the more-than-human world, eco-philosopher Anna Tsing suggests that the 'social' is made in entangling relations with significant others, a definition that recognizes that living beings other than humans are fully social with or without humans (2013: 27). As I will show, some 'nature' board games imply just such a recognition in their disclosure of the internal and external relations of more-than-human beings, modelling these relations through the game system and mechanics. In *Photosynthesis* (2017), designed by Hjalmar Hach, for example, nonhuman 'social' relations are elaborated in rules that govern interactions between individual trees, between trees and sunlight, and between fully grown trees and their seeds. In modelling such relations, board games intimate the social being of more-than-human actors.

In the scientific domain, emerging research offers further co-ordinates for an evaluative framework aimed at interrogating and designing 'nature' games. Alenda Chang has already begun the work of bringing ecology and game studies together, drawing on Erle Ellis and Navin Ramankutty's notion of the 'anthrome', or, an anthropogenic biome, to understand video game worlds (Chang 2019: 7–8; Ellis and Ramankutty 2008). The anthrome is a provocation to ecologists and game designers alike because it jettisons the idea that there are 'natural' ecosystems that humans 'disturb' and acknowledges the human influence on global ecosystems. These are 'human systems with natural ecosystems embedded within them' and require modes of investigation and understanding that integrate human and ecological systems (Ellis and Ramankutty 2008: 49). The very idea of a natural ecosystem or biome is a fallacy based upon a false divide between humans and nature that does not hold, especially not as the globe experiences anthropogenic climate change. If, as Chang suggests, games act as 'mesocosms' (2019: 21), that is, as experimental enclosures that model ecological states, relations and agencies, then they are mesocosms in which the 'natural' and the 'human' are thoroughly entangled. Entanglement is also the watchword in developmental biology, as work by Scott Gilbert, Jan Sapp and Alfred Tauber (2012) attests. Their thesis that 'we have never been individuals' challenges the classical biological conception of the organism: 'Animals cannot be considered individuals by anatomical or physiological criteria because a diversity of symbionts are both present and functional in completing metabolic pathways and serving other physiological functions. Similarly [. . .] new studies have shown that animal development is incomplete without symbionts' (Gilbert, Sapp and Tauber 2012: 325). Just as human systems are entangled with 'natural' ones, so are human bodies and those of other animals entangled with one another. Finally, in the field of forest ecology and management, the work of Suzanne Simard and others has suggested cross-species collaboration at scale in woodland ecosystems as trees share resources through a network of fungi and microbes in the soil, affectionately known as the 'wood wide web' (Beiler et al. 2009; Simard 2021). New paradigms in ecology and biology, then, are shifting a popular understanding of 'nature' as a site of a pseudo-Darwinian and Hobbesian contest and competition towards a state of collaboration and cooperation.

These ideas from philosophy and science are not necessarily a good fit with contemporary board game design, but there are some potential synergies. The games in my sample fall into the category of 'eurogames', which, rather than being immersive simulations, reveal themselves as games (Woods 2012: 83). That is, they invite players to pay attention to the rules and mechanics and encourage experimentation with different approaches through replayability, wherein each (re)play offers possibilities for adopting different strategies within the written rules. Replayability encourages systemic thinking about and reflection on the different modes of interaction modelled in the game world. In what remains of the chapter, then, I interrogate the possibilities inherent in contemporary 'nature' board games through a series of short case studies. I explore the potentials for synergy with, as well as areas of tension between, ethical, philosophical and scientific ideas that decentre the human while making clear our embeddedness in 'nature'. I apply the co-ordinates taken from Sicart and the MDA framework (distilled previously as rules, mechanics and aesthetics) alongside an ethical framework for evaluating games that is emerging from this tangle of cross-disciplinary ideas. In summary, the framework evaluates games according to the following principles:

1. That they engage players with the moral considerability of more-than-human beings, inclusive of 'individual' organisms, however contingent that individuality, to whole ecosystems, without erasing difference.
2. That they extend concepts of sociality and agency beyond the human.
3. That they explore the ways that agency is distributed across networks and assemblages, rather than being a property held by an individual. Indeed, I contend that distributed agency is a necessary condition for solidarity between lifeforms.
4. That they disclose collaboration as a fundamental condition for the development of life.
5. That they complicate neat distinctions between human and 'natural' systems.

Using these principles, I examine how three games engage human players with different kinds of actors and relationships at different scales, from tree species to an ecosystem, to the biosphere of a planet.

Speak for the trees? Arboreal agency in *Photosynthesis*

'Speak for the Trees' (2014) is a song by young climate activist Xiuhtezcatl Martinez and Earth Guardians. In the song, Martinez exhorts the listener not only to protest deforestation on behalf of trees but to imagine that they themselves are trees: that their bodies are Gardenia, their hearts its seed, to identify with the Baobab, Redwood and Pine. Martinez's call for interspecies solidarity suggests that climate action depends on more than just understanding the science of climate change, acting sustainably or engaging in protest; it requires imaginative acts of solidarity with a more-than-human world. In the board game *Photosynthesis*, players take on the role of a species of tree in what seems to be a ludic answer to Martinez's call. The publisher, Blue Orange, boasts climate-friendly production and an ecocentric promise with its flagship game that recognizes trees as vital actors in a time of climate crisis.

The rules set up a competitive game in which players vie for dominance in the forest, which is represented by a hexagonal board on which there are concentric circles of placement spots for individual trees. The sun moves around the board, bestowing 'light points' on players depending on the relative position and height of their trees. Those not shaded by other trees gain light points that can be exchanged for seeds, or to grow saplings into larger trees. The game is directly competitive because players must dominate the hexagon vertically, shading other trees in order to capture more light, and concentrically, because the trees growing at closer to the centre of the forest net the most points in the endgame. This account of the rules of *Photosynthesis* immediately points to a mismatch between the game and the framework. It provides an example of how contemporary board games owe much of their design to wargames, which were the earliest forms of hobby gaming (as we know it today) to emerge (Woods 2012). The wargames that were developed in the 1960s and 1970s, and which preceded the type of board game of which *Photosynthesis* is an example, were simulations that relied on abstraction and simplification. Typically, wargames coordinate play on boards divided up into hexagonal grids, representing terrain, with units, represented by tokens, expected to vie for control of this terrain (Woods 2012: 22). Though the 'zones of control' that characterize wargames are not inherently militaristic (Harrigan and Kirschenbaum 2016: xvii), the logic of the acquisition, and control, of territory on a board is an abstraction that persists in eurogames and is hardly complementary to the eco-ethical framework I have sketched in this chapter. This design legacy creates curious tensions, especially for games that purport to be about trees. As a game whose rules operate on the logic of wargames, *Photosynthesis* might easily be re-skinned such that its tree avatars were represented by military units and the forest floor a field of conflict. Elsewhere, in other tree games, such as *Forests of Pangaia* (2022) designed by Thomas Franken, this problem persists. The promotional video for the game suggests that players will grow a magical forest, awaken earth spirits and 'expand' their 'territory'. The animist and symbiotic aesthetics comingle uneasily with the mechanics of control and competition. Designed within a humanistic conception of play, games tend to privilege the human actor offering mastery of terrain as the ultimate lusory goal, even if the prelusory goal is, say, to grow a living forest. Woods notes, for example, that the majority of eurogames take place on a miniaturized representation of a real-world geographical location, or a stylized rendering of an imagined setting (2012: 81). This aesthetic representation of terrain emphasizes the mechanics of expansion, area control, contest and competition, all of which hardly inculcate players into a sense of their own embeddedness in nature.

The rules of *Photosynthesis* also reveal that games tend to favour mechanics that mimic colonial-capitalist ideologies. Chang notes that video games 'lure us to play with the unspoken promise that we will always gain, and the reassurance that we can only level up' (2019: 73). She adds that such a 'disturbing' promise does little to counter a paradigm of capitalist growth that has fuelled climate change (2019: 73). Woods's description of eurogames also suggests that they revolve around the over-arching goal of accumulation (2012: 98). Many of the mechanics serving this goal are present in *Photosynthesis*, the aim of which is to grow the largest trees that can be removed at the end of the game for the most points possible. This aim requires engaging with mechanics of area control, resource taking and collection, 'buying' and upgrading, all which position 'nature' as a passive resource for human management, and so potentially divorce players aesthetically from imaginative engagement with the more-than-human beings represented in the game. The rulebook of *Photosynthesis*, for example, describes players 'buying' seeds with their light points, which hampers identification with the trees *as* trees and instead frames them as units of resource. Nonetheless, the game also makes apparent constraints to growth that challenges the mechanics of endless gain Chang identifies in video games. The hexagonal board provides a constrained play area, bringing the different tree species into competition. Though the emphasis on competition belies the collectivity of woodland ecosystems, it provides limits to territorial expansion and might encourage players to reflect on the real-world effects of habitat constriction. As Peter Wohlleben notes, the 'triumphal march' and migration of trees is negatively affected by human interference and climate change (2015: 190).

The rules of *Photosynthesis* evoke the conditions of real forests in other ways, too, offering an abstraction of the chemical process of photosynthesis. Light points allow players to buy seeds and grow saplings but distributes this growth across the species in a way that reflects how real trees distribute nutrients across a community rather than harbouring them within individual units (Wohlleben 2015: 16). Such cooperation does not extend far, however, since there is no sharing of resources between species, and tall trees will deny light points even to their compatriots. This belies the 'extraordinary generosity' of the woodland, which is an ecosystem that connects trees in a 'web of interdependence' (Simard 2021: 11, 12). In terms of competition for light, the basic rule of *Photosynthesis*, many species actually require the older members of the community to shade the young so the latter will grow slowly and develop strength. Beyond its rules, the mechanics of *Photosynthesis* further render the woodland as a site of competition rather than collaboration. Mechanically, players gain dominance by sacrificing weak individuals (trees of the same species that have been poorly placed) and crowding out other species entirely. These mechanics operate contrary to the biodiversity of the woodland, in which trees of different species need one another and smaller plants for survival (Simard 2021: 109–10). As Wohlleben notes, 'survival of the fittest' is not the doctrine of the forest (2015: 17). The game does not wholly capitulate to the mechanics of competition, however. At least until the final phase, when the largest trees are removed from the board for points, *Photosynthesis* suggests that trees are not objects but living processes. Players 'manage' their species only by nurturing seeds into sapling and saplings into mature trees, which can generate seeds. The process is cyclical and one of dependency and exchange with an environment rather than of individual striving.

My framework also asks whether a game evokes and sustains the subjectivity and agency of the 'natural' beings it represents. In this respect, *Photosynthesis* is ambiguous. The resource management rules usefully reveal a tension between individualism and eco-centrism, since both the species and the individual trees operate as agents. However, the codified rules about seed distribution and sapling growth necessarily erase difference, belying the varying strategies of distinct species in real woodland ecosystems. However, the most disruptive effect of the mechanics on the game's evocation of trees as agents is the slippage from a tree-like perspective (growing your seeds into saplings in the early game) to a forest management perspective (harvesting the large trees for points in the endgame). As Simard suggests, forest management from the human perspective tends to be a zero-sum game, emphasizing competition for light, water and nutrients in its quest for efficient and swift manufacture of timber (2021: 204). As I have suggested,

Photosynthesis draws on some of the aspects of this zero-sum game in its mechanics of competition, which coalesce in the final stage of the game when the largest trees must be removed for points. The game rules describe this as ending the 'life cycle' of the tree, but the mechanics suggest it is also a kind of harvesting or consumption: trees for points. It is also possible that the feeling the game evokes here of the player inhabiting not the role of a species, but that of forest manager, emerges from a human mindset that struggles with imagining itself as a tree. The multiple resource tokens of seeds, saplings and large trees also forestall the possibility of identifying with them as avatars of a species, further encouraging this ascendant trajectory whereby the human player is abstracted from the game as an external manager.

The tensions in the aesthetics of the game also revolve around whether the trees are allotted moral considerability as subjects. On the one hand, in inviting players to be trees, the game counters anthropocentric thinking which has, as Michael Marder notes, consistently failed to allot interiority and intentionality to plant life (2013: 25). Contra anthropocentric thought, *Photosynthesis* invites players to occupy the role of the tree as a subject, inhabiting a species mind that is intentional and perceptual. Player actions affectively identify with the trees' *conatus* for nourishment and propagation. Yet, as discussed, this engagement culminates in the accumulation of points through the harvesting of your tallest trees, suggesting a tree is valuable only once it is removed from the forest, rather than as a living subject with interiority. Again, the game is at odds with emerging scientific research on woodland ecology. Simard suggests the value of the 'biggest, oldest timbers' lies not in the girth of their trunks but in the fact that they are the source of fungal connections, connecting all neighbours, young and old; they 'serve as the lynch pins for a jungle of threads and synapses and nodes' (2021: 14). These synapses and nodes are, of course, under the soil, which is an area of the woodland in which *Photosynthesis* has no interest. The rules and mechanics hinge on the revolving sun, suggesting a transcendent view of trees as beings that culminate in a crown of leaves high above the canopy. In this respect, *Photosynthesis* misses an opportunity to engage players with a subscendent view of nature in which diverse agencies comingle as soily beings.

'Nature' as a field of relations: *Ecosystem*

Where *Photosynthesis* is weak on modelling interspecies collaboration and woodland biodiversity, *Ecosystem* (2019), designed by Matt Simpson, founds its rules and mechanics on just such principles. In this set collection and card placement game, players draft cards from randomly shuffled sets into their 'ecosystem', represented by a 5 × 4 grid of cards. Scoring rules for card placement suggest ecological principles of the food web and of trophic cascades, with bears thriving (i.e. scoring points) when placed adjacent to rivers and foxes only scoring where they are not in competition with other predators. Individual cards score based on their placement and the whole ecosystem scores biodiversity points, where fewer 'gaps' in animal types equals more points. Elements of direct competition occur in rules for rivers and wolf packs: only the players with the most of these cards gain points. Players can also deny a relevant card to their competitor by placing it into their ecosystem before passing along the hand. Although the highest scoring ecosystem wins, the ecosystems are not otherwise in direct competition, either for space or resources. The rules of *Ecosystem* reveal the social experience of board games, making clear the collaborative and collective dimensions of play even when a competitive element remains. The rules also offer abstractions of scientific ideas about ecosystems, as I will discuss, but the metagames that emerge through the social experience of playing the game are useful for challenging paradigms about nature as a passive resource and a stable background for human activity.

The mechanics of the game encourage players to allot moral considerability to individual animals and to plan for their well-being in the layout of the ecosystem. The aesthetics compliment this aspect of the game with soft-lit visages of foxes, wolves, deer and bears gazing out of the cards. Some of these animal cards represent individuals (an individual wolf appears on a card, for example, and multiple wolf cards comprise a wolf pack). Others represent bigger collectives on a single card, such as a stream or meadow. On one hand, the mimetic artwork prompts players to appreciate the beauty of nature, but all bears, wolves and so on are represented by the same image, which suggests the game allots their moral considerability in terms of their species belonging, rather than as individual beings. On the other hand, the mechanics allow for a range of placement options for each animal, such that individual cards (and animals) function in distinct ways within the ecosystem. This use of the cards suggests the need to allow for moral considerability at different scales, from individuals to species collectives, and from species to habitats. This encodes an ecocentric ethical perspective into the game and the slippage between the agency of an individual and of the species is, as in *Photosynthesis*, a provocative element of gameplay.

The fact that biodiversity is coded into the scoring is important for challenging anthropocentric thinking on the climate crisis. Rules for card placement scoring suggest that species well-being is entangled in complex ways, rather than dependent on the competitive survival of individuals. The inclusion of wolves, bears and fish in the game recalls the famous reintroduction of wolves to Yellowstone in 1995, which improved the populations of bears, songbirds and beavers, reversing the erosion of the riverbank and the heating of the river. Trophic cascade – the effect of the behaviour of the apex predator on the ecosystem – is intimated in the rules and mechanics of *Ecosystem* in ways that allows for complex relationships between predators such as bears and wolves without recourse to Hobbesian (and capitalist) notions of ruthless competition. Both the Yellowstone experiment and the game reveal that biodiversity is beneficial. This has been emphasized by climate scientists, who argue that biodiversity renders ecosystems more resilient to climate change. Indeed, *Ecosystem* presents us with what Ingold describes as a 'field of relationships' (2000: 4). This field is comprised of relations of interdependence, which are sometimes competitive and sometimes collaborative, and always unfolding, never stable. The game's replayability intimates just such a continually unfolding field of relationships, inviting players to find new ways to create diverse ecosystems each time they play.

Although the layout of *Ecosystem* is a 5 × 4 grid of rectangular cards, its mechanics and aesthetics gesture to a conception of 'nature' as an entangled field of relationships rather than a static habitat or stable background for the activity of organisms. The river cards, for example, structure the ecosystems along what Ingold calls a 'line of growth' (2006: 13–14). Ingold argues that organisms are not self-contained 'balls' that propel themselves from place to place but constituted in a 'meshwork' of interwoven lines (2006: 13–14). In such a conception of 'nature', the environment is not what surrounds a lifeform, 'since you cannot surround a web without drawing a line around it', but the entanglement of the lines of growth themselves (2006: 14). A comparison between *Ecosystem* and *Renature* serves to illustrate Ingold's comments. Like *Ecosystem*, *Renature* asks player to place counters (dominoes) representing specific species on a grid in order to produce diverse habitats capable of sustaining life. However, the placement rules are arbitrary, rather than tied to specific species and their relationships in nature, and competitive. The board is divided by orthogonal lines, representing rivers, along which dominoes are placed. Rather than serving as lines of growth, these rivers surround the habitats, cutting them off from one another. The competitive dimension renders some habitats barren as players abandon them when their ability to net points is hampered. The rivers of *Renature*, then, are not lines of growth, and the board does not represent a field of relationships but a terrain of spoils to be managed and divided.

Biospheric thinking: *Planet*

Where *Ecosystem* asks players to consider the entangled well-being of groups of animals and habitats by placing cards in a two-dimensional grid, *Planet* (2018), designed by Urtis Šulinskas, requires you to build a habitable planet by placing tiles on a three-dimensional planet core. Players receive a habitat objective card that dictates which type of habitat to prioritize for points at the end of the game before taking turns to pick magnetic habitat tiles to attach to their planets. Further scoring occurs after turn three, when 'life' appears on the planet and players can pick animal cards. These are collected when players have met their conditions, which include having the most of one kind of region, or the biggest region which either is or is not in contact with a specified habitat. There are multiple animal cards with different conditions and the aim is to 'welcome' as many animals onto the planet as possible. These mechanics shift the perspective on nurturing and sustaining life to the level of the biome, that is, distinct biological communities with shared climates.

The tendency towards human mastery coded in hobby gaming is apparent in *Planet* as players take charge of a whole globe that they can hold in their hands. In this respect, the game literalizes Latour's description of the earth as a Galilean object seen from an unknown vantage point in space: the ultimate transcendent and objectifying conception of our planetary home. *Planet* thus belongs to the genre of 'god' games popular in video games. However, the mastery accorded by the god perspective is frustrated by the random allocation of continent tiles and scoring cards: there are none of the resource management mechanics common to eurogames here, nor are the pentagonal tiles 'zones of control' in the sense of wargame simulations. Indeed, the three-dimensional planet core and pentagonal continent tiles make management of the globe tricky because they deny an at-a-glance view of which regions are biggest or in contact with which other regions, required for scoring.

The planetary scale of this game, along with its rules governing the interactions of biomes, also suggests the kind of shift in scalar awareness Clark advocates in confronting the Anthropocene. Indeed, if *Photosynthesis* positions players within the subjectivity of the species, *Planet* positions you within the subjectivity of Gaia, as you take on the role of a self-regulating system to create the conditions for life. Lovelock's Gaia hypothesis conceptualizes biodiversity and mutualism at scale and *Planet* engages players in systemic thinking at just this scale. As with *Ecosystem*, replayability necessitates you consider the planet as a complex and ever-changing system: there is no single way to score points and each planet you construct will be different from the last.

Perhaps the major pitfall of *Planet* is that there are no people. Your completed planet is an idealized blue and green globe, each biome free from human habitation and interference. At the same time, the human agent is abstracted from the world even as it manages the placements of biomes and animals. *Planet* thus encapsulates the strange tension apparent in contemporary 'nature' board games: their exhortation for players to identify with a more-than-human world while also idealizing that natural world as separate from humans. I agree with Chang that games have the 'potential to marry both subjective and objective features of experience, and to render the nonhuman accessible' (2019: 134), and we have seen how shifts in perspectives enacted in these games might provide such access. Nonetheless, the rules and mechanics of *Photosynthesis*, *Ecosystem* and *Planet* elide the ways in which human lives are always already entangled with more-than-human lives at different scales.

Conclusion

While games that explicitly tackle the climate crisis, such as *Tiny Footprint* and *Carbon City Zero*, focus on sustainability, planning and lifestyle decisions at the level of the human individual, household and community, *Photosynthesis*, *Ecosystem* and *Planet* focus on the natural world as though it were distinct from the human world. A hybridization of such approaches is needed in game design. Can we make and play games that help us see the ways in which the human and the more-than-human are entangled? Can we reorient games towards the 'terrestrial' such that they reveal how the social and political relations of human and more-than-human actors intersect in complex ways? This is the challenge for board game design in troubled times.

This chapter has suggested ways forward for such a project, building an eco-ethical framework for analysis and providing a critique of a sample of contemporary 'nature' board games that identifies the problems as well as possibilities that are coded in the rules, or else expressed in gameplay as mechanics and aesthetics. I conclude by suggesting that a step change is required in game design to complement a much-needed interrogation of the concept of 'nature' that persists across the political, social and environmental imaginary. Board games can contribute to the transformation of the way in which human situate themselves with respect to 'nature', playing with our positionality, inviting us to play as various kinds of interconnected agents, and by effecting perspectival shifts in scale. With the right 'nature' games we might, finally, understand that humanity and nature comprise a single field of relationships.

Note

1   I am grateful to Paul Wake for his comments on drafts of this chapter, which improved the analysis and contributed to the development of the framework it sets out.

References

Alaimo, S. and S. Heckman (2007), 'Introduction: Emerging Models of Materiality in Feminist Theory', in S. Alaimo and S. Hekman (eds), *Material Feminisms*, 1–22, Bloomington: Indiana University Press.

Alam, S. (2008), 'Majority World: Challenging the West's Rhetoric of Democracy', *Amerasia Journal*, 34: 87–98.

Backe, H. J. (2017), 'Within the Mainstream: An Ecocritical Framework for Digital Game History', *Ecozon@*, 8 (2): 39–55.

Baumgarten, A. G. (1750–8), *Aesthetica*, Frankfurt: Ioannis Christiani Kleyb.

Beiler, K., D. Durall, S. Simard, S. Maxwell and A. Kretzer (2009), 'Architecture of the Wood-Wide Web: Rhizopogon spp. Genets Link Multiple Douglas-fir Cohorts', *The New Phytologist*, 185: 543–53.

Carbon City Zero (2020), [Board game], Designers: S. Illingworth and P. Wake. UK: 10:10 Climate Action.

Chang, A. (2019), *Playing Nature: Ecology in Video Games*, Minneapolis: University of Minnesota Press.

Clark, T. (2015), *Ecocriticism on the Edge: The Anthropocene as a Threshold Concept*, London: Bloomsbury.

Cronon, W. (1996), 'Introduction: In Search of Nature', in W. Cronon (ed.), *Uncommon Ground: Rethinking the Human Place in Nature*, 31–91, New York and London: W. W. Norton.

Ecosystem (2019), [Board game], Designer: M. Simpson, USA: Genius Games.

Eisenack, K. (2013), 'A Climate Change Board Game for Interdisciplinary Communication and Education', *Simulation & Gaming*, 44 (2–3): 328–48.

Ellis, E. C. and N. Ramankutty (2008), 'Putting People in the Map: Anthropogenic Biomes of the World', *Frontiers in Ecology and the Environment*, 6 (8): 439–47.

Fjællingsdal K. S. and C. A. Klöckner (2020), 'Green Across the Board: Board Games as Tools for Dialogue and Simplified Environmental Communication', *Simulation & Gaming*, 51 (5): 632–52.

Forests of Pangaia (2022), [Board Game], Designer: T. Franken, Germany: Pangaia Games.

Gilbert, S. F., J. Sapp and A. I. Tauber (2012), 'A Symbiotic View of Life: We have Never Been Individuals', *The Quarterly Review of Biology*, 87 (4): 325–41.

Groves, C. (2019), 'Sustainability and the Future: Reflections on the Ethical and Political Significance of Sustainability', *Sustainability Science*, 14 (4): 915–24.

Haraway, D. (2003), *The Companion Species Manifesto: Dogs, People, and Significant Otherness*, Chicago, IL: Prickly Paradigm Press.

Haraway, D. (2016), *Staying with the Trouble: Making Kin in the Chthulhucene*, Durham, NC: Duke University Press.

Harrigan, P. and M. G. Kirschenbaum (2016), 'Introduction' in P. Harrigan and M. G. Kirschenbaum (eds), *Zones of Control: Perspectives on Wargaming*, xv–xxxii, Cambridge, MA: The MIT Press.

Hunicke, R., M. LeBlanc and R. Zubek (2004), 'MDA: A Formal Approach to Game Design and Game Research', AAAI Workshop – Technical Report.

Ingold, T. (2000), *The Perception of the Environment: Essays on Livelihood, Dwelling and Skill*, London: Routledge.

Ingold, T. (2006), 'Rethinking the Animate, Re-animating Thought', *Ethnos*, 71 (1): 9–20.

Keep Cool. (2004) [Board game], Designer: K. Eisenack and G. Petschel-Held, Germany: Spieltrieb.

Kwok, R. (2019), 'Science and Culture: Can Climate Change Games Boost Public Understanding?', *PNAS*, 116 (16): 7602–4.

Lahsen, M. and E. Turnhout (2021), 'How Norms, Needs, and Power in Science Obstruct Transformations Towards Sustainability', *Environmental Research Letters*, 16 (2): 025008.

Latour, B. (2017), *Facing Gaia: Eight Lectures on the New Climatic Regime*, trans. C. Porter, Cambridge: Polity Press.

Latour, B. (2018), *Down to Earth: Politics in the New Climatic Regime*, trans. C. Porter, Cambridge: Polity Press.

Lovelock, J. (1972), 'Gaia as Seen Through the Atmosphere', *Atmospheric Environment*, 6 (8): 579–80.

Lovelock, J. and L. Margulis (1973), 'Atmospheric Homeostasis by and for the Biosphere: The Gaia Hypothesis', *Tellus*, 26 (1): 2–10.

Marder, M. (2013), *Plant-Thinking: A Philosophy of Vegetal Life*, New York: Columbia University Press.

Martinez, X. (2014), 'Speak for the Trees' [Song]. Lyrics from "This Week Climate Song for Paris COP 21"', *United Nations Climate Change*, 8 July 2015. Available online: https://unfccc.int/news/8-july-2015-this-week-climate-song-for-paris-cop21 (accessed 15 December 2021).

McKibben, B. and S. Diehn (2015), 'McKibben: We Won the Climate Argument, Now We Have to Win the Fight', *DW.Com*, 10 December. Available online: https://www .dw.com/en/mckibben-we-won-the-climate-argument-now-we-have-to-win-the -fight/a-18909959 (accessed 22 June 2021).

Mert, A. and S. Van der Hel (2016), 'Meaning-making in Climate (Video) Games: An Appraisal Framework', *Centre for Global Cooperation Research*, 12: 41–51.

Morton, T. (2016), *Dark Ecology: For a Logic of Future Coexistence*, New York: Columbia University Press.

Morton, T. (2017), *Humankind: Solidarity with Nonhuman People*, London: Verso.

Photosynthesis (2017), [Board game], Designer: H. Hach, France: Blue Orange.

Planet (2018), [Board game], Designer: U. Šulinskas, France: Blue Orange.

Renature (2020), [Board game], Designers: M. Kiesling and W. Kramer, Germany: Deep Print Games.

Sicart, M. (2008), 'Defining Game Mechanics', *Game Studies*, 8 (2). Available online: http://gamestudies.org/0802/articles/sicart (accessed 22 June 2021).

Sicart, M. (2014), *Play Matters*, Cambridge, MA: The MIT Press.

Simard, S. (2021), *Finding the Mother Tree: Discovering the Wisdom of the Forest*, New York: Alfred A. Kopf.

Tiny Footprint (2019), [Board game], Designer: M. Jargarden, Sweden: Gaard Games.

Tipping Point (2020), [Board game], Designer: R. Smith, Switzerland: Treecer.

Tsing, A. (2013), 'More-than-Human Sociality. A Call for Critical Description', in K. Hastrup (ed.), *Anthropology and Nature*, 27–42, London: Routledge.

UNDP (2021), *United Nations Development Programme: The Peoples' Climate Vote*. Available online: https://www.undp.org/publications/peoples-climate-vote (accessed 22 June 2021).

Vetlesen, A. J. (2019), *Cosmologies of the Anthropocene. Panpsychism, Animism and the Limits of Posthumanism*, Oxon and New York: Routledge.

Williams, R. (2015), *Keywords: A Vocabulary of Culture and Society*, New Edition, Oxford: Oxford University Press.

Wingspan (2019), [Board game], Designer: E. Hargrave, USA: Stonemaier Games.

Wohlleben, P. (2015), *The Hidden Life of Trees*, London: HarperCollins.

Woods, S. (2012), *Eurogames: The Design Culture and Play of Modern European Board Games*, Jefferson, NC: McFarland.

IV

Cultures

9

Contested spaces, velvet ropes, exclusion zones

The pleasures and dangers of face-to-face play in analogue gaming spaces

Tanya Pobuda

It is the fall of 2014, and my partner and I are walking down the dark, dank stairs of a basement games shop in the north of our Canadian city. The stairwell is papered over with posters of comic book heroes: muscle-bound men and scantily clad women. We were in this place to attend a Thursday-night tabletop role-playing (TTRPG) meetup for the very first time. The owner is pleased and welcoming and walks us over to several large folding tables filled with mainly men of various ages, from teens to middle age. Another woman who is roughly my age walks over to me and beckons us to walk with her. She introduces my partner and I to a seated group of young men, and in turn introduces them as the beginner's table: a place that would be perfect for newcomers like us. She then turns to a young man seated at the centre of the group and hisses, 'You be nice to her or I'll murder you.' I laugh nervously, and thank the woman for the kind introduction, and my partner and I sit down. There are some mumbled and downcast hellos. Our appearance seems to have deflated this close-knit group. At no point during the game does the Dungeon Master (DM) look me in the eye, instead directing instructions to only the people he knows, my questions, quips and character points go unanswered. There are in-jokes, quiet asides and boisterous laughter out of nowhere. It feels like junior high all over again, with the sniggering happening at my expense. Throughout the game, it is made clear to us this experience isn't for us, and we aren't in on the jokes. I realized we were marginalized in the game before we began.

Long (and painful) story short, my dwarven hero opted to pitch herself overboard from the riverboat in which our adventuring party found ourselves.

When asked by the group if my character would like to be revived by a cleric, I said, 'No, I'm great.'

Spoiler alert: we never returned to TTRPG night. Taking stock of the evening in later months, I thought to myself. Would I have gone to that meetup without my partner? The honest answer would have to be: absolutely not. The basement location was musty, poorly lit. The photos on the walls were filled with images that would have looked at home on a heavy metal- and pinup-loving fourteen-year-old boy's bedroom wall. Women on their knees and bent over in diaphanous, skimpy clothing. There was a lingering odour of unwashed hair and skin in the air, as much attributable to the crowding of bodies into long, crowded play sessions, as it was to the poor ventilation, and limited air conditioning in these industrial park locations, selected presumably for their low rents for large, open spaces. This friendly local game store (FLGS) had an unspeakably horrible small washroom with a broken lock on the door. This space and others like it are often dominated by tight cliques of men who stare a little too hard at the women, and other marginalized identities who dare enter their preserve. Most of the analogue gaming spaces in my Canadian major city have a similar feel. Crowded with mainly men having animated conversations about *Magic: The Gathering* single prices and 'fat packs' full of cards wrapped in crinkly shiny plastic wraps, scattered around the store like discarded candy wrappers. I have played *M:TG* myself, and greedily opened sealed boosters during drafts, amassing a huge collection after an obsessive purchasing jag that ended in early 2019. Now, I have boxes and unopened booster packs currently shoved under my bed. A middle-aged woman asking for a *M:TG* booster box generated some odd looks, some eye rolls, pedantic corrections, and often I got ignored outright. Every time I entered these stores, particularly alone, I felt like I was committing a transgressive act; I felt like I was somewhere I shouldn't be.

Physical gaming spaces in the analogue and video game hobby are often dominated by white men. Early video game arcades, with their bright lights, and 8-bit white noise, were similarly dominated by white, middle-class men. Studies into video game enculturation have examined the gender-based divides in physical gaming spaces. In early video game studies conducted in the mid-1980s, even kindergarten-aged female children were conditioned to believe that video games were a boy's pastime (Wilder, Mackie and Cooper 1985). Other studies noted that while women and girls reported that they enjoyed games, they made up only 20 per cent of the arcade players (Kaplan 1983). Kocurek (2015) plotted the rise of the early marketing idea that boys and men were not only the ideal targets for video games but often the only imagined audience for early video games. Arcades in the 1980s and early 1990s, which I was also known to frequent, were dominated by men. The moral panic around video games, worries about the morality of such gaming spaces, played a role in keeping these gaming spaces homogeneously male. I was told repeatedly that 'good girls' didn't frequent arcades, the implication being that gaming spaces were dangerous spaces for girls and women.

Of course, the history of men's dominance in gaming parlours, arcades and chess clubs goes back further than the late 1970s and 1980s. The entirely analogue gaming worlds and spaces described in foundational gaming scholarship texts of Huizinga (1955) and Caillois (2001) were the rarefied preserves of gentlemen of social and economic privilege (Montola 2009). The reality that games and gaming were for men of a higher socioeconomic class is not surprising. What do you need when you game? You need time; you need the physical space. Players of campaign games like *Pathfinder: The Adventure Card Game*, *HEXplore It* and *Gloomhaven* understand that you need a really large table that can remain untouched for days, even weeks at a time. All of these elements require a certain access to financial means, the privilege of playing without interruption, the literacy and skill to play these games. You need the time to think, practice and experiment. Our material realities impact our access to play. In early Canadian and US cultures, white men tended to check these boxes and have these luxuries of material wealth and thus have full command over their time, more often than other identities. And of course, the games played, critiqued and referenced by Huizinga and Callois were entirely analogue, board, card and sports games (Torner, Trammell and Waldron 2014).

While not the only way to play analogue games, face-to-face or embodied play can form some of the necessary conditions for the play of board games. As the hobby and sector continue to grow, there are increasing options for board game players. Today, you can play board games solo, online with other virtual players or against artificial intelligence (AI) on a phone, tablet or computer. Simulators such as *Tabletop Simulator*, *Board Game Arena* and *Tabletopia* can provide digital multiplay affordances through dealing cards, throwing dice, laying tiles, placing game pieces and turn-taking. In some cases aspects of the tabletop itself are simulated as in *Tabletop Simulator* where you can even flip the entire table to show your displeasure (PankakeManceR 2015). While there is a growing movement towards solo gaming (Castle 2020) and digital board gameplay, most board games require the physical gathering of fellow players in the material meatspace to achieve the necessary conditions for maintaining the game state (Donovan 2017b; Arnaudo 2017). Analogue games are, often, all about tactility. Physical board games see players rolling the physical pieces in their hands, moving meeples, pushing block infantry, pawns and tiles into position on a board, on a table in a room filled with other living, breathing people. It is about embodied play, with the materiality of the pieces as representative stand-ins for people, animals, places and things. While this material dimension of games is important, this chapter, however, focuses on what happens to a human body in analogue gaming spaces. I explore the pleasures and dangers of being an embodied player in board gaming spaces. What happens when players enter board game spaces such as FLGSs, meetups and conventions? What happens when you are not a member of the affinity in-group of board gamers, the so-called real gamers who invariably tend to be white, middle-class players who are men. Those identities that do not conform to the outward identities of the in-group, what kind of a welcome do they receive in these spaces? I combine accounts of my own experiences in gaming spaces with the online survey data I collected during my doctoral dissertation research, which focused on gender and racial representation in board gaming, to answer these questions.

Indeed, one of the pleasures of board gaming is embodied play. There is an escape from the everyday that gaming affords us, offering us time away from mobile phones and the cares of regular life and work. Board games can offer a respite from the, at-times, adrenaline-filled digital world. Indeed, this is often the way that board games are often marketed as a way to connect with others, lock eyes, watch the micro momentary emotions on an opponent's face, a slight curl of the lip when disappointed, a flicker of an eyebrow when a 'good' card is drawn. There is also a vulnerability, an exposure, entailed in entering these gaming spaces. Some argue that board games recall a simpler time before the inundation of the digital age, where we can focus on one another, learn and engage in some pleasurable and shared problem solving (Arnaudo 2017; Donovan 2017a; Pilon 2015). As Donovan suggests, board games provide players with access to 'normal face-to-face interaction without the distraction of smartphones or happening via screens. And I think that's healthy' (2017a: n.p.). The return to the nostalgia of a pre-digital world is a common argument for board games. Others also recognize the risks and threats inherent in entering into these intimate physical encounters. Gaming spaces can involve an element of risk for some identities more than others. Games scholars and commentators of the gaming hobby have documented that gaming environments can be unpleasant and even dangerous for women, non-binary, Black, Indigenous, Persons of Colour (BIPOC) or LGBTQiIA+ gamers (Kocurek 2015; Sheldon 2016; Hova 2014; Davis 2013). Physical spaces reserved for gaming offline, such as board game cafés, stores, conventions and other public gaming events can be unwelcoming spaces for women, LGBTQiIA+ and BIPOC players (Sheldon 2016; Hova 2014; Davis 2013). Because of the lack of scholarly focus on board games, much of the research and commentary often come from hobbyist or journalistic sources; as such, my research has to draw heavily from these sources. To date, the toxicity of gaming platforms and spaces is better documented in digital and video games scholarship than it is in board gaming. One such video game study, Fox, Tang and Gilbert (2018), looked at multiplayer online games and outlined the ways in which gamers identifying as women needed to adopt coping strategies to avoid harassment in virtual multiplayer games, including gender masking or disguising their gender identities. This kind of avoidance strategy used by women in digital spaces simply is not readily available to analogue players. Other online gaming affordances, such as remote gaming or gaming with a male ally, as identified by Jenson et al. (2007), might be similarly difficult to maintain for those engaging in the board game hobby. Analogue, digital game commentators and other members of the game hobby have contended that gaming, both online and offline, is an overwhelmingly male dominated in terms of representation and encircled by white male gatekeepers (Pobuda 2018; Sheldon 2016; Davis 2013; Williams et al. 2009; Shaw 2014).

The board game experience is not enjoyed nor practised by everyone. While there has been a demographic shift in gaming, the progress has happened, based upon the available evidence, mostly in the video game space. It has been noted that the digital gaming is a nearly 50/50 split (Teague 2016: 4). Women are, today, a significant demographic segment in digital gaming, representing 46 per cent of gamers in the United States (Gough 2019). Pew Research (2017) found that 24 per cent of Black respondents reported playing video games often and 21 per cent reported playing them sometimes; 18 per cent of Hispanics reported playing often and 29 per cent reported playing sometimes (Duggan 2015). The average age of self-reported gamers in Canada is thirty-nine years, with the demographic split evenly between those who identify as male and female, at 50 per cent and 50 per cent respectively in Canada (ESAC 2018). By contrast, board gaming players, based on publicly available player demographics, seem heavily skewed towards whiteness and maleness. A *Daily Worker Placement* survey had only 6.1 BIPOC participation in a demographic survey. Another 2016 poll of members of *PAXsims* saw male-identified participants at 99 per cent (Brynen 2016). A Stonemaier Games (2019) registered users survey identified that 81.1 per cent of men participated in the demographic poll. A recent survey conducted by Booth (2021) found that a survey of tabletop players represented participation from 27 per cent women and 11 per cent BIPOC, or only 89 respondents identifying as BIPOC from a total sample of 837.

If these numbers represent the current state of the hobby, what is keeping gamers of colour and women away from board gaming and board gaming spaces? How does limited representation and diversity impact board game enthusiasts in spaces where gaming is practised, including public gaming events and conventions? I conducted a peer-reviewed, ethics-approved online survey to find some answers. In this wide-ranging doctoral study, one of the key areas I wanted to drill into is the physical realities of analogue play in board game conventions, friendly local game stores, cafés and other public gaming meeting places. What did the respondents think and feel about these embodied experiences?

A survey of avid board gamers: Methodology

First, I want to explain my research promotion and recruitment strategies. The survey, part of a wider doctoral dissertation, was posted and promoted on Twitter, Reddit and BoardGameGeek (BGG). I saw the most traction on BGG, resulting in some of the BGG respondents taking it upon themselves to post links to the survey on other local forums and Facebook sites. The result was feedback from 320 board game hobby and industry professionals who can best be described as long-time, passionate and *avid* gamers due to their self-reported length of time in the hobby and their self-reported tendency to play board games at least weekly at a rate of 70.7 per cent. Respondents with eleven years or more in the board gaming hobby made up the majority of the sample at 53.5 per cent (Pobuda 2021). Respondents with thirty-one or more years in the hobby made up 15.1 per cent of the sample. Newcomers with less than one year's worth of experience in the hobby made up 1.6 per cent (see Figure 9.1).

While I gathered voluminous and precise data about the anonymous participants of this online survey conducted for my doctoral dissertation, everything from gender identity to household income to gaming preferences, for the purposes of this chapter, I will simply share some of the main highlights. The respondents were most likely to hail from North America (Canada and the United States specifically), were mostly in their thirties and forties and more than half of the respondents identified as women, including trans women. Respondents were mostly white and slightly likely to identify as LGBTQiIA+. Respondents were also more likely to be in a relationship with another person or persons than be

What selection below best describes the length of your participation in the board gaming hobby?

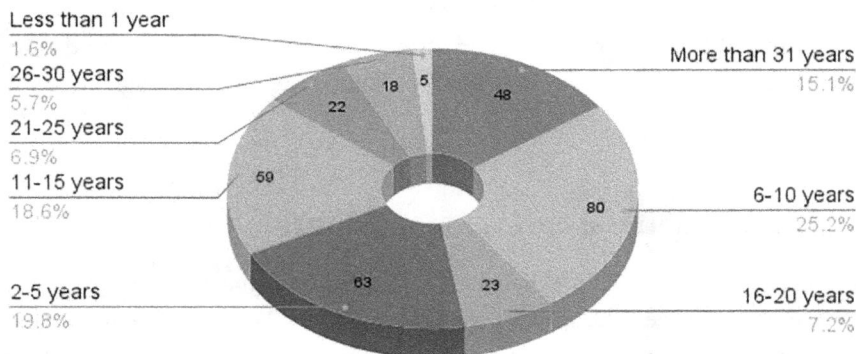

Figure 9.1. What selection below best describes the length of your participation in the board gaming hobby?

single. Respondents were highly educated, have full-time employment and have household incomes of 50,000 dollars or more. The following is a snapshot list of the characteristics of my online survey respondents:

- 73.8 per cent currently live in North America
- 67.8 per cent reported being in their thirties or forties
- 74.9 per cent identified as white
- 20.4 per cent identified as BIPOC
- 60.4 per cent identified as women
- 25.3 per cent identified as men
- 9.4 per cent identified as non-binary
- 52.8 per cent identified as LGBTQiIA+
- 78.9 per cent reported being in a relationship with another person(s)
- 81.8 per cent completed some form of postsecondary education
- 58.5 per cent reported household incomes higher than 50,000 dollars

(Pobuda 2021)

My extensive online survey asked many questions about equity, diversity, inclusion and representation in the board gaming hobby, asking about the relative levels of agreement with questions about the importance of seeing BIPOC and women game designers, diversity in artwork and representation's impact on play and purchase behaviour. I asked respondents to think about their time in the physical spaces in which board gaming is practised. I also presented high-level conceptual statements to assess levels of agreement and disagreement based on psychometric Likert scales on a continuum of 'strongly agree' to 'strongly disagree'. One such conceptual statement was 'The board gaming industry is dominated by white men'. I read a strong level of agreement in the data to that statement with 89.6 per cent of respondents agreeing or strongly agreeing (Figure 9.2).

Women as minority in board gaming industry

I wanted to interrogate how entering gaming spaces made certain people of certain identities feel. The survey posed the statement 'Women are a minority in the board gaming industry' and saw similar strong agreement to the 'white male domination' statement that women were a perceived minority in the labour of games at 89.4 per cent, with 40.3 per cent at 'agree' and 49.1 per cent at 'strongly agree'. One respondent disputed that women were a minority in the gaming industry, writing: '[F]rom what I see from multiple conventions, women are involved. I truly believe that the industry is becoming closer to 50% men and 50% women.'

BIPOC as minority in board game industry

There was an 88.4 per cent overall agreement that BIPOC participation in the board game industry is low, and BIPOC participants formed a minority in the

The board gaming industry is dominated by white men.

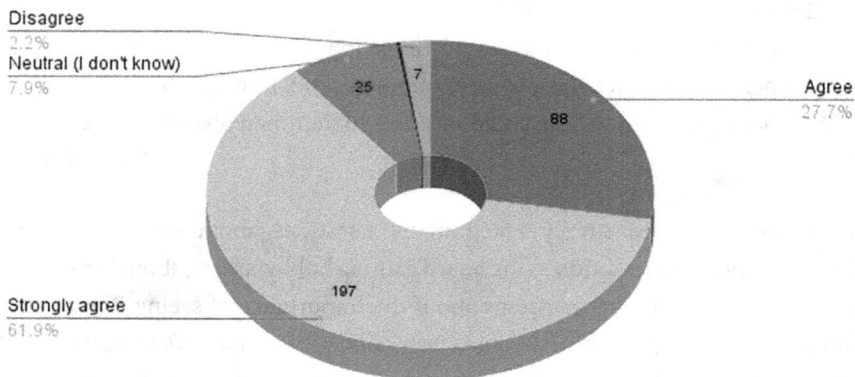

Figure 9.2. The board gaming industry is dominated by white men.

business of board games, with 29.6 per cent selecting 'agree' and 58.8 per cent selecting strongly agree. Outside of professional and industry roles, respondents similarly agreed that women and BIPOC identities were minorities in gaming rooms where games are played, talked about and purchased. The respondents shared that they agreed or strongly agreed at 89.4 per cent, with 40.3 per cent at agree and 49.1 at strongly agree. Some respondents shared personal stories of the feeling of being a minority in these spaces:

> I have been going to gaming stores for decades. I used to get all the eyes on me like I was an alien from Mars in the stores. Didn't stop me from going. Eyes less so now and I regularly see younger women with a significant male other in the stores. They are discussing games and making choices together which tells me these women are gamers too. Wonderful to see. While some of the staff can still be overly helpful – like I am a non gamer, it is well meaning and not offensive to me. So I guess it is a special, secret pleasure when I buy something like 40K minis and blow their minds. :)

Another anonymous participant shared that progress, however slow, is happening across gender lines:

> I've been in this hobby for nearly 40 years. As a girl, I was frequently the only female at the table. These days, that is very rare. I have rarely experienced incivility or -ism during gameplay with a notable exception last year at a convention by someone I know.

BIPOC as minority in hobby

Respondents felt BIPOC players were a minority in the hobby, with 76.7 per cent selecting 'agree' or 'strongly agree'. There were slightly higher levels of agreement here by 6.3 percentage points than the statements about women in the hobby. The biggest piece of the pie were respondents who strongly agreed at 42.9 per cent, with those selecting 'agree' following at 33.8 per cent. Only 4.1 per cent disagreed, and 1.9 per cent strongly disagreed. An anonymous participant wrote this at the end of the survey:

> Thankfully, it seems like the industry and hobby have changed for the better in the last few years, but it still isn't enough. In my teens and early-mid twenties it was way worse. Lately it has been easier to find kinder, more inclusive spaces (although it didn't erase the bad ones in their place). Gender diversity is more prevalent than racial diversity, though.

Another anonymous respondent shared this:

> We have no Black or Hispanic players in my large local club, which does have
> multiple LGBT and handicapped players. Prior to #BLM, I never considered
> racial representation in the hobby or game art.

One survey respondent wrote, 'I've attended conventions in Vermont where
my friends and I are the only people of colour, and we did stand out, compared
with my experiences in Vancouver, Calgary, Seattle, and Portland where there
are definitely more BIPOC in the hobby.' This remark from a respondent gets
to the heart of how one's embodied gaming experience can differ in different
physical contexts. The experience can differ regionally and in different kinds of
spaces.

Behavioural barriers: What are the issues?

What about behaviours that might keep certain identities away from gaming
spaces? There are many written accounts of FLGS horror stories, issues at board
game conventions and other gaming meetups (George 2014;; Teague 2016;
Weidling 2016 as cited by Teague 2016). Board game enthusiasts have reported
that some attendees at major conventions were decked out in Nazi regalia, and
white supremacist paraphernalia was featured for sale at booth in events like Gen
Con (George 2014; Kessock 2013), creating unwelcoming, toxic environments
for attendees.

To locate levels of agreement among respondents about behavioural barriers,
I asked about issues of incivility, harassment and discrimination. I posed the
statement to respondents: 'Before the global pandemic, I was often the only
player who identified as a woman at the table.' The respondents who agreed
or strongly agreed numbered 30 per cent of the overall sample, with 22.8 per
cent agreeing and 7.2 per cent strongly agreeing with the statement. Those who
selected 'I don't identify as a woman' numbered 31.6 per cent.

Treated differently due to gender

Were respondents treated differently due to their gender identity while playing
board games? This question yielded some interesting feedback with 41.1 per
cent of the respondents sharing either agreement or strong agreement. This
particular question reflects a slight issue in my approach. I was looking for

any feedback here, asking those who identify as men, women and non-binary to share their experiences. I sought an undifferentiated approach. In peer review, this statement and its responses were rightly called out as one might hypothesize that this perspective might see more agreement from those who identify as women, something that was reflected in the write-in comments I received in the survey. The largest segment was respondents agreeing with that statement at 33.5 per cent. It is important at this point to recall that more than half of the respondents identified as women at 60.4 per cent, a total that is inclusive of trans women at 4.9 per cent. Of the 25.3 per cent who identified as men, of which 1.3 per cent were trans men. This question was posed to every respondent, from every gender identity. One of the anonymous respondents talked about feeling that others don't have the same levels of acceptance in the hobby:

> I have personally seen other folks struggle with being accepted into the board gaming hobby because of their gender (whether the gender assigned at birth or otherwise) and race, and I'd love to see that change.

Another survey respondent wrote:

> Due to how women in the hobby are perceived, I often feel defensive about games I like or collect, or that I have to perform and pretend I enjoy different games than I do in order to defy the gender expectation placed on women. The merits of a game like that are dismissed, and if I like or defend it, I am dismissed for the same reason. This makes me less likely to share publicly about my love of the hobby, or my collection of games.

Discrimination due to gender

Beyond being treated differently, I wanted to see if that different treatment translated into overt discrimination. We can see the slightly lower response here from the previous responses, with 35.4 per cent agreed or strongly agreed in total. In this case, more disagreed and strongly disagreed with that statement at 45.9 per cent. Some shared a generally optimistic view of the hobby:

> Yes, there are guys there who don't believe me at first and make it tough . . . but when they realize I am the only one with the answer they needed they realize that I am not as dimwitted as they thought. Don't get me wrong, it took me years to get to that point. It has not tainted my view of the industry nor do I believe that women aren't present.

Another respondent shared that they are dismissed as an authority due to their gender identity:

> At another con, a man who had a 'teacher wanted' sign dismissed me as a teacher when I offered. I said ok and pointed out an easily missed rule. He said 'huh I guess you have played this'. I couldn't fathom why he would think I had lied.

Only BIPOC at the table?

I wanted to determine what the experience of BIPOC players was like. Respondents at 15.7 per cent agreed or strongly agreed that they were the only BIPOC at the table in some gaming spaces. 20.4 per cent of the respondents self-identified as BIPOC, making that fifty of the sixty-five respondents who self-identified as BIPOC reported being the only BIPOC player in some of their experiences in gaming environments. This translates into a majority of those who identified as BIPOC tending to be the 'only' in board gaming at 76.9 per cent. This feeling was described in a blog post, entitled 'Gaming's Race Problem' written by George (2014), who talked about their experience as a BIPOC participant at Gen Con, one of board gaming's largest events:

> I saw almost no one who looked like me. By far, the most visible minorities at Gen Con were the hired convention hall facility staff who were setting up, serving and cleaning up garbage for the predominantly white convention-goers. . . . Acceptance meant being white. (George 2014: n.p.)

Treated differently due to race?

Are BIPOC participants treated differently in board gaming contexts because of their racial identity? The same challenge exists in this Likert scale assessment of this particular statement as it did with the 'treated differently due to gender'. I posed this question to all respondents, not only the sixty-five BIPOC respondents, with the hopes of getting the perspectives of all respondents. In this, I did not want to assume that all gaming spaces were white-dominated, thus the blanket ask of all respondents whether they were white or BIPOC. Again, in peer review, this statement and its responses were quite rightly called out as one might hypothesize that this perspective might see more agreement from those who identify as BIPOC, something that was also reflected in the write-in comments I received in the survey. Only 9.8 per cent of the respondents agreed or strongly agreed, signalling low levels of agreement with this statement and experience. It is important to recall here that this sample was majority white, at 74.9 per cent, and this question was posed to the entirety of the respondents.

Similarly, there were similarly relatively low levels of agreement with the statement, 'I have faced discrimination in board gaming because of my racial identity.' Those respondents who agreed represented 6 per cent of the responses. Those who selected 'strongly agree' numbered only four responses or 0.6 per cent of the response. Those who disagreed or strongly disagreed represented 75.3 per cent of the responses. Again, 74.9 per cent of the sample identified as white. Respondents who selected neutral (I don't know) represented 11.7 per cent; those who preferred not to answer were 2.2 per cent.

Incivility in the hobby

By contrast, the statement, 'I have experienced incivility (being interrupted, talked over, talked down to, dismissed, ignored)' saw higher levels of agreement. Those who agreed or strongly agreed with the statement rested at 66.4 per cent. Those who disagreed or strongly disagreed represented 27.5 per cent, with 9.5 per cent strongly disagreed, and 18 per cent disagreed. One respondent described the issues in this way, 'It's a hobby permeated by obnoxiousness, and I have a decent local friends-group kernel with a positive attitude, and I try to protect and nurture that (yay for the socialized focus on nurturing!).' Another said there were issues in the hobby but wouldn't describe the issues as 'discrimination' with this comment:

> Many times, it's hard to be sure why one is being treated poorly – people are sometimes just jerks. I don't *talk* about my sexual orientation, so I don't think I experience discrimination because of it . . . but that not talking about it might itself be a response to perceived safety. White privilege means that I see my race represented all over the place; I really don't need to see it represented in a game. This does not mean I don't think those with less privilege should feel the same. The intersection with disability is non-trivial for me. It's harder to get into places, so more commitment when I do; I need to ask men to move out of the way if I want to access another area.

Another said they are cautious now about new gaming experiences as the result of some bad past experiences:

> One of my first gaming experiences was with my husband and another couple. The other couple did a poor job explaining the game, ganged up on me and then ridiculed me for making poor decisions. I still can't play Catan without feeling ashamed. Luckily, husband didn't give up and slowly introduced me to other

board games that I love. But it's this experience that won't allow me to attend events unless I know the organizer and am reassured people with good teaching skills are available.

Gendered name calling and insults

One commenter wrote in response to the question of gendered name calling, 'I've been called a "Dick", a "Cunt", and a "shithead." Does that qualify?' Another wrote: 'I have not been the target of gendered name calling & insults, but I have observed them being directed at women & LGBTQ.' Still another shared, 'If it has happened, I've not noticed or perhaps cared enough to notice.' Overall, this saw roughly three in ten of the respondents agreeing or strongly agreeing with the statement, 'I have experienced gendered name calling and insults about gender while participating in board gaming.' Respondents at 32.9 per cent selected 'agree' or 'strongly agree', with strongly agreed representing 8.5 per cent, and those who agreed at 24.4 per cent. It is worth noting here that 25.3 per cent of the respondents self-identified as men.

Racial slurs and insults

There were low levels of agreement with the statement, 'I have experienced being called racial slurs or insults about race while participating in the board gaming hobby.' Respondents disagreed or strongly disagreed at 82.5 per cent. Those who agreed or strongly agreed represented 7 per cent of the sample. One of the rare respondents who reported being of Russian descent, and who selected 'strongly agree', shared that they had been called 'squatting slav', 'commie', 'damn eastern European' and 'mother Russia' during gameplay. Some respondents selected 'disagree' but noted that comments were never directed at them as 'this in a very homogenous environment'. Another selected 'agree' and shared, 'I am white but have sadly seen/heard this happen. It has even occurred when only white people are around and somehow I guess they felt it's okay to discuss which it wasn't.' Another respondent, rightly, asked for an expansion of the categories to include disability:

While most people I know at uni would never use racial, sexual, or homophobic slurs, and would rightly call people out for them, they are very comfortable with slurs like 'retarded'. Disability needs to be considered equally alongside race, gender, and orientation, or it will continue to be overlooked and regarded as a 'fair target' for discrimination.

Homophobic remarks

The prevalence of homophobic slurs saw higher levels of agreement across the respondents (Figure 9.3). More than one-third of respondents agreed or strongly agreed that they had experienced homophobic remarks while playing games represented 31.3 per cent. Those who disagreed or strongly agreed represented 57.9 per cent, and 30.7 per cent strongly disagreeing and 27.2 per cent disagreeing with the statement. Some contextualized their selections by adding in written remarks such as 'Strongly Disagree currently. However, it was definitely a thing thirty years ago, and it happened to me then.' Others wrote, 'No to me, but around me' and 'I've been told to stop being "a fag" and make a move. It was funny, especially coming from a gay man.' Another wrote, 'Since I came out as Lesbian, married a same sex partner and more recently owned being non binary, I haven't gamed in a group.'

Unwelcome sexual advances

Approaching three in ten of the respondents agreed or strongly agreed with the statement 'I have experienced unwelcome sexual advances while participating in the board gaming hobby'. Exactly 26.6 per cent of respondents were in agreement or strong agreement that they had experienced unwanted sexual advances. Those who strongly agreed made up 10.1 per cent; those who simply agreed represented 16.5 per cent. Those who disagreed or strongly disagreed with the statement

I have experienced homophobic remarks while participating in the board gaming hobby.

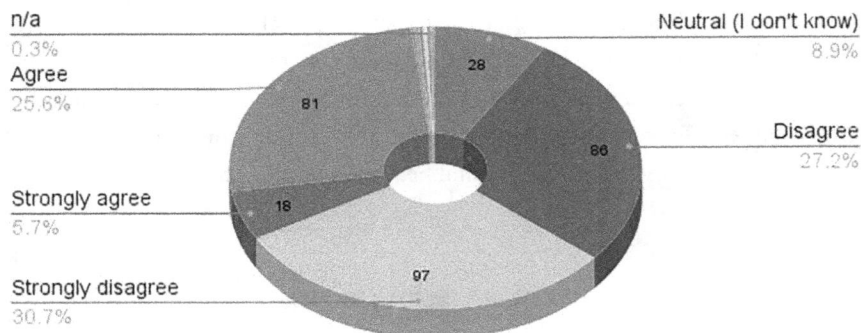

Figure 9.3. I have experienced homophobic remarks while participating in the board gaming hobby.

represented 64 per cent, with 35.8 per cent strongly disagreeing. Some of the respondents wrote in comments such as 'I have not, but my friends have', and another respondent shared a chilling account of their experience at a convention:

> While walking to a con from my hotel, I had a guy get off a bus many stops early to walk with me. He made strange comments alluding that he'd been previously watching me and when I dismissed his advances repeatedly he said he would still come by my booth at the end of the day. It was quite frightening and definitely weighed in the back of my mind all day while I demoed games.

Sexual assault in the hobby

There have been many accounts of violence, both sexual and physical, in the hobby. Sexual violence tends to be underreported in Canada and the United States. To help put this section's numbers into broader context, I pulled numbers from Canadian statistics. There were 460,000 sexual assaults reported to law enforcement in Canada each year (University of Ottawa 2021). That means only 0.012 per cent of the population in Canada reports a sexual assault. When respondents were presented with the statement 'I have experienced sexual assault while participating in the board gaming hobby in public and private spaces (homes)', I found that agreement and strong agreement rested at 3.7 per cent, with 3.4 per cent or eleven respondents selecting agree and one respondent at 0.3 per cent selecting strongly agree. One respondent wrote: 'A guy massaged my head without consent and tried a second time. Don't know how broadly Canada defines sexual assault.' Another wrote, 'I've encountered a couple of creepy guys in role-playing, but the GM has stepped in with both to ensure my safety.'

When asked about physical violence, there were lower levels of agreement, 'I have experienced physical violence (i.e. pushing, punching, slapping, shoving) while participating in the board gaming hobby in public and private spaces (homes).' Only 2.4 per cent or eight respondents, with one respondent selected strongly agree. One respondent wrote, 'Guy waved a knife around and threatened people. He was in the midst of a mental health crisis though.'

Avoiding public events

Do any of these factors or others play a role in limiting the way respondents engage with the hobby? Do the respondents report that they avoid public board gaming events? Over a third of the respondents agreed or strongly agreed that they avoided public board gaming events, pre-pandemic, at 36.4 per cent, with 23.4 per cent agreeing and 13 per cent strongly agreeing. More disagreed at 27.5 per cent who said they strongly disagreed, and 27.3 per cent disagreed. Some respondents wrote in lengthy comments regarding this section:

> The gender inequality, as well as racial inequality make me feel uncomfortable when attending board gaming events. Others tend to make things uncomfortable through passive aggressive comments, or make sexually based comments that are unnecessary. People also assume that I am only there because a boyfriend MUST have brought me. It is frustrating.

Other respondents talked about their barrier to gaming more, and getting more involved in the community came down to issues around 'bigotry, whether dressed as racism, sexism or queerphobia'; still another respondent commented that they could not game as much as they liked due to issues around '[f]inding friends to play with because I don't feel comfortable at game shops'. Another wrote, '[a]s for the community, I have no desire to engage in it.' Others talked about having to hide their identities to be accepted, 'I haven't been out for very long, so I haven't engaged with the board game community outside of personal friends [while] presenting female.' In a similar vein, another wrote, 'I am not open about my gender identity.'

State of play: The implications of the data

What can these findings tell us about gaming spaces and the experiences of marginalized gamers? My goal with this research was to find out what barriers, challenges or dangers in gaming and gaming spaces might exist for women, non-binary, BIPOC or LGBTQiIA+ gamers. I found that for some respondents in this representative sample of avid gamers there are some significant impediments to their full enjoyment of board gameplay and unfettered, uncomplicated access to gaming spaces. Notably, given the relative whiteness of my sample, at 73.8 per cent, I was struck by those respondents who discounted discrimination, name calling simply because it wasn't happening to them, writing in that they selected disagree or strongly disagreed, with some noting that their communities were homogenous. This was one challenge with getting to the heart of the issue. In addition, board game researchers, like myself, really only have access to the people who have decided to stay or self-identify as qualifying to answer questions about board games. Thinking back to my own experience in that basement one Thursday night, trying to engage in TTRPG play, I wonder what about the people who didn't find the hobby compelling enough to stick it out. My sample was made up of people who had decided that board gaming was enough of a compelling draw to them, such that they opted to frequent BGG forums, the r/boardgames discussion board or were a few nodes away from my social network on Twitter. Yet, they exist within the community with some strong feelings of discontent, as well as hopes for its improvement.

What about the people who didn't stay, who didn't make profile accounts on BGG, who had a bad experience, or no experience with, nor access to board games, and gaming spaces due to a variety of socioeconomic factors? What about people who would never step foot in a games store, a café or a convention? What about their feedback?

Who gets access to games and gaming spaces? One of the catalysts for this research was from my past life as a communications professional at a mental health non-profit organization. I attended a youth event to discuss the racist practice of police carding in my Canadian city, which disproportionately affects BIPOC people. One of the stories from the youth leader presenting at this anti-carding event was that of a group of his friends who were playing *Dominoes* in a public park by his apartment complex. He and his friends loved this analogue gaming experience, and they would spend hours doing it. It was a break for his friends and community. But access to the commons, in this case a public park, is not equal, as this youth leader argued. The picnic tables he and his friend used for gaming were removed and never replaced by the city after neighbourhood association and law enforcement complaints. At the time, and to this moment, this story made me absolutely furious and underlines the inequitable access to play, games and gaming spaces. We do not all have equal access to play, to games, to the places where gaming is practised. For some of us, gaming is a transgressive act that is actively punished with symbolic violence, and worse.

This die-hard, passionate group of gamers I was able to connect with through my online survey provides us with an interesting picture and snapshot view into the current state of board gaming. I was struck by a level of passion in some of the responses. There were high levels of agreement with the notion that women and BIPOC people were a minority both in the business and hobby sides of board gaming. There was a very strong level of agreement with the statement that 'board gaming was dominated by white men'. There was less agreement with abstract concepts such as the notion of 'discrimination' on the basis of gender or race. There were much stronger levels of agreement when specifics were provided, such as incivility with examples of being talked over, interrupted and being on the receiving end of unwanted sexual advances. Homophobic and gendered slurs were reported as occurring more frequently than racial slurs, but again, many respondents pointed out that their gaming groups tended to be quite racially homogeneous, tending towards gaming groups who were mostly or entirely white.

Despite intentionally recruiting for diversity, I generated only 20.4 per cent BIPOC participation. This is a finding in and of itself. And there are some possible wider dynamics at play here. One of my brilliant graduate school colleagues researches DNA kits and noted at a conference that white people were more willing to engage with these kinds of invasive, intimate disclosures with limited reserve or caution, whereas BIPOC communities are significantly less likely to participate in this level of disclosure (McGeachie 2019). The result is that 90 per cent of Caucasian/white DNA in the United States will be mapped in only a few more years, because of white people's unquestioning use of ancestry kits (Murphy 2018). The same issues at play in other areas of our lives might be at play here. BIPOC, LGBTQiIA+, women and non-binary people understand the importance and pitfalls of disclosure. It is possible that some demographic groups approach online surveys with some caution. Given my story about youth trying to play games and facing law enforcement intervention, one might understand why. Play can be transgressive, dangerous and forbidden for some identities.

Whenever a labour group, fandom or gaming population doesn't map to population levels, you have to ask yourself: Why? A reference sample should roughly reflect its wider population unless some significant force or forces are acting against it. When I look at population statistics in the United States and Canada, I can see that more than half of each nation's population is women at 50.5 and 50.4 per cent respectively (World Bank Group 2020; Statistics Canada 2020). The non-Hispanic, white population in the United States, based on the 2020 census, has declined to 57.8 per cent of the overall population (N.A. 2020). Statistically speaking, Black, Indigenous and People of Colour represent over 80 per cent of the world's population (Campbell-Stephens 2020). In this context, the skew towards whiteness and maleness means there are barriers surrounding gaming spaces for players who are not white nor men. These findings provide game scholars additional an few puzzle pieces or clues to help us discern a broader and slightly clearer picture of the challenges and barriers, and give us a view into the current state of analogue gaming and the experiences of embodied play for marginalized gamers.

References

Arnaudo, M. (2017), 'The Experience of Flow in Hobby Board Games', *Analog Game Studies*, 4 (5). Available online: https://analoggamestudies.org/?s=the+experience+of +flow (accessed 8 August 2020).

Booth, P. (2021), *Board Games as Media*, London: Bloomsbury Academic.

Brynen, R. (2016), 'Women and Wargaming: The Good, the Bad and the Ugly', *PAXsims*. Available online: https://paxsims.wordpress.com/2016/03/09/women-and -wargaming-the-good-the-bad-and-the-ugly/ (accessed 12 August 2020).

Caillois, R. (2001), *Man, Play and Games*, trans. M. *Barash*, Urbana: University of Illinois Press.

Campbell-Stephens, R. (2020), 'Global Majority; Decolonising the language and Reframing the Conversation about Race', Leeds Beckett University. Available online: https://www.leedsbeckett.ac.uk/-/media/files/schools/school-of-education/final -leeds-beckett-1102-global-majority-9221.docx (accessed 9 October 2021).

Castle, S. (2020), 'Board Game Types Explained: A Beginner's Guide to Tabletop Gaming Terms', *Dicebreaker*. Available Online: https://www.dicebreaker.com/ categories/board-game/how-to/board-game-types-explained (accessed 23 July 2020).

Daily Worker Placement (2016), 'Survey Results #1: Who Are We?', *The Daily Worker Placement Website*, 19 February. Available online: http://dailyworkerplacement.com /2016/02/19/survey-results-1-who-are-we/ (accessed 11 June 2020).

Davis, E. (2013), *Women and Gaming Preliminary Research Report*, Unpublished Report. Available online: https://docs.google.com/file/d/0BxMj6fVK -hglOGtrMFR5c1dVdFk/edit (accessed 14 August 2018).

Donovan, T. (2017a), *It's All a Game: The History of Board Games from Monopoly to Settlers of Catan*, New York: St. Martin's Press.

Donovan, T. (2017b), 'Why Old-fashioned Board Games Thrive in the Internet Age', *Wharton Business Daily*. Available online: https://knowledge.wharton.upenn.edu/ article/why-old-fashion-board-games-thrive-in-the-internet-age/ (accessed 23 July 2020).

Duggan, M. (2015), 'Attitudes Towards Video Games', Pew Research, Available online: https://www.pewresearch.org/internet/2015/12/15/attitudes-about-video-games/.

ESAC. (2018), *Essential Facts about the Canadian Video Game Industry 2018*. Retrieved from: http://theesa.ca/wp-content/uploads/2018/10/ESAC18_BookletEN .pdf.

Fox, J., M. Gilbert and W. Y. Tang (2018), 'Player Experiences in a Massively Multiplayer Online Game: A Diary Study of Performance, Motivation, and Social Interaction', *New Media and Society*, 20 (11): 4056–73.

George, A. A. (13 August 2014). 'Gaming's Race Problem: GenCon and Beyond', Tor .com. Retrieved from: https://www.tor.com/2014/08/13/gamings-race-problem-gen -con-and-beyond/ (retrieved 14 August 2020).

Gough, C. (2019), 'U.S. Computer and Video Gamers from 2006–2019, by Gender', *Statista*. Available online: https://www.statista.com/statistics/232383/gender-split-of -us-computer-and-video-gamers/ (accessed 17 April 2020).

Hova, G. (2014), 'Women in Gaming vs. Invisible Ropes', *Formal Ferret Games*. Available online: https://gil.hova.net/2014/10/27/women-in-gaming-vs-invisible -ropes/ (accessed 14 August 2018).

Huizinga, J. (1955), *Homo Ludens: A Study of the Play-Element in Culture*, Boston, MA: Beacon Press.

Jenson, J., S. de Castell and S. Fisher (2007). 'November. Girls Playing Games: Rethinking Stereotypes'. In *Proceedings of the 2007 conference on Future Play*, 9–16. ACM.

Kaplan, Sidney J. (1983) 'The Image of Amusement Arcades and Differences in Male and Female Video Game Playing', *The Journal of Popular Culture*, https://doi.org/10 .1111/j.0022-3840.1983.1701_93.x DO - https://doi.org/10.1111/j.0022-3840.1983 .1701_93.x SP.

Kessock, S. (2013, August 12), 'Can't Swing A Con Badge Without Hitting A Nazi, Shoshana Kessock [Blog]'. Retrieved from: https://shoshanakessock.com/2013/08/21 /cant-swing-a-con-badge-without-hitting-a-nazi/ (retrieved 23 July 2020).

Kocurek, C. A. (2015), *Coin-operated Americans: Rebooting Boyhood at the Video Game Arcade*, Minneapolis: University of Minnesota Press.

McGeachie, E. (2019), [Conference Talk] 'Spy Games: Corporate DNA Surveillance, and Canadian Privacy and Security', Futures Conference. Available online: https:// www.ryerson.ca/content/dam/graduate/programs/comcult/NewsAndEvents/ Future_Comms_2019_ConferenceSchedule_Dec11.pdf (accessed 20 September 2021).

Montola, M., J. Stenros and A. Waern (2009), *Pervasive Games: Theory and Design*, London: CRC Press.

Murphy, H. (2018), 'Most White Americans' DNA Can Be Identified Through Genealogy Databases', *The New York Times*. Available online: https://www.nytimes .com/2018/10/11/science/science-genetic-genealogy-study.html (accessed 12 September 2021).

N.A. (2020), *Census Statistics Highlight Local Population Changes and Nation's Racial and Ethnic Diversity (2020)*. Available online: https://www.census.gov/newsroom/ press-releases/2021/population-changes-nations-diversity.html (accessed 12 August 2020).

PankakeManceR (2015), 'How do I Flip the Table?', *Steam* [Tabletop Simulator Discussion Board]. Available online: https://steamcommunity.com/app/286160/ discussions/0/541906989406282126/ (accessed 23 July 2020).

Pilon, M. (2015), '*Monopoly* Was Designed to Teach the 99% About Income Inequality', *Smithsonian Magazine*. Available online: https://www.smithsonianmag.com/arts -culture/monopoly-was-designed-teach-99-about-income-inequality-180953630/ (accessed 8 August 2020).

Pobuda T. (2018), 'Inclusivity or Invisibility?: Gender and Racial Representation in Top-Rated *BoardGameGeek* Games', *Analog Game Studies*, 5 (4). Available online: https://analoggamestudies.org/2018/12/assessing-gender-and-racial-representation-in-top-rated-boardgamegeek-games/ (accessed 20 September 2021)

Pobuda, T. (2021), '"I Didn't See Anyone Who Looked Like Me": An Analysis of Gender and Race in Board Gaming', PhD Thesis, X and York University, Toronto.

Shaw, A. (2014), *Gaming at the Edge: Sexuality and Gender at the Margins of Gamer Culture*, Minneapolis: University of Minnesota Press.

Sheldon, S. (2016), 'BackTalk 16: Inclusive Gaming' [Video File], *Dicetower*, 21 November. Available online: http://www.dicetower.com/game-video/backtalk-16-inclusive-gaming (accessed 20 September 2021).

Statistics Canada (2017), 'List of Ethnic Origins 2016'. Available online: https://www23.statcan.gc.ca/imdb/p3VD.pl?Function=getVD&TVD=402936&CVD=402937&CPV=2&CST=18092017&CLV=1&MLV=3 (accessed 11 July 2020).

Statistics Canada (2020), Table 17-10-0005-01 Population estimates on July 1st, by age and sex.

Stonemaier, J. (2019), '5 Revelations from Our 2019 Demographic Survey', *Stonemaier Games*. Available online: https://stonemaiergames.com/5-revelations-from-our-2019-demographic-survey/ (accessed 13 July 2021).

Teague, E. (ed.) (2016), *Girls on Games: A Look at the Fairer Side of the Tabletop Industry. Eliza Teague* [Self-Published].

Torner, E., A. Trammell and E. L. Waldron (2014), 'Reinventing Analog Game Studies', *Analog Game Studies*, 1 (1). Available online: http://analoggamestudies.org/2014/08/reinventing-analog-game-studies/ (accessed 23 July 2020).

University of Ottawa (2021), *Sexual Violence: Quick Facts*. Available online: https://www.uottawa.ca/sexual-violence-support-and-prevention/quick-facts (accessed 12 September 2021).

Wilder, G., D. Mackie and J. Cooper (1985), 'Gender and Computers: Two Surveys of Computer-Related Attitudes', *Sex Roles*, 13 (3): 215–28.

Williams, D., N. Martins, M. Consalvo and J. D. Ivory (2009), 'The Virtual Census: Representations of Gender, Race and Age in Video Games', *New Media & Society*, 11 (5): 815–34.

World Bank (2020), 'Population – Female'. Available Online: https://data.worldbank.org/indicator/SP.POP.TOTL.FE.IN?locations=US (accessed 13 November 2020).

10

'Hands, face, space'

The material turn in board gaming during Covid-19

Esther MacCallum-Stewart

In the early months of 2020, the coronavirus pandemic meant millions of people around the world had to change their daily behaviours with immediate effect, often with no real indications of when 'normality' (whatever that was) would return. Fundamental alterations in social, physical and cultural norms occurred overnight. Millions of people were confined to their homes or near home environments. The deadly invisible pandemic was here, and it was taking our lives away, both literally and figuratively. In retrospect, perhaps we should have realized what living through a global pandemic might be like, but the fiction imagining such disasters shows either the direct moments of an outbreak, as in such texts as Max Brooks's *World War Z* (2006) or Emily St John Mandell's *Station Eleven* (2014), or the world as it recovers in the years afterwards, as in such texts as Robert Kirkman's *The Walking Dead* comic series (2003–19) and Namwali Serpell's *The Old Drift* (2019). It is perhaps unsurprising, then, that we were less prepared for what might happen during the months, possibly years, of a viral outbreak, for which there was no immediate vaccine.

Fiction gives us multiple, apocalyptic futures, but it does not usually depict the slow grind towards that vision, which is how 2020 felt to many. Staying indoors, keeping away from other people, socializing remotely and reconfiguring our daily working lives caused an almost unthinkable upheaval – except it was happening right now, and we all had to do it to save each other. The world was thrown into disorder, regimented even more visibly along class lines than it had been previously and punctuated with violent acts of civil disorder around the world. Yet, it also felt as time itself had stuttered and was being re-ordered around an obsessive refreshing of news feeds as we spent long hours with only ourselves for company.

I acknowledge that this chapter necessarily excludes the experiences of essential workers, or those who could not afford to remain inside. Class and racial divisions, when compared with infection rates around the world, present a stark picture of privilege and an ongoing lack of equality. These issues continued to periodically burst to the surface as the pandemic persisted. For the more affluent sections of the world, however, the switch to virtual social technologies to manage day-to-day life was almost instantaneous. Working, teaching, learning and socializing were facilitated through online platforms and applications that allowed people to see each other, even if they could not physically be present. This pivot online has come at a point not only where virtual technologies are heavily embedded in global society but when a material turn within gaming and other media technologies has become a well-established critical and commercial motif. In areas where public health initiatives such as 'Shelter in Place' or full lockdown of local populations occurred, the majority of people not in key work positions had to shift daily practices to within the confines of their own homes.

In this chapter I explore how materiality was challenged during this pivot through gaming technologies. I focus on the playing and consumption of board games. If the world outside our front doors seemed to be drastically stuttering from crisis to crisis, the sense of displacement inside drew players towards games that provided them with escapism, allowing them to jump away from this world into others. This was not without difficulty, however, as it involved a radical reconfiguration of how players were used to interacting with board games.

Board gaming is a multibillion industry, which was worth $7.2 billion in 2017, $13.1 billion in 2019 and is still growing exponentially (Seetharaman 2020). Rather than slumping during the pandemic, the gaming industry attracted new consumers and began investing in platforms that replicated material gameplay experiences online. Older, more traditional titles, such as Hasbro's *Monopoly* and *Connect 4*, saw a huge rise in sales, as those indoors hearkened back to nostalgic conceptions of happy, domestic life. The image of a nuclear family gathered around a board game was central to this depiction, particularly in popular news media coverage (Smith 2017).

A crucial element of board gaming popularity has also come from spectated playthroughs, both live and recorded, which emphasize the sociality of games. Shows such as *TableTop*, *Dice Tower* and *Shut Up and Sit Down* are not only immensely popular but present board games to an upcoming generation of players. These shows are consumed as artefacts in their own right as performed sessions with no accompanying need for viewers to play along or take part in any way. They also present games as intensely social. The banter of the invited guests (who are often highly experienced players, as well as popular performers and media personalities) is as important to the audience as the game the guests are playing.

Board games helped many people cope with enforced lockdown, giving them a sense of positive, if artificial materiality, in these early months. The sense that materiality was created by these games was enhanced by their often mundane themes; shopping, building, collecting and socializing. Board games are by nature tactile, often comprising hundreds of individual pieces which are handled and shared between players. These pieces often represent signifiers of material goods – wooden and plastic chunks representing bread or coins, cards depicting paints or animals, and images of locations such as shops. All of these aspects point directly to material activity and sometimes sharing in the world outside, all of which had been radically curtailed or restricted by the pandemic. This artificial material activity therefore became a touchstone for behaviour that had been removed from social activity beyond the household. Both board games and tabletop role-playing games (TTRPGs), which are cousin to the board game and have also experienced many of the same online shifts during the pandemic, additionally provide a physical linguistic delineator of location, 'board' and 'tabletop' both being indicative physical signifiers of where the play takes place. Wizards of the Coast, a game company whose online pivot is discussed later, take this further, emphasizing in-person tournaments where card games are played together, and offering modes of play which involve new packets of cards being opened and passed between players. Opening packets of cards together and sharing their contents is obviously a lucrative element of play for the company, but it also makes explicit links between material sharing and healthy socialization – see, for example, their cheerful guidelines for people wishing to host a tournament on their website (Wizards of the Coast 2021), which emphasizes the link between material play and good sportspersonship. The experience of recreating such material satisfactions in an online space is a key focus of this chapter.

However, the places where board games are played have changed since their rise in popularity. There has been a move away from play within family units towards play with larger groups of people (friends and fans), playing socially and publicly together, often sharing game titles collectively due to cost. A social environment of cafés, pubs willing to host players and gaming shops with allocated space for play has evolved around this newer mode of board game play, allowing an opportunity for players to 'try before they buy' and to play with friends as a social event. The evolution of board games as a lucrative media has evolved around this social and economic context, changing the content and price point of games as a result. For example, game shops quickly realized that understanding rules is a barrier to entry, and therefore trained their staff to be able to demonstrate and explain these as part of a sale (or social event at the shop).

These newer ways of board gaming conflicted with health guidelines during Covid-19, which forbade extensive social contact and advised against touching objects to avoid transmission. Thus, board games and their communities of players reconfigured themselves. I explore how groups chose to adapt, and how this affected the material play of a genre which effectively fetishizes the importance of physical (and virtual or imaginary) artefacts. While traditional representations of play in the media adopted a nostalgic and highly problematic direction, presenting the materiality of play as idealized within domestic spaces, modern audiences changed their habits, overcoming proprioceptive demands via a highly successful 'needs must' series of apps and virtual platforms. Despite this, gamers still yearned for the physical play and for the playful artefacts that the developing community had begun to create, compensating in other ways while still utilizing virtual technology during play. The next section examines how board games used pre-existing motifs of play to develop and overcome the restraints of the pandemic by taking two radically different directions. In media representations, board games were presented as a physical signifier of familial unity and strength, with many popular news articles reverting to traditional, stereotypical depictions of board gaming and the family to encourage healthy indoor relationships. For players, however, the reality of lockdowns meant that modes of play were frequently removed, and alternative modes of interaction had to be sought. Both aspects drew from, and reinterpreted, the materiality of the board game as a physical artefact that had to be repurposed when groups of people were suddenly unable to touch or interact in person. As Scott Beattie remarks, '[b]efore we lived with the reality of a global disease outbreak, *Pandemic* was just the title of a series of board games' (2020: n.p.). Games took on a new purpose, becoming both physical and virtual articulations of what could and could not have a material presence in this new world.

Fun for all the family

When the pandemic began and people headed inside, an idealized family unit sheltering in solidarity together was pushed to the forefront of the popular imagination. An image of coziness in the household was enforced in media representations by a systemic and unconscious adoption of the kyriarchy, regressing to dated, linear preconceptions of the family unit. This normality often reinforced retrospective images of solidarity and togetherness. For example, the UK government changed a national holiday in May 2020 to coincide with VE (Victory in Europe) Day and also used the term 'Business As Usual' throughout government propaganda during the early months. It is worth noting the superficiality of these propagandist actions. 'Business As Usual' was a term used initially during the First World War, specifically to mask the economic disaster unfolding in the UK, and VE Day occurred during a period of governmental crisis in the UK, when an exhausted population were growing increasingly disillusioned after five years of war and rationing. Board gaming had a role to play in this depiction of unity and pretend normality, with its persistent imagery of togetherness, healthy cooperation, fun and material interaction with others. This section briefly examines this configuration and why it re-emerged, counterpoised with the reality of sales and board game consumption during the pandemic.

Although the board games industry is experiencing massive growth, board games also have a very specific ideology attached to them as objects of play in the media. The same tired titles persist in the popular imagination as indicative of board gaming play: *Monopoly* (Parker Brothers 1935), *Scrabble* (Selchow and Righter 1952), *Cluedo* (Waddingtons 1949) and *Catan* (Kosmos 1995). These titles are ideologically presented as the epitome of family 'togetherness'. Advertising of such games, as well as media stories about their popularity, persistently show an archetypal family unit (heterosexual cis female mother, cis male father, two children, all white) gathered around a board, with expressions of joy and celebration on their faces. This image also frequently contains Yule iconography such as festive decorations or clothing, supporting the idea that games are played once a year after the Christmas (Christian) meal. Men are shown in active positions, leaning forward or taking turns, while women are shown with approbation on their faces. In these images, board games are also frequently played on the floor, signifying that they are more toy than game.

A rapid resurgence in lifestyle articles promoting these cultural stereotypes and linking them to board game play proliferated during the first months of the pandemic, intensifying during the peak buying period before Christmas and coinciding with a second wave of the pandemic in the United Kingdom and United States. Stock images of families depicted in this way proliferated in articles where the source material was unavailable, perpetuating the idea of an idealized family as the board game playing unit. *Hello Magazine*'s December 2020 feature on board game recommendations is typical of this construction (Bull 2020). A selection of old, 'classic' or easy-to-play games is presented. The article recommends several trivia games, the trinity of *Scrabble, Monopoly* and *Cluedo* (*Clue* in America) and two games aimed specifically at very young children. This list is typical in its scattershot approach to recommendations and is indicative of someone who does not know the genre, its players, or how gaming has developed in recent years. Many of the titles suggested have little sustained gameplay nor are they indicative of the plethora of more playable (and age-appropriate) titles available. They are also not 'family friendly'; they do not encourage sustained group play and several could not be played by all ages. For example, trivia games have limited playability (once you know the answers, the game lacks excitement), many children's games are not interesting for adults, and the classic games such as *Scrabble* rely on a developed vocabulary that may not be available to all. While the article is nominally about recommending titles to play, it reinforces gameplay stereotypes of family unity and short-term play. These stereotypes are apparent in the recommendation of the trivia tie-in 'Mr and Mrs' with the statement 'how well do you know your partner?', the comment that *Monopoly, Friends The TV Series* (Hasbro 2018) will provide 'a few hours' entertainment, and comments suggesting that the recommendations are to keep children 'busy'. These articles, although plentiful, are often met with considerable aspersion from people looking for recommended titles. *The Guardian*'s 14 December 2020 article on board games to buy over Christmas and play during the pandemic (Irving 2020) attracted scathing comments concerning its lazy, dated recommendations. In the comments online, Cally777 accurately summarizes the article: 'It's very like a video games enthusiast being told that the height of this or her hobby is playing *Space Invaders*.'

The presentation of classic board games as a panacea to boredom and fraught relationships in the household is problematic for many reasons, not simply for the presentation of archaic, exclusionary representations of family units, but because board games were shown to be extremely physical in nature. Such stock images of families reinforce the idea of closeness, proprioception and physical intimacy and of games as a play activity, more akin to toys than games. We see the hands of each participant nearly touch, and the game they are playing comprises dozens of pieces as well as the board itself. The material presence of the game is undeniable. The identification with 'family', alongside the subtext that of board games are an activity that everyone secretly loathes and only plays during one set point in the year, puts board games into a position where they become a figurehead for awkward physical play. Fortunately, this type of representation is not borne out by sales, recent board game design, player behaviours or increasingly more liberal attitudes to board gaming and play (Woods 2012; Booth 2021). Importantly, board game design and sales are not consumed by a catch-all 'family' unit, but instead lie predominantly within the twenty-five to forty-four age group (Booth 2019). Young professionals with greater disposable incomes fall into this demographic and they are also a group more likely to share accommodation with other people in their age range than with their parents.

A key element overlooked by the many articles suggesting games to play during lockdown was that many buyers did not hail from a traditional family unit and that these people were also looking for things to do indoors for entertainment. Just as families were navigating the tensions of being confined to their homes, other people were experiencing the tensions of living in close quarters with housemates. This latter demographic of players was previously more likely to play board games in social spaces away from the home, such as board game cafés, at large expos and in pubs. With a much stronger cultural awareness of available titles and changes in board gaming design, this group spent heavily on games during lockdown. The board game industry experienced a 240 per cent increase in sales during the first week of the UK lockdown (Butler 2020) and consistent growth throughout the next year. The demographic comprising board game fans contributed to this growth but had to find alternative play spaces. Often, socializing had to shift to virtual spaces. The last section of this chapter will discuss how this group transformed their material play on a 'needs must' basis, negotiating mediated play online.

Touch and trace

Board games are extremely tactile. Components come in a vast array of shapes and sizes, and most games involve the movement of these elements, from playing a card to destroying a city populated with dozens of wooden 'meeples' using a wooden dinosaur (*Terror in Meeple City*, Repos 2013). Even non-physical games such as *Werewolf* (1986) or *Two Rooms and a Boom* (Tuesday Knight Games 2013) have retail versions which provide cards, tokens and props for each game. As Paul Wake argues:

> In the manifest physicality of their paper, card, wood, and plastic technology, analog games might make a claim to be better placed to engage with the senses

of their players than their digital counterparts. Characterized by the high production values of their components and artwork, contemporary board games appeal directly to the senses of touch and sight and on rare occasions to taste. (Wake 2019: n.p.)

In their paper 'The Materiality of Board games', Rogerson et al. assert the undeniable importance of a material presence in board gaming (2016). Despite online alternatives, the players they surveyed actively chose to physically interact with the board games they played and with other players. This is a persistent theme in the trio's research: later work finds that players frequently engage in practices such as the customization of individual elements and pieces in order to make them both unique and interesting for others (Rogerson, Gibbs and Smith 2016, 2020). Game pieces can be friable, and wear and tear can break a game entirely if cards are scuffed or otherwise marked. Thus, a thriving aspect of the board games industry is the supply of protective components such as boxes, bags and protective card 'sleeves', as well as individualistic markers such as interestingly coloured dice, moulded figures, apparel and storage items.

The integral nature of physical components, and the fetishization of these (just ask a TTRPG player how many sets of dice they own to see an example of this), is not the only reason that players like to be present when playing. The social ethos that has developed around board games is a result not only of the community growing but also of the ways in which games encourage players to communicate while playing. Board games often involve discussions, debate and sometimes intense social interactions (especially apparent in games with a traitor mechanic, for example, where one person is deliberately deceiving the others). They have a complexity that often involves one or more people needing to verbally explain the rules to others, or are cooperative, requiring verbal communication and agreement on how an individual turn will take place, and what its benefit to the group might be. Finally, cost (a large boxed board game in the UK often costs between £50 and £90) means that players tend to pool their resources. One person will buy a title and bring it to an event to play collectively with others or develop a circle of friends who share their copies of games. Players enjoy being present when they play together, even if virtual alternatives exist. The growth of board game events and conventions is a testimony to this, with thousands of people attending events such as UKGE (21,000 attendees in 2019) and Gen Con (anticipated 70, 000 in 2021) (Morrus 2019; Hall 2021). Prior to lockdown, Rogerson et al. discussed the availability of online platforms and apps which allowed board game play online, but consistently found that players eschewed them for material play (Rogerson, Gibbs and Smith 2015, 2018, 2020). Going into the pandemic, therefore, the core board game purchasing demographic was much more attuned to virtual and online technologies in daily life but absolutely preferred physicality in their play.

The Covid-19 pivot changed this by necessity. Players could not meet in their regular groups, visit communal spaces nor take part in events like conventions where new titles are showcased. Both sales and play had to move online. Fortunately, an existing infrastructure already exists in the form of websites and platforms that replicate games or allow board game play online. From March 2020, existing sites like *Tabletopia*, *Tabletop Simulator*, *Board Game Arena* and *Roll20* saw an immediate and dramatic increase in usage. Steam saw an increase from 5,069 users in February 2020 to 36,793 in April 2020. *Board Game Arena* saw a 600 per cent growth, with over 5 million users in 2020. In January 2021, *Board Game Arena* was bought out by board gaming giant Asmodee (Jarvis 2021), suggesting a level of long-term investment in the platform, alongside an expectation that many players would retain their subscriptions on a long-term basis.

The board game fan communities demonstrated a flexible attitude to losing the materiality of shared play in larger groups, both capitalizing on the growth in virtual sites and buying more physical copies. Interestingly, despite the huge growth in online play, sales of physical board games continued, with similar massive increases in sales as those seen online. This is borne out by pre-pandemic buying habits, where playing virtual copies of a game results in more physical sales. Famously, sales of the online version of *Ticket to Ride* caused commensurate increases in the sales of the physical copy (Melby 2013), bringing it to new audiences through apps and other online versions, but boosting physical copies alongside these purchases. This success also meant that Asmodee was already committed to creating copies of their board games in a robust online format. While this was intended to drive physical sales as well, it meant that their developer team was already established, with a track record of existing titles that had been converted successfully to a virtual form.

Case study: Wizards of the Coast and the online pivot

Wizards of the Coast makes an interesting case study in how pre-existing attitudes towards online play fed into the rapid pivot needed to market their games. Although it is a card game, *Magic: The Gathering* (*M:TG*) (Wizards of the Coast 1993) is not only sold alongside board games but is considered a compatible/comparable activity by players. Many board/card games blur the lines between the two genres to the extent that it is difficult to separate where a game-like *Fort* (Rodiek 2020) falls on the spectrum. The similarities in material presence – many items that are picked up, shared and act as ludic components, as well as the communities that engage in play – mean that this chapter sees card and board games as generically interwoven to the point that separation is extremely hard.

Companies such as Wizards of the Coast, who rely on in-person tournament sales for games like *M:TG*, rapidly pivoted their sales to online versions of the game. Tournament play, which is a lucrative and popular element of *M:TG*, is specifically tailored towards in-person events where players often need to buy unopened packs of cards to play on the day. After cancelling their in-person events and setting up contingencies for winning players to have their rankings rolled forwards, Wizards of the Coast created a series of online tournaments that required similar purchases but were played entirely virtually. They also shifted their marketing onto Twitch streams – a direction they were already moving into – and launched a 'Stay at Home, Play at Home' marketing campaign. As with Asmodee, and probably because of the transmedial literacies of their purchasing audience, the company was not only starting to explore the potential of online content but had a pre-existing development team and an awareness of how online and physical sales can dovetail. For example, robust video game conversions of *Magic the Gathering*, including pre-existing elements like card cover assets, game development and competitive play, already existed, which they could draw on when creating the content for competition play in an online arena.

Dungeons & Dragons, the largest TTRPG franchise, also owned by Wizards of the Coast, pivoted its marketing to support remote play. While this is a TTRPG and not a board game, the implementation of *Roll20* is a comparable example of the rapid transformation of gaming habits to *Tabletopia*, *Tabletop Simulator* and other board game conversion sites. In the first and second quarters of 2020, Wizards of the Coast deployed a massive push towards their digital platform, *D&D Beyond*. *D&D Beyond* was launched in 2017 to revitalize *D&D 5ed* in a virtual context. The platform is largely free to use, with purchasable content comprising more tools for players and storytellers (a term I use here to promote more inclusive language during play), access to supplements and new manuals, and online content which helps players taking part in virtual campaigns and games. It provides many resources for players and storytellers, with a specific remit to endorse 'homebrew' content (games created by players and not taken from official scenarios). While the platform not only saw growing usage prior to 2020 it also saw unprecedented and immediate levels of growth in March 2020, with players shifting both regular and new games to an online space. The 'Stay at home, Play at home' promotion supported freebies, support packages and online play in general, pushing the player base towards *D&D Beyond*.

D&D has also seen a recent move to online spaces through both official and unofficial endorsement from high profile 'actual play' Twitch streamers and podcasters, which is also highly symptomatic of the trend in gaming to spectate as well as play. *Critical Role* frequently uses *D&D Beyond* during play to quickly look up for information. *The Adventure Zone* used the adventure included in the *D&D 5ed Starters Guide* in a less official capacity as the basis of their first game 'Here be Gerblins'. These shows support a more casual participation mode whereby viewers spectate or listen to live or edited versions of games by skilled players, including voice actors and comedians. Both shows are at the forefront of a huge wave in the act of viewing or listening to others play games as well as playing them, moving the game into a spectated position easily consumed from virtual devices. Board game sites such as *Shut Up and Sit Down*, *Dice Tower* and *Tabletop/Geek and Sundry* promote both the celebretization of play and are seen as key sites of endorsement by the industry. A recommendation on *Shut Up and Sit Down* is currently seen as a 'golden ticket' to success, as with their recommendation of Anthony Conta's *FunEmployed* (Iron Wall Games 2013), a card-based party game, which took the game from relative obscurity to sell out success as soon as the video review was published.

This last aspect of game culture, whereby play is seen from the perspective of fandom, highlights the last, possibly surprising element of pandemic play. Game sales of physical copies continued to boom. Despite the heavy promotion of existing virtual paratexts such as the online platforms, streaming shows and virtual resources, Wizards of the Coast advertising encouraged gamers to buy physical copies alongside virtual ones. *Candlekeep Mysteries* (Wizards of the Coast 2021), a game supplement for *D&D* released on 16 March 2020 is a good example of this. The supplement provides resources and guidance for newer players, containing seventeen short adventures for low-level characters, specifically targeting new players and providing them with short, detailed adventures to play. The supplement was heavily advertised as both an online and physical artefact. While the virtual copy of *Candlekeep Mysteries* came with a unique set of digital dice, physical copies were promoted in tandem, including a limited collector's edition of the supplement. Advertising stressed the dual purchase options with local game stores pre-eminent on this list: 'Pre-order now at your local game store, bookstores such as *Barnes & Noble*, *Books-a-Million*, or online retailers like *Amazon*. Also available for pre-order at *D&D Beyond*, *Fantasy Grounds* and *Roll 20*' (Wizards of the Coast 2021).

This blending of the physical and the digital in terms of consumption and sales is fascinating. To an extent, the drive to push sales of physical elements is a long-term finance strategy, keeping the 'local game store' afloat by bolstering a financial model that has afforded the board games industry rising success. Offering this support to the smaller retail outlets and promoting larger distributors, Wizards of the Coast can appear supportive and suggest a guaranteed alternative. This is a win-win situation for them in terms of sales and retaining fans. However, the focus on the materiality of the product, for example its different covers, its assumed place alongside others on a player's bookshelf, tangible inclusions such as a pull-out map included in the contents and the emphasis on simply owning a copy, are central elements of the advertising. The classic image of a storyteller poring over a manual is a pose that is rather more difficult in virtual space. Overall, the expansion is defined by its material presence.

This trend for owning a tangible version, often fetishizing the ownership of such, is reflected in sales across the board games and TTRPGs. Not only did these games sell in both a physical and virtual capacity, but sales of single-player and two-player games increased. The first reason for this is obvious: people were alone or living together in smaller units, therefore they sought playable games. However, the idea of duplication also appears here. Some people, like myself, invested in more than one copy of a game so that they could play a physical version of a game in tandem with a remote partner, but others appear to have succumbed to the same desire as with *Ticket to Ride* in 2011 and bought a physical copy to own alongside the virtual one.

For me, using virtual board gaming and role-playing platforms enhanced my ability to play because my usual gaming group live in Ireland and I am an inhabitant of the UK, but this was a fairly unusual circumstance. Nevertheless, I too found myself absolutely in thrall to compensating for online play through physical gestures and purchases. I found myself consuming physical artefacts alongside the virtual ones, buying copies of board games I could not physically play, and gaming manuals that were more effective to use in their virtual iterations. I loaned physical copies of my board games to my neighbours and took a lot of satisfaction in knowing they would be played in person. I bought new dice, continued to buy an escape room board game that I was fond of, despite having no one to play it with, and invested in the next iteration of *Gloomhaven*, called *Frosthaven* (Cephalofair Games 2022) on Kickstarter, which was the first crowdfunded project I had spent money on for years. Many conversations with my gaming group consisted of lengthy discussions of what we would play when we saw each other again, sometimes at the expense of completing any kind of meaningful play online. These daydreams became an important locator for our social activities, 'when we meet in person' becoming an extension and an elision of the fact we were all gathering more frequently than we ever had done previously, and that I was in a different country. I found myself going further, buying physical copies of role-playing games, and mailing them to my gaming group in Ireland (a ridiculously cumbersome way to purchase titles for them!), even when we were playing together on Discord and pooling PDFs and website resources. When I sent a 'gelatinous cube soap' containing dice to a friend, she reciprocated by sending me a set of spell cards, we realized our buying had transcended necessary gaming elements and become entirely cosmetic (it was good soap, though). Overall, these activities show a tension between the desire to continue touch-based, in-person activities and adaptive techniques to overcome these. We liked the virtual versions of games, but we connected by sending physical accompaniments, reminding ourselves of the times we shared experiences in the same space. I do not think this part of my experience was particularly unusual and contend that a strong identification with material activity is part of our social make-up. The materiality of these game-related items and their proprioceptive nature – such as flicking over a spell card, feeling the sensation of the dice emerging from the soap and stashing a manual on my bookcase – made up for the lack of touch, contact and face-to-face communication that we had lost.

Conclusion

The activities described in this chapter demonstrate an adaptation to material requirements in the Covid-19 pandemic, rather than an abandonment of them. Our need to touch, possess and hold items peeks through the virtual iterations of play that were necessary during lockdown. Material play is shown to be important but not essential, yet it is still discarded with some regret or with a residual need to have the best of both. Heidi Tyni and Oli Sotamaa argue that '[a] lot of the play experiences now available to us are more or less hybrid experiences, combinations of physical and digital elements' (2014: 12), and it was perhaps because of this that players pivoted online so quickly. However, their lasting desire to materially interact with both the games and people they were playing with was still a pervasive element in their play.

Lockdown demonstrated a strengthening of physical desire, rather than a release of it, even when the virtual provided an almost identical version of the game, and, often, a more streamlined one, for players to gather around. Conscious of what was missed, groups met online to replicate idealized versions of physical connections, although they also developed and strengthened these aspects of play to extend beyond their non-material presences. The fantasies played out in board games, with their clear definitions of winning and losing, and the triumphant worlds of role-playing games, all saw a dramatic surge that reflected not only the need for escapism but also the need to replicate material connections in liminal spaces. None of this was necessarily problematic. Rather, it reveals a reliance on materiality which persisted and was repurposed, with an understanding that both physical and non-physical interactions might move gaming forwards and the realization that they were surprisingly interchangeable. The desire for both modes of play, evident in buying a physical copy of a board game one was also playing online, demonstrated a fascinating blur between materiality both within the game and as an essential comfort in the tangible world.

References

Beattie, S. (2020), 'Playing Pandemic – The Hit Board Game about the Very Thing we're Trying to Avoid', *The Conversation*, 29 April. Available online: https://theconversation.com/playing-pandemic-the-hit-board-game-about-the-very-thing-were-trying-to-avoid-137009 (accessed 15 November 2021).

Booth, P. (2019), 'Who's at the Table – Board Game Players and Communities', *Meeple Mountain*, 27 August. Available online: https://www.meeplemountain.com/articles/whos-at-the-table-board-game-players-and-communities/ (accessed 15 November 2021).

Booth, P. (2021), *Board Games as Media*, New York: Bloomsbury Academic Press.

Brooks, M. (2006), *World War Z*, New York: Penguin Books.

Bull, M. (2020), '15 Best Family-Friendly Board Games to Play with Kids during the Second Lockdown: *Cluedo, Trivia* and More. A Fun Way to Keep Everyone Entertained', *Hello Magazine*, 8 December. Available online: https://www.hellomagazine.com/healthandbeauty/mother-and-baby/2020040287351/popular-family-board-games-for-children-and-adults/ (accessed 15 November 2021).

Butler, S. (2020), 'Sales of Board Games and Jigsaws Soar during Coronavirus Lockdown', *Guardian*, 1 April. Available online: https://www.theguardian.com/business/2020/apr/01/sales-of-board-games-and-jigsaws-soar-during-coronavirus-lockdown (accessed 15 November 2021).

-r

Candlekeep Mysteries (2021), [Tabletop Role-Playing game], Designers: G. Barber, K. L. D'angelo, A. Huang, M. Hulmes, J. Kretchmer, D. Kwan, A. Lee, A. Levitch, S. Madsen, C. Perkins, M. Polkinghorn, T. Rehman, D. Ruiz, K. Shaw, B. Stoddard, A. Vorpahl and T. Winslow-Brill, USA: Wizards of the Coast.

Catan (1995), [Board game], Designer: K. Teuber, Germany: KOSMOS.

Cluedo (1949), [Board game], Designer: A. E. Pratt, UK: Waddington, Ltd.

Connect 4 (1974), [Board game], Designer: N. Strongin and H. Wexler, USA: Milton Bradley.

Critical Role (2015 to present), [Twitch stream]. Available online: https://critrole.com/ (accessed 15 November 2021).

Fort (2020), [Board game], Designer: G. Rodiek, USA: Leder Games.

Frosthaven (2022), [Board game], Designer: I. Childres, USA: Cephalofair Games.

FunEmployed (2013), [Board game], Designer: A. Conta, USA: IronWall Games.

Gloomhaven (2020), [Board game], Designer: I. Childres, USA: Cephalofair Games.

Hall, C. (2021), 'Gen-con is Back with an In-Person Convention this September', *Polygon*, 17 March. Available online: https://www.polygon.com/2021/3/17/22336640/gen-con-2021-moved-to-september-badges (accessed 15 November 2021).

Jarvis, M. (2021), 'Board Game Arena has been Bought by Catan, Pandemic and Ticket to Ride Maker Asmodee', *Dicebreaker*, 11 February. Available online: https://www.dicebreaker.com/companies/board-game-arena/news/board-game-arena-asmodee-acquisition (accessed 15 November 2021).

Kirkman, R. (2003–2019), *The Walking Dead*, Portland, OR: Image Comics.

Magic: The Gathering (1993), [Card game], Designer: R. Garfield, USA: Wizards of the Coast.

Melby, C. (2013), 'Ticket to Ride: How the Internet Fuelled a New Board Game Powerhouse', *Forbes*, 18 March. Available online: https://www.forbes.com/sites/calebmelby/2013/03/18/days-of-wonder-how-the-internet-fueled-a-new-board-game-powerhouse/?sh=41c3741e41d1 (accessed 15 November 2021).

Monopoly (1935), [Board game], Designers: C. Darrow and E. J. Magie, USA: Parker Bros.

Monopoly: Friends the TV Series (2018), [Board game], USA: Hasbro.

Morrus (2019), 'UK Games Expo Attendance up 18% Maintains World #3 Spot', *Enworld.org*, 6 June. Available online: https://www.enworld.org/threads/uk-games-expo-attendance-up-18-maintains-world-3-spot.666399/ (accessed 15 November 2021).

Rogerson, M., M. Gibbs and W. Smith (2015), 'Digitising Board Games: Issues and Tensions', *Proceedings from DIGRA 2015: Diversity of Play: Games – Cultures – Identities*. Lüneburg.

Rogerson, M., M. Gibbs and W. Smith (2016), 'I Love All the Bits', *Proceedings of the 2016 CHI Conference on Human Factors in Computing Systems*, May, 3956–69.

Rogerson, M., M. Gibbs and W. Smith (2020), 'More than the Sum of their Bits: Understanding the Gameboard and Components', in D. Brown and E. MacCallum-Stewart (eds), *Rerolling Board Games*, 88–108, Jefferson, NC: Macfarland & Co.

Scrabble (1948), [Board game], Designer: A. Mosher Butts, USA: Selchow and Righter.

Seetharaman, S. (2020), 'How Big is the Board Game Market', *Pipecandy*, 6 September. Available online: https://blog.pipecandy.com/board-games-market/ (accessed 1 November 2021).

Serpell, N. (2019), *The Old Drift*, London: Vintage.

Shut Up and Sit Down (2015), 'Let's Play *Funemployed*', *Shut Up and Sit Down*. Available online: https://www.shutupandsitdown.com/videos/susd-play-funemployed/ (accessed 4 June 2021).

Smith, Q. (2017), 'SU&SD Presents: Board Gaming's Golden Age! (2017 Update)', *Shut Up and Sit Down*, 19 April. Available online: https://www.shutupandsitdown .com/videos/susd-presents-board-gamings-golden-age-2016-update/ (accessed 1 November 2021).

St John Mandell, E. (2014), *Station Eleven*, London: Picador.

Terror in Meeple City (2013), [board game], Designer: A. Bauza, Belgium: Repos Production.

Two Rooms and a Boom (2013), [board game], Designers: A. Gerding and S. McCoy, Tuesday Knight Games.

Tyni, H. and O. Sotamaa (2014), 'Material Culture and *Angry Birds*', in *Proceedings of the Nordic DiGRA 2014 Conference*. Available online: http://www.digra.org/digital -library/publications/material-culture-and-angry-birds/ (accessed 4 November 2021).

Wake, P. (2019), 'Token Gestures – Towards a Theory of Immersion in Analog Games', *Analog Game Studies*, 7 (2). Available online: http://analoggamestudies.org/2019 /09/token-gestures-towards-a-theory-of-immersion-in-analog-games/ (accessed 1 November 2021).

Werewolf (1986), [board game], Designers: D. Davidoff and A. Plotkin, USA: Mayfair Games.

Wizards of the Coast (2020), 'Wizards of the Coast Response to COVID-19', *Wizards .com*, 17 September. Available online: https://company.wizards.com/article/news/ wizards-coasts-response-covid-19 (accessed 1 November 2021).

Wizards of the Coast (2021), 'Community Tournament Guidelines', *Wizards.com* , 25 October. Available online: https://company.wizards.com/en/community -tournament-guidelines (accessed 1 November 2021).

Woods, S. (2012), *Eurogames: The Design. Culture and Play of Modern European Board Games*, Jefferson, NC: Mcfarland & Co.

V

Hybridity

11

The cult of new (stuff)

Kickstarter's digital/material tensions

Paul Booth[1]

It has become a truism in board game research that Kickstarter has revolutionized the playing field as one of the most consistently popular, funded categories on the site (see Roeder 2015; Werning 2017; Brown and MacCallum-Stewart 2020; Buttice and Noonan 2020). Perhaps the most oft-cited example of the Kickstarter/analogue game connection is *Exploding Kittens* (Ad Magic 2015), a card game designed by Elan Lee and Shane Small, with artwork by *The Oatmeal*'s Matthew Inman. The game has been noted as the 'Most-Backed Project of All Time' on Kickstarter (Kickstarter 2015: n.p), with 219,382 individuals pledging $8.78 million to the cause (see Torner 2018; Werning 2017). *Exploding Kittens* is far from the largest dollar amount for board games, however: Isaac Childres's *Frosthaven* (Cephalofair 2021) holds that honour, with almost $13 million pledged for the sequel to *Gloomhaven* (Cephalofair 2018, also a Kickstarted game).

   In this chapter, I unbox the connection between board games and Kickstarter to examine the effect that Kickstarter is having on the material reality – the ludo-textuality – of board games. In this chapter, I assume that board games are what I've called a 'ludo-textual' combination of material physicality and immaterial play experience (Booth 2021). The material reality of board games is made up of the actual physical components as well as the imaginative interaction with those components during gameplay. As a medium for board game financing, Kickstarter is a key node in an oppositional-yet-contingent connection between the immaterial and the material in board gaming. It balances a tension between the highly digitized world of board game creation and the physical realities of board game play, highlighting how the *ludo-textual* can be a useful methodology for board game analysis.

Kickstarter itself emphasizes this divide between the material and the immaterial. Kickstarter's stated mission is to 'make ideas into reality' (Kickstarter 2021: n.p.) by helping to connect designers with investors. In other words, Kickstarter promises an actualization ('reality') from the immaterial ('ideas') via the production of material goods. But in promising to turn the immaterial actual, Kickstarter privileges the material – after all, why bother to 'materialize' ideas if dreams are enough? This privileging of the material maps onto the board game landscape: the logic of Kickstarter seems to imply that the physical 'object-ness' of the game preempts the game's experiential play. But if board games exist always as an object/experience amalgam, then Kickstarter's insistence on the material deemphasizes the immaterial reality of gameplay experience.

Kickstarter is a crowdfunding site, where users ('backers') can pay a certain amount of money to help fund a particular campaign. In exchange, they (usually) get a reward if the campaign meets its minimum goal – in the case of board game Kickstarters, the reward is usually some variant of the game, plus 'unlocked' stretch goals and optional add-ons (which may or may not be game materials). As I demonstrate, Kickstarter's digital platform undergirds and shapes this transaction. As Aaron Trammell establishes, 'analog games are emerging as a cultural phenomenon in our present moment because of their explicit relationality to the digital' (2019: n.p.). The digital nature of Kickstarter affects not only the physicality of the games that get funded but also the board game market as a whole. It does this by normalizing the (over)production of material components (e.g. miniatures) as well as making such production seem generically necessary. In other words, and as Stefan Werning notes, Kickstarter has incentivized particular '"formulae" rather than the exploration of new ideas' (2017: 69); analysing these formulae helps us better understand the contours of the industry and the games that get produced.

Werning's work on Kickstarter and the board game renaissance focuses on software studies (he examines Kickstarter as a platform). In contrast, I am interested in the impact of Kickstarter on the materiality of games produced. What, I ask, is the connection of the digital platform and the material games that are realized? And how does this affect the games we play? To that end, I examine a selection of games funded via Kickstarter for the way the physical objects become part of the promotional system and add to the use-value of the game, 'enhancing games through upgraded, special edition, or custom components' (Rogerson, Gibbs, and Smith 2020: 89). As of the writing of this chapter (January 2021), more than 1 in 5 (21 per cent) of the top 200 board games on *BoardGameGeek* are the results of successful Kickstarter campaigns. At the same time, in an apparent push back against the introduction of too many physical components, a wave of digital content – often fan-produced – has been created to augment or even replace the physical in analogue games. This chapter considers these developments through both textual analysis of Kickstarted board games and ethnographic interviews with game designers, players and online content creators about the influence of Kickstarter on analogue game production.

Board games and materiality

Kickstarter's funding model is now well established. The creator of a campaign for Kickstarter seeks a minimum amount of money. Each backer pledges an amount that puts them at a particular 'tier' – that tier will offer a reward if the campaign makes that minimum amount. If the minimum amount is not achieved, the campaign is not funded and no backer spends money. If a campaign meets its goal, then it is funded and the backers' money is split between the campaign and Kickstarter (which takes 5 per cent). In 2020 alone, '[s]uccessful campaigns for tabletop games and accessories earned more than $233 million . . . up from $176.3 million in 2019 – an increase of more than 32%' (Hall 2020: n.p.). Usually, different amounts of money unlock different 'tiers', which offer different 'rewards'. In the case of board games, most tiers offer some format of the game – either a regular edition, a special edition, some extra minis and so on. Each campaign lasts a specific time limit (usually around a month).

While sometimes posited as opposites in the analogue gaming world (Rogerson, Gibbs and Smith 2020: 104), board gaming relies on digital technology (Trammell 2019 gives an authoritative overview). From design, to playtesting, to digital versions of games, to playing online during a pandemic, board games today are always intimately tied to digital technology (and that goes beyond the many games that require digital apps to function). On the one hand – and quite obviously – Kickstarter is an intermediary digital platform: it facilitates the relationship between game producers and buyers. Yet, on the other hand, the 'design affordances of the Kickstarter platform characteristically foster a design focus on materiality' (Werning 2017: 77). That is, one of the greatest enticements of helping fund a Kickstarter is the very materiality of board games – and Kickstarter creators know that more material elements help spur backers.

On Kickstarter, the use of miniatures in promotional materials has contributed to the success of some campaigns as well as increased the price of many games. As Werning notes in a content analysis of board game Kickstarters:

'miniatures' is one of the most common terms with 239 occurrences, which disproportionately cluster in the most successful campaign pages. This appears plausible because projects involving miniatures are usually more expensive; however, it also applies to projects with the highest funding ratios . . . suggesting that – inversely – games involving miniatures appear to be particularly appealing on Kickstarter. (2017: 71)

Melissa J. Rogerson, Martin Gibbs and Wally Smith agree with this assessment of the appeal of miniatures, noting that the categories on Kickstarter that receive the most funding also have the greatest physical/table presence of the game. For instance,

the game *Scythe* (Stonemaier 2016) – which offered four different support levels, each with its own deluxe components, and raised US\$1.8 million – sold more copies of the \$99 "Collector's" edition than it did of all the other available levels together. The base game, which featured metallic (silver) foil on the box for all copies ordered through the Kickstarter campaign, cost only \$59 but sold well under half as many copies as the Collector's edition, which cost nearly twice as much. (2020: 95)

This pattern is repeated over and over again: in an analysis of successfully Kickstarted board games in the Top 100 on *BoardGameGeek*, I found that 90 per cent (20/23) that offered a higher tier with more stuff included had more people backing at that amount. The 2021 Kickstarter campaign for Simone Luciani and Nestore Mangone's board game *Darwin's Journey* (ThunderGryph 2021) serves as a key example. More than 16,000 backers pledged over one million Euros to bring this game to life (Bisi 2021: n.p.). There were two-tier levels for the campaign: 1,034 people pledged €45 to get a copy of the game, including all the stretch goals not available for the retail product, while 14,311 people pledged €70 to get the game, stretch goals, an expansion, and a number of 'special items': metal coins and soft plastic wax seals. Some campaigns had more expensive tiers that did not offer more 'things' but instead offered signed copies or creator visits. For example, the campaign for R. Eric Reuss's *Spirit Island* (Greater than Games 2017) offered a signed copy of the game along with a map and a game mat for an additional \$80. Far fewer people backed at that higher level. Similarly, the number of backers for Jamey Stegmaier and Alan Stone's *Viticulture* (Stonemaier 2013) did not vary too much between tiers when those tiers included items that would not contribute to gameplay, like wine glasses or the chance to visit with the creators (although these in-person events were strictly limited to just a few people, they had fewer than half of these options backed). Backers seem more interested in multitudes of gameplay stuff rather than exclusive merchandise or in-person events.

But what do I mean by 'gameplay stuff'? Generally, *stuff* comes in many forms but can be described as the physical objects that make up our everyday life (Miller 2013). For board games, stuff includes all the things that make up the tangible nature of gameplay. This can be miniatures (plastic, resin, metal, etc.), cards (of various stocks), game mats, the game boards, and even more trays to hold all this extra stuff. Some stuff (miniatures, for example) is directly related to the game diegesis and thus affects actual gameplay. Other stuff can be non-diegetic to the game, handling what Elias, Garfield and Gutschera call 'busywork' (2012: 185): stuff like the instruction manual or game mats. Finally, there is ancillary stuff that is more paratextually related to the game (see Gray 2010): the wine glasses from *Viticulture*, a book about the making of a game (*Anachonry*, Mindclash 2017), signed art (*Spirit Island*), promotional materials (*Architects of the West Kingdom*, Garphill Games 2018), or even different games from the same publisher (*Brass: Birmingham*, Roxley 2018). This non-gameplay stuff seems less interesting to a majority of Kickstarter backers. In fact, of the three games mentioned earlier that did not have more backers at the higher tier rate, two of them included such non-gameplay stuff in their Kickstarters (*Nemesis*, Awaken Realms 2018, offered an art book and *Through the Ages*, CGE 2015 offered a different game from the same publishers). It appears that stuff matters, but only when it matters to the gameplay.

The success of Kickstarter as a production hub for board games is undisputed. Small companies have been able to promote and produce at an unparalleled rate. Large companies can ensure the viability of their products to a mass audience. Ironically, though, Kickstarter itself is a *digital* 'media distribution platform' that, for board games, relies on physical components to entice backers (Werning 2017: 65). Werning goes on to note that Kickstarter actualizes the connection between digital platform studies and game studies. Platform studies is a diverse field that explores 'the connection between platform technologies and creative production to be investigated' (Bogost and Montfort 2009a: 1, 2009b). In other words, one thing it examines is the way the particular affordances of a software constrain the users of that platform. For example, Kickstarter 'imposes its own mode of governance on the developers, both formally through its functionality as a software application as well as layers of terms of use' (Werning 2017: 68–9). As a platform, then, Werning offers four ways that Kickstarter has been designed affects board game campaigns (and the games that emerge from them):

(1) The 'infinite scroll' allows for a seemingly-endless stream of new content, contributing to a *cult of the new* mentality;

(2)   The writing constraints force the written copy to fit into particular categories, which over time 'become stable categories in users' minds';

(3)   The stream of FAQs, Comments, and Updates aims to create a sense of community, leading to stronger bonds between gamers; and

(4)   The quantification of backers algorithmicises and enumerates the popularity of a game, leading to the success of games being measured in dollars and backers rather than in gameplay or innovation. (Werning 2017: 72–3)

The effect of all this quantification is to foster 'the creation of games that are easily communicable and exhibit a characteristically 'modular' design approach' (Werning 2017: 76) – that is, games in which the core gameplay can accommodate new elements (e.g. new characters, new locations, new game modes). One Kickstarted game appears a lot like another Kickstarted game. For Werning, then, the platform affects material production.

But what does this look like for gamers? For one, the material elements of board games are just as crucial to the players whether the game has been Kickstarted or not. Rogerson, Gibbs and Smith reveal that 'Modern boardgames are known for the attention that publishers pay to their components' (2020: 90). Werning indicates that the outside influence Kickstarter generates affects new games, even if they had not been Kickstarted: in other words, game players expect more materiality in games today, regardless of where they come from. In my own *Board Games as Media* (2021), I describe how the actual, physical components of a board game are enticing elements for players: in a survey of over 900 players, 'table presence' was consistently named as one of the most important elements to consider when choosing games to play. As Marco Arnaudo describes, 'The material nature of analog board games can contribute to make their content particularly vivid' (2018: 21). In other words, for some players, the material presence of games makes them more 'real': they become more immersive and detailed, and they allow for deeper immersion in the gameworld. As mentioned earlier, to set the gameplay experience apart from the material object-ness of the game is a false dichotomy; the two are intimately connected. Games are as 'real' as players imagine them to be.

By the same token, the material elements of a board game 'shape . . . players' experiences and practices' (Wasserman 2020: 73). They take on an oversize role in the meanings that players create when they play a game (Booth 2021). Board games are textual objects that have textual objects within them. The objects in games construct 'a bounded experience' which can create 'an alternate world for viewers/players to mindfully inhabit' (Booth 2021: 8). The cubes, meeples, cards and minis create and replicate cultural meanings. Characters may be designed in particular ways, which shapes the interpretation players give them. Studies of race and gender in games (see, e.g., Johnson 2016; Pobuda 2018; Robinson 2014; Trammell 2018) have shown that board games often reproduce cultural stereotypes about identities (e.g. women characters are often highly sexualized in art and figurines). Material elements can also enhance the *play* aspect of gameplay, increasing the 'ludic complexities . . . from the physicality of boardgames as a played entity' (Brown and MacCallum-Stewart 2020: 3). The tangible aspects of gaming can complicate how the game itself is played: players with disabilities may find it more difficult to move pieces, roll dice, draw cards or play tiles. All this is to say that material elements of board gaming do not just separate analogue games from their digital counterparts: they can create an entirely new gaming experience. The larger point here, though, is that the physical makes a significant difference to any board game – not just those that have been crowdfunded – and thus it should come as no shock to learn that the business model of Kickstarted games to entice players with more physical elements has found its way into other aspects of contemporary board gaming.

Furthermore, in an article about the user's rationale for backing crowdfunding campaigns, Colistra and Duvall (2017) have shown that there is significant evidence that backers are attracted to 'Kickstarter-exclusive rewards', which for board game Kickstarters are usually additional material elements. Kickstarter campaigns tend to frame material quality as an 'upgrade' for pre-existing games (Werning 2017) or as a 'premium' edition (Rogerson, Gibbs and Smith 2020: 94) – substituting metal coins for cardboard ones, for instance – lending perceived authenticity and a sense of realism to the game and as 'enticements to encourage purchasers to commit to buying the game (and to pay for it) before it is produced' (Rogerson, Gibbs and Smith 2020: 94). When we play games with metal instead of cardboard, wood instead of plastic, or wax instead of paper, it is not just weightier in our boxes, it also replicates the different textures and sensual experiences of our everyday lives.

Playing a board game is an ephemeral experience: it is bounded by the beginnings and endings of the play session, and will be 'vastly different from one player to another' (Booth 2021: 104). In some ways, an emphasis on materiality in Kickstarter games might encourage game players to view the game in a more tangible way. By purchasing a lot of content, players actualize their passion, offering money for tangibility. And the more games purchased means the more games to play (or, at least, to anticipate playing).

In other words, when backers pay more for a diverse set of material elements, or for more miniatures or physical objects in a game, they are emphasizing the game as an object rather than experience, or, rather, the game as textual being. Like Kickstarter's mission statement, the material reality supersedes the immaterial ideas. But, if games, as I have argued, are *both* texts and experiences *at the same time*, then conceptualizing games as objects suggests a more passive being than does conceiving of games as experiences. The experience of the game, although filtered through the objects on the board, seems less important than the objects themselves. However, because objects have meanings, backers are also making the game more meaning-*full*, thus linking the monetary value of the game to the use-value, or value of the experience, of the games (see Booth and Jones 2020). Crowdfunding for board games becomes 'affective labour' that not only helps the board game manufacturers but also facilitates emotional value for the player (see Trammell 2019). We pay for our own material reality, turning our imaginative experience tangible.

Board game players have differing opinions on the influence of Kickstarter on the hobby. For *Board Games as Media*, I conducted a survey of over 900 board gamers about their experiences in the hobby. In analysing the responses, I was able to identify key elements relating to the tension between the digital and the analogue in Kickstarter. Using comments from these players, creators and influencers, I note the conflicted tension around Kickstarter from the board game community itself.

One tension identified within the interview subjects was what they termed the 'cult of the new'. As Arnaudo describes, gamers 'enjoy the challenge that comes from absorbing often complex new sets of rules that require time and energy to memorize, let alone to implement effectively. This factor alone means that the "stretching" of one's mind in the play of a new hobby game is more likely to occur' (2017: n.p.). By virtue of the sheer number of games available to fund on Kickstarter – and the rapid turnover between campaigns, which generally last less than a month – there is almost always something new and exciting to fund on the site. Some hobbyists enjoy the constant stream of newness emerging on Kickstarter. According to one participant (all quotes are anonymous as per my Institutional Review Board requirements), Kickstarter offers:

> new themes and art and ideas and mechanics into board games; i.e., less toy manufacturers going for the lowest common denominator, more cranky geniuses turning out material for weird and/or marginal communities.

But, as another notes, at the same time:

New games come out every week, and every week there are reviewers saying that this week's games are great(!). I think that this is inflating FOMO [Fear of Missing Out] and it is clouding the consumer's judgment. As a result, we have a lot game going to print, and being purchased that otherwise wouldn't be. . . . The hobby can continue to grow without a new 'must-buy' game coming out every week.

On the one hand, 'it is the new "hotness" of a game which inspires me to play a game', while on the other hand, 'people are constantly buying new games, many of which never get played because there's always a new hotness around the corner'. At the same time, 'the "cult of the future" attitude is a real turn off. People seem to talk more about games that are coming out in six months vs. games that we already have and enjoy. I'm like, here's this 4-year-old game that I really like, is it worthy of being played please?'

Interviewees commented on other aspects of crowdfunding as well. Kickstarter's reach and influence allows it to promote/develop new board game creators and can get 'unique indie games published'. However, 'Big companies [still have] a monopoly on sales due to their recognized name . . . selling mediocre products'. Indeed, some players feel strongly that Kickstarter

needs to better define what they are. Originally a means for unknowns or non-publishers to get their game out there, it now is a pre-order system that is replacing distributors and retailers. Bright Shiny Objects – In this age of CMON [Cool Mini or Not, a major game developer using Kickstarter] it seems like the game with the most minis is the winner.

When these large companies run Kickstarter campaigns, it often feels like 'nothing more than a pre-order system, bringing a fully to near fully developed game to Kickstarter'. My review of the top 200 games revealed this as well: some big game companies ran their campaigns as if the games were already completed and backers were simply pre-ordering content.

With more campaigns appearing complete from the start, smaller companies that may need funding to get off the ground may suffer. This level of commitment means a company needs to come to Kickstarter with a lot of the product already developed: 'If you bring an idea that is still in the early stages of development, it is far harder to succeed. Without a minimum of 3D renders of the game, a draft of the rulebook, box contents etc. consumers will pass you up.'

At the same time, players feel as though Kickstarter has had an indelible effect on innovation in the board gaming hobby. For instance, 'the rise of Kickstarter has brought so many budding designers to the table'. Kickstarter has provided a way for new designers to find a niche, to 'get out of the bubble', 'making board games more accessible and accepted than ever before'. However, some find this overwhelming:

> now the market is flooded with barely-tested thrown-together games with a shelf life of nil contrasted with huge box, ultra-long pricey games stuffed with miniatures and flashy app-based gameplay. The middle-budget projects are dying because they don't have the mass appeal or the niche demand.

This brings us back to the focus of this chapter: the physical presence of games. As Kickstarter has bifurcated into small, indie games and huge blockbusters, the games often become synonymous with table presence. As one participant in my study said, 'Often Kickstarter games that generate a lot of hype tend towards games with extra bling (figurines, scale, extra boxes, etc.)'. Another remarked on the 'fancy components' that the creators design. When all these minis and meeples produce a larger game, they become incentive for the backers. But the preponderance of extra pieces does not just affect the final amount the campaign raises: these extra pieces and game elements need to be stored and made accessible. Players need more space to store and even show off games (see the 'shelfies' – photos of gamers' shelves – that users post on their social media). Some games have added modular storage elements to help players with all the additional pieces: in the 2020 *Anachrony Infinity Box* (Mindclash) campaign (the game's second Kickstarter campaign), a separate instruction booklet was included with the game that told players how to store all the pieces in more than fifteen plastic trays.[2] And all these material elements create environmental concerns as well, as the amount of plastic, cardboard, wood and other elements (not to mention the increased weight and its requisite increase in shipping) can contribute to wasteful production.[3]

Materiality and games

As we have seen, one effect of Kickstarter has been an increasing materialization of board games – it is now considered not only normal but de facto that games will create more and more material objects. While this has many different effects, there are two that I want to discuss here. First, the production of more stuff allows backers to see the fruits of their investment. Second, increasing the physical presence of the board game more tangibly grounds the game within the real-world. Creating more material goods within a Kickstarter campaign literalizes the game and creates a one-to-one ratio between the amount of money pledged and the physical, tangible, material presence of the game.

First, more money pledged at higher tier levels rewards backers with greater returns. For example, the campaign for *Anachrony* featured one pledge level at $59 that offered cardboard versions of the main 'exo-suits' in the game, while the next tier level up ($79) offered 24-plastic minis for the game. Notably, 74 backers pledged at the lower tier while 4,239 people backed at the higher level. A second way the campaign can increase tangibility is through stretch goals, specific milestones reached after a campaign hits its goal but before it has officially been completed. At these milestones, which are usually but not always monetary points, the creators release new content for backers (often, tiers are listed as earning 'all unlocked stretch goals' to make a mutable experience). *Anachrony*'s first Kickstarter campaign had fifteen stretch goals, all of which were achieved, including upgraded cardstock for the board and pieces; double sided boards; upgraded materials for pieces (from cardboard to resin); metallic ink and embossed box top; and a new module with additional minis. A third way campaigns can increase tangibility is with 'add-ons': additional components that do not automatically come with a pledge but can be bought afterwards. For instance, *Dark Souls – The Board Game* 'not only offered stretch goals but also un-lockable "add-ons", that require backers to increase their pledge level' (Werning 2017: 76). Other add-ons can diversify the types of materials garnered by backers: expansions to games, additional components or even backstock of a company's older games.

All these additional ways to spend money deepen the socioeconomic divide in game player purchasing (add-ons can become expensive very quickly). As board games include more physical components, attendant increases in prices places some outside the reach of those hobbyists for whom the cost is too high. If, as many already believe, the board gaming hobby is alienating to non-privileged identities (see Booth 2021; Johnson 2016; Pobuda 2018), aligning gameplay with more and more expensive material elements furthers that divide.

For those that can afford it, offering more stretch goals and providing a physical augmentation to the game brings a sense of tangibility to the investment. If I increase my pledge from $59 to $79, I actually see the results. While this may not seem particularly avant-garde (after all, that is how Kickstarter is supposed to work) it does shift the focus away from the idea of *donation* to one of *purchase*. This is made literal with the 'add-on' content: as a donor, I receive additional product. I am not investing in an idea; I am buying a product. The effect of this is to literalize the transactional nature of Kickstarter. In contrast, one could imagine a campaign where the increase in payment came with a social good rather than a material good: with, say, the funding of a scholarship for underrepresented people to have a position at the company, or the use of environmentally sound production practices. These intangible extras might be a boon for the game, company or culture – but would not be visible to players. It is telling that the material is highlighted rather than intangible social goods.

A second effect of materialization in Kickstarter is to more tangibly ground the game within the real-world. In *Board Games as Media*, I argued that 'the [board] game itself, as a mutable, textual, tangible object, does not come into being without the addition of player agency' (2021: 9). All board games exist in two states – as an object and as an experience determined (but not entirely) by the state of that object. Therefore, despite Kickstarter's emphasis on the object-ness of the board game as mentioned earlier, any understanding of a board game must come not just from the objects within the games themselves but also from the players and their experiences with those objects. To analyse this game-object/player interaction, I introduced the term 'ludo-textual analysis', which focuses on the individual (and particular) use of objects within a game. A cube in one game might represent money; in another, it might represent poverty. We can read objects within games for their social, cultural or ideological (*representational*) value, but their *ludo-textual* value does not come into being until players actually interact with (play) the game.

While the game-object/player tension is not a stable ratio (some games may have very few components and others may take very little player action), there has to be a balance between the two. A game with no components is not 'analogue' and an object with no player interaction is not a 'game'. In this way, the increase in the material elements via Kickstarter seems to be deliberately shifting the balance towards the game-object. This is not to say that players no longer interact with the game (far from it) but rather than the increased material presence of games reduces the imaginative load of players. I no longer need to imagine that this red cube is a disease if I have a small plastic or resin model of a virus in its place. The ludo-textual becomes more textual, more grounded in reality than present as imaginative growth.

Ultimately, then, the material components of board games work in multiple ways on players: they not only offer a significant use-value but also ground the game within the lived experiences of the players. The game becomes more real. But, in contrast, some players may find that the relentless focus on materiality changes how they play the game. More pieces can mean more complications:

while replacing a cardboard standee with a plastic miniature does not change the gameplay very much, adding additional characters or more complicated scenarios might affect what players need to keep track of. This increased complexity has led some players to eschew all the extra physical pieces entirely, especially as 'new technology has made games more accessible and easier to create' (response from survey). These players find digital apps to replace these material elements, streamlining some part of the game while effacing others. For these players, the difference between gameplay 'stuff' and non-gameplay 'stuff' does not seem vast.

Digital technology can clean up the table, reducing the material presence of the game; it turns the reality into immateriality. For example, there are many things to keep in mind with Cephalofair's game *Gloomhaven*: turn order, how monsters focus, how monsters attack, how much damage to track, how to calculate range and even how to calculate what level you play at requires some math. With an estimated 1,000+ hours of play, and often played solo (see Booth 2021; Leorke 2018), *Gloomhaven*'s many material components make the game (especially when first played) complex and difficult to understand. The 95+ scenarios are detailed in a book and on 30 modular boards, monster attacks are summarized on randomized cards, damage is tracked on character dials and monster cards, multiple monsters are controlled through stat cards, elements are conjured by players and monsters and tracked on a third board, the footprint of the game is immense and there can be a lot of 'stop and start' as the 'unstructure' forces players to need to check the rulebook or online FAQs (see Booth 2015).

In response, a number of homemade or amateur apps have arisen that automate much of the mathematics of the game. At the time of writing, the Google Play store lists fifteen non-Cephalofair created 'Gloomhaven' apps, including *Gloomhaven Helper*, *Gloomhaven Campaign Tracker*, *Gloomhaven Scenario Viewer* and *Gloomhaven Attack Deck*. These apps reduce the amount of material presence on the table, digitizing much of the mental work that goes into the games. The digital here supersedes the physical because of the ease of access and accessibility but lost in translation is that lived reality of the game (Wake 2019). The game seems less grounded, less fixed. Players outsource the mental for the material.

Conclusion

It has never been a better time to be a board gamer. Many thousands of new games are released annually. New board game cafés and stores are opening around the world. A thriving community of players on *BoardGameGeek* and other sites make gaming more widespread and social. Thousands of new games are released every year. And as more players join the table, the social interaction engendered by board games invites engagement. Whether this is a board game bubble about to burst or a sustained renaissance in gaming remains to be seen. But one result of this clear shift in the culture of board gaming is a strong emphasis on the materiality of games, emphasized and encouraged by the abundance of Kickstarter-funded games.

As we have seen, examining the Kickstarter platform reveals some key attributes that have affected the types of games that get funded: the tier-based model emphasizes the production of material elements and tangible, game-related goods. Evidence from successful Kickstarted games reveals that backers support more tangible elements when they are specifically game related, rather than more general 'add-ons'. And interview data suggests that not all players are supportive of the Kickstarter revolution: it may support a greater number of indie game developers, but it also leads to game bloat and a fear of missing out.

Another attribute that leads to a shift in the types of game produced is the emphasis on *completed* (or near-completed) games. The most successful Kickstarted board games tend to have the most developed content: 3D-rendered computer-generated gameplay graphics; detailed rulebooks and playthrough videos, near-finished art and models. Backers want to know that the money that they are investing will result in a fulfilled pledge. One of the best ways to demonstrate how 'complete' a game is, is to show the physical components for the backers. This, however, crowds out those indie developers who might be using Kickstarter as a jumping-off point, and instead rewarding those who already have enough funding to make a complete game. Kickstarter becomes a pre-order system.

The stretch goal system is a third platform attribute that contributes to the materiality of Kickstarted games. Stretch goals become enticements for backing and for spreading the word about campaigns: if a campaign can make more money, they can produce new objects for the backers. The more money pledged, the more elements that can be added. The infrastructure of Kickstarter here facilitates the physical growth of a game.

In this chapter, I discussed the way the material development of board games seems to stem from two intersecting ideas: the use-value of a game increases, as does the lived reality of the game. This chapter has focused on the increased materiality of board games from a more theoretical perspective, and more work should be done on how individual games integrate physical objects into the gameplay. Additional, more ethnographic work on the use-value of physical objects in games might reveal more reasons why physical components are popular in games. Finally, there needs to be more ecological scholarship done on the ramifications of all this material production in games. As plastic consumption increases – and has a deleterious effect on our planet's climate and ecosystem – the production of even more miniatures comes at a cost.

If you ask any board game hobbyist what the pleasures of gaming are, they might regale you with stories of 'come-from-behind' victories and the pleasure of group social interaction. Or, perhaps, they will tell you of the unique pleasure of opening a fresh game, punching out the cardboard pieces, pulling the miniatures from their plastic containers and moving them around the board, or the tactile feeling of 'clicking' a HeroClix model. Board games are analogue. They exist in our world, as objects *and* as experiences. The sensual pleasures of the game go beyond the mental: they are pleasures of touch, of feel, of being. They are the pleasures of being human.

Notes

1 My thanks to DePaul University's University Research Council for the leave to write this project and Rebecca Woods for the research help.
2 It took this experienced researcher two hours to properly store everything in the box.
3 Some companies, like BlueOrange, make eco-friendly games part of their sales pitch.

References

Arnaudo, M. (2017), 'The Experience of Flow in Hobby Board Games', *Analog Game Studies*, 4 (5). Available online: https://analoggamestudies.org/2017/11/the -experience-of-flow-in-hobby-board-games/ (accessed 1 October 2021).

Arnaudo, M. (2018), *Storytelling in the Modern Board Game: Narrative Trends from the Late 1960s to Today*, Jefferson, NC: McFarland& Co.

Bisi, G. A. (2021), 'Darwin's Journey', *Kickstarter*. Available online: https://www .kickstarter.com/projects/gonab/darwins-journey (accessed 1 October 2021).

Bogost, I. and N. Montfort (2009a), 'New Media as Material Constraint: An Introduction to Platform Studies', HASTAC. Available online: http://bogost.com/ downloads/bogost%20montfort%20hastac.pdf (accessed 1 October 2021).

Bogost, I. and N. Montfort (2009b), 'Platform Studies: Frequently Questioned Answers', *UC Irvine: Digital Arts and Culture*. Available online: https://escholarship.org/uc/item/01r0k9br (accessed 21 October 2021).

Booth, P. (2015), *Game Play: Paratextuality in Contemporary Board Games*, New York: Bloomsbury.

Booth, P. (2021), *Board Games as Media*, New York: Bloomsbury.

Booth, P. and C. O. Jones (2020), *Watching Doctor Who: Fan Reception and Evaluation*, New York: Bloomsbury.

Brown, D. and E. MacCallum-Stewart (2020), 'Introduction', in D. Brown and E. MacCallum-Stewart (eds), *Rerolling Board Games: Essays on Themes, Systems, Experiences and Ideologies*, 1–14, Jefferson, NC: McFarland & Co.

Buttice, V. and D. Noonan (2020), 'Active Backers, Product Commercialisation and Product Quality after a Crowdfunding Campaign: A Comparison between First-time and Repeated Entrepreneurs', *Internationals Small Business Journal*, 38 (2): 111–34.

Colistra, R. and K. Duvall (2017), 'Show Me the Money: Importance of Crowdfunding Factors on Backers' Decisions to Financially Support Kickstarter Campaigns', *Social Media + Society*, 3 (4). Available online: https://journals.sagepub.com/doi/full/10.1177/2056305117736942 (accessed 1 October 2021).

Elias, G. S., R. Garfield and K. R. Gutschera (2012), *Characteristics of Games*, Cambridge, MA: MIT Press.

Gray, J. (2010), *Show Sold Separately*, New York: New York University Press.

Hall, C. (2020), 'Games Broke Funding Records on Kickstarter in 2020, Despite the Pandemic', *Polygon*, 22 December. Available online: https://www.polygon.com/2020/12/22/22195749/kickstarter-top-10-highest-funded-campaigns-2020-video-games-board-games (accessed 1 October 2021).

Johnson, A. (2016), 'Positionality and Performance: A Player's Encounter with the Lost Tribes of Small World', *Analog Game Studies*, 3 (5). Available online: http://analoggamestudies.org/2016/09/positionality-and-performance-a-players-encounter-with-the-lost -tribes-of-small-world/ (accessed 1 October 2021).

Kickstarter (2015), 'Exploding Kittens Is the Most-Backed Project of All Time', Kickstarter, 20 February 2015. Available online: https://www.kickstarter.com/blog/exploding-kittens-is-the-most-backed-project-of-all-time (accessed 1 October 2021).

Kickstarter (2021), 'Our Mission Is to Help bring Creative Projects to Life', Kickstarter. Available online: https://www.kickstarter.com/about (accessed 1 October 2021).

Leorke, D. (2018), 'Solo Board Gaming: An Analysis of Player Motivations', *Analog Game Studies*, 5 (4). Available online: https://analoggamestudies.org/2018/12/solo-board-gaming-an-analysis-of-player-motivations/ (accessed 1 October 2021).

Miller, D. (2013), *Stuff*, Cambridge: Polity Press.

Pobuda, T. (2018), 'Assessing Gender and Racial Representation in the Board Game Industry', *Analog Game Studies*, 5 (4). Available online: https://analoggamestudies

.org/2018/12/assessing-gender-and-racial-representation-in-top-rated -boardgamegeek-games/ (accessed 1 October 2021).

Robinson, W. (2014), 'Orientalism and Abstraction in Eurogames', *Analog Game Studies*, 1 (5). Available online: http://analoggamestudies.org/2014/12/orientalism -and-abstraction-in-eurogames (accessed 1 October 2021).

Roeder, O. (2015), 'Crowdfunding is Driving a $196 Million Board Game Renaissance', *Five Thirty Eight*, 18 August. Available online: https://fivethirtyeight.com/features /crowdfunding-is-driving-a-196-million-board-game-renaissance/ (accessed 1 October 2021).

Rogerson, M. J., M. Gibbs and W. Smith (2020), 'More than the Sum of Their Bits', in D. Brown and E. MacCallum-Stewart (eds), *Rerolling Board Games: Essays on Themes, Systems, Experiences and Ideologies*, 88–108, Jefferson, NC: McFarland & Co.

Torner, E. (2018), 'Just (the Institution of Computer) Game Studies', *Analog Game Studies*, 5 (2). Available online: https://analoggamestudies.org/2018/06/just-the -institution-of-computer-game-studies/ (accessed 1 October 2021).

Trammell, A. (2018), 'Representation and Discrimination in Role-Playing Games', in S. Deterding and J. Zagal (eds), *Role- Playing Game Studies: Transmedia Foundations*, 440–7, New York: Routledge.

Trammell, A. (2019), 'Analog Games and the Digital Economy', *Analog Game Studies*, 6 (1). Available online: https://analoggamestudies.org/2019/03/analog-games-and-the -digital-economy/ (accessed 1 October 2021).

Wake, P. (2019), 'Token Gestures: Towards a Theory of Immersion in Analog Games', *Analog Game Studies*, 6 (3). Available online: https://analoggamestudies.org/2019 /09/token-gestures-towards-a-theory-of-immersion-in-analog-games/ (accessed 1 October 2021).

Wasserman, J. (2020), 'Materially Mediated: Boardgames as Interactive Media and Mediated Communication', in D. Brown and E. MacCallum-Stewart (eds), *Rerolling Board Games: Essays on Themes, Systems, Experiences and Ideologies*, 71–87. Jefferson, NC: McFarland & Co.

Werning, S. (2017) 'Conceptualizing Game Distribution, *Kickstarter* and the Board Game "Renaissance"', La Valle Dell'Eden. Semestrale Di Cinema e Audiovisivi, 31: 65–82.

12

The logic of analogue adaptation

Nathan Altice

Analogue game adaptations rarely appear in either popular game histories or critical game studies. When they do, they are either highlighted as curiosities – for example Milton Bradley's *Super Mario Bros. Game* (1988) (Altice 2020) – or referenced as a sidebar to their source game (Demaria 2019: 83, 165; Kent 2001: 215, 224). And this holds true whether the subject matter is video games or board games. In *The Oxford History of Board Games*, for example, David Parlett relegates adaptations to a category he calls 'pulp games', describing them as 'ephemeral games designed to cash in on current trends, fads, and fashions, entirely based on TV programmes or characters merchandized from the world of showbiz and popular entertainment' (1999: 347). Adaptations unite the analogue and digital domains of game studies, but they are summarily ignored by both.

Granted, critical oversight is not unique to game adaptations. No matter the media, adaptations are routinely passed over and commonly disdained. Meanwhile, creators keep making them and audiences keep reading, watching and playing them. And that relationship hasn't changed much throughout the course of media history. Humans love to hear stories told and retold, revisit well-known characters and inhabit familiar worlds in endless theme and variation. Just look around. In our contemporary popular media ecology, for better or worse, adapted comic books have enjoyed a decade-plus reign in film and television. Even video game adaptations of Lego adaptations of film adaptations of comic books sell millions (Calvin 2016).

Digital-to-analogue game adaptations are equally ubiquitous. In 2016, UK video game industry trade magazine *MCV/Develop* heralded 'the rise of video games-themed board games' (Dealessandri 2016), citing recent and upcoming adaptations of *Civilization* (Fantasy Flight 2010), *The Witcher* (Fantasy Flight 2014), *XCOM* (Fantasy Flight 2015), *Doom* (ADC Blackfire 2016), *Dark Souls*

(Steamforged 2017), *Plague Inc.* (Ndemic 2017), *This War of Mine* (Awaken Realms 2017), *Minecraft* (Ravensburger 2019), *Bloodborne* (CMON 2021) and *Street Fighter* (Jasco Games 2021). 'Players', the article reports, 'want to experience different worlds in as many formats as possible – if they love a video game, they'll be eager to learn more about its universe through a board game, which will allow them to see its subtleties from another perspective' (Dealessandri 2016).

Of course, highlighting the 'rise' of adaptations might give the impression that such games are a new phenomenon, but the history of analogue/digital adaptation is long and bilateral. The history of digital games, especially in its formative years, is heavily populated by adaptations of sports and board games, from *Tennis* (1972) and *Hockey* (1972) on the Magnavox Odyssey to *Video Chess* (1979) and *Video Checkers* (1980) on the Atari 2600.[1] But the history of board and card game adaptations of video games is nearly as long. Some of the first include Bandai's クレイジークライマ [*Crazy Climber*] (1981), Milton Bradley's *Donkey Kong* (1982) and Entex's *Defender* (1982). Since then, games as varied as *Wizard of Wor* (Ideal 1983), *Dragon's Lair* (Milton Bradley 1984), *Gradius* (Bandai 1986), *Double Dragon: The Board Game* (Tiger Electronics 1989), *Sim City: The Card Game* (Mayfair Games 1994) and *Myst* (University Games 1998) are just some of the hundreds of analogue adaptations released in the past forty years.

Linda Hutcheon's cross-media study of adaptation, *A Theory of Adaptation*, is driven by this paradox of adaptations 'continuing popularity' and 'critical denigration' (2013: xiii–xiv). She takes adaptations seriously *as* adaptations and creates a theoretical framework to understand them, both in relation to their source media and as a product and process that is its own 'palimpsestic thing' (2013: 9). Following Hutcheon, my goal is not only to point out that digital-to-analogue game adaptations exist, and have for many decades, but to give them serious critical attention. I build on *A Theory of Adaptation* to understand *how* these adaptations operate and *what* precisely gets adapted in the transposition from digital to analogue. Game adaptations share some features of adaptations in other media, but a game adapting a game has different considerations than a game adapting a film or graphic novel. And an *analogue* game adapting a *digital* game adds specific material constraints to that process.

To examine these constraints, we will first need to understand how Hutcheon's theory works, how it incorporates games, and tease out some limitations that require modification. Hutcheon's case studies largely focus on literary examples, so her framework tends to isolate story as a primary unit of transposition between adapted works. Games tell stories too, but that is not all they do, and in the specific case of game adaptations, isolating story does not always help us understand what games transplant and refashion from other games. Rather, there are other, more fundamental elements underlying analogue adaptations.

Beyond story and world

Part of what is novel about Hutcheon's *A Theory of Adaptation* is how it counters many common misapprehensions about its subject. The most persistent and critically corrosive is the idea that adaptations are forever temporally doomed to be derivative seconds to an originary first. Hutcheon reconfigures that relationship, arguing that adaptations are 'repetition but without replication, bringing together the comfort of ritual and recognition with the delight of surprise and novelty' (2013: 173). Being secondary is a mere fact of chronology. Adaptations are derived from an acknowledged prior work, but they are still creative works. They are meant to function both in conversation with their predecessors and as works in and of themselves, since no author can be guaranteed that their audiences will be familiar with the adapted source.

Additionally, chronology does not foreclose a reciprocal relationship between the old and the new. Adaptations serve many purposes – homage, parody, critique, commentary, economic opportunism – but, in all cases, they recontextualize the source work without erasing it. 'An adaptation', Hutcheon writes, 'is not vampiric: it does not draw the life-blood from its source and leave it dying or dead, nor is it paler than the adapted work. It may, on the contrary, keep that prior work alive, giving it an afterlife it would never have had otherwise' (2013: 176). In other words, *Bram Stoker's Dracula* (1992) cannot kill Bram Stoker's *Dracula* (1897). In many cases, audiences may encounter adaptations prior to – or in absence of – the original. And doing so may send the new audience back to the old media.

Hutcheon also skirts two common pitfalls in adaptation criticism – medium specificity and fidelity criticism – by taking a different tack, classifying adaptations according to three different 'modes of engagement': telling, showing and interacting (2013: 22). In general, poems and novels tell us stories, film and theatre show us stories, while video games and other new media invite us to interact with stories. Hutcheon's tripartite classification allows her to keep a medium's formal and material contours in mind – a play is, after all, different from a film, so medium specificity is not without value – while also highlighting important similarities between media, especially those that might otherwise seem distinct. Video games and theme park rides, for example, despite their apparent differences in material, scale and design, share the mode of interactive engagement. Both a *Pirates of the Caribbean* video game and a *Pirates of the Caribbean* theme park ride let us engage with their shared fictional world.

However, the interactive mode of engagement, while easy to categorize, proves to be the least amenable to intermedia comparison. As Hutcheon admits, there is something *different* about the interactive mode versus the other two: 'We can be told or shown a story, each in a range of different media. However, the perspective, and thus the grammar, changes with the third mode of engagement; as audience members, we interact *with* stories in, for instance, the new media, from virtual reality to machinima' (2013: 22). Hutcheon is clear that this is not a rehash of the claim that new media are more immersive than old media. Rather, this change in the mode of engagement's 'grammar' involves a particular kind of kinesthetic involvement that is absent in the showing and telling modes (2013: 23). Whether our bodies are strapped in and carried about by a theme park ride or our fingers gesture idly across a smartphone, the interactive mode's embodied engagement is a fundamental fulcrum of difference.

The complication that arises for adaptation is how that fulcrum shifts the balance of engagement away from the unit of transposition so common in adaptive criticism: story. Video games and other interactive media certainly have stories, but in many cases the story is 'no longer central or at least no longer an end in itself' (2013: 13). Hutcheon aims to expand adaptations' critical language to consider at least one other unit of transposition, arguing that what often gets adapted in the interactive mode of engagement is, 'a heterocosm, literally an "other world" or cosmos, complete, of course, with the stuff of a story – settings, characters, events, and situations. To be more precise, it is the "*res extensa*" of that world, its material, physical dimension, which is transposed and then experienced through multisensorial interactivity' (2013: 14). In other words, even lacking substantive or meaningful stories, games can still construct substantive and meaningful worlds. The flimsy narrative structure of, say *The Legend of Zelda* (1986), isn't as important as the characters, flora and fauna that make Hyrule a lively and inhabitable world.

Hutcheon's recognition of the 'intensity of cognitive and physical engagement' and 'sensory presence' aided by audio-visual-haptic spectacle in video games, along with games' propensity to enfold those intensities into a real and coherent world, demonstrates an attention to the nuances of games as media that many media scholars elide (2013: 13, 51, 131). And it is commendable that Hutcheon acknowledges games in the ecosystem of adaptation at all, more so that she does so both frequently and seriously. Nonetheless, *A Theory of Adaptation* implicitly foregrounds story as its primary unit of transposition and analysis. When video games appear as examples, they are predominantly described in those terms, like when *Silent Hill* is described as a 'survival horror story' (2013: 51). Board, card and role-playing game adaptations of film or literary works appear only a handful of times and never with specificity.[2] And, unsurprisingly, analogue adaptations of digital games are never mentioned.

Digital-to-analogue game adaptations deserve closer attention, not only due to their enduring ubiquity within the ecosystem of games and media but also because they allow us to make further refinements and modifications to adaptation theory. A theory of adaptation should encompass all media, in all modes of engagement, regardless of their specific 'grammar' or articulation, and when edge cases arise, we should take them seriously. Game-to-game adaptations in particular require both a de-centring of story and an expansion of the possible units of transposition beyond the heterocosm. Board game adaptations tell stories and construct worlds, but they transpose other units of expression, and they do so with specific considerations of form and material, a tactility that resonates with Hutcheon's description of interactive media's 'physical, enacted dimension' (2013: 133), but put into play through wood, paper, plastic and cardboard.

The logic of game adaptation

Consensus around precise terminology to describe what games are made of has been a longstanding matter of debate. For decades, designers and scholars have used the term 'mechanics' to help understand games' 'atomic structure' (Brathwaite 2009: 25). Definitions of the term vary broadly, ranging from the programmatic, as with Miguel Sicart's 'methods invoked by agents, designed for interaction with the game state' (2008), to the grammatical, as in Anna Anthropy and Naomi Clark's 'game verbs' (2014: 15), to Robert Zubek's more recent multi-part description, which comprises pieces to be manipulated, actions that can be performed with them, and rules to govern those actions (2020).

As with many matters of semantic precision, the irony is that mechanics are simpler to identify than define. A game's rules are helpful in this regard because they articulate, both explicitly and implicitly, a player's range of possible actions. *Pandemic*'s rule book tells its players that they can move, build, treat, share and discover, and those verbs map neatly to most definitions of mechanics (2008). But even without overt rules, play and observation can tell us a lot about a game's mechanics. In *Donkey Kong*, we jump and climb and hammer. In *Doom* we strafe and shoot. In *Catan* we build and trade and buy. In Chess we move and capture. And in *Minecraft* we mine and craft.

It is sensible to shift the target of adaptive transposition from story or heterocosm to mechanics because they are so straightforward to identify. But games are more than a catalogue of mechanics. Often what is more intriguing in games than their base actions is the purposeful aggregation of mechanics into complex systems (Sellers 2017). In *Pandemic*, the individual actions of drawing cards, travelling from city to city and treating diseases can be satisfying in isolation, but it is the careful balance of mechanical interactions exhibiting systemic emergence that both drives players to make harrowing strategic decisions and emphasizes the game's theme – namely, avoiding crossing the delicate tipping point that will trigger an unstoppable global pandemic.

But systems, like mechanics, have inconsistent definitions among designers, and they certainly aren't exclusive to games. Weather systems, economic systems and political systems are all highly complex aggregates of multiple interacting agents that exhibit emergent behaviours, many of which cannot be predicted by the actions of any individual component. Likewise, in the analysis and pedagogy of game design, mechanics and systems tend to be decoupled from their concomitant communicative roles – not only how they look, sound or feel but also what they mean. I can describe, for example, the mechanics of *Sagrada* (2017) in formal analytic terms: draft dice and arrange them in specific patterns to earn points. I could also isolate and replicate those mechanics in another context, effectively 'cloning' *Sagrada*'s form and function without transposing its representational elements (and, in fact, this kind of formal replication is one way that game genres develop and propagate). But doing so strips *Sagrada* of the meaning it aims to communicate to players. The game's colourful, translucent dice represent facets of a stained-glass window, and the patterns they form are more than mere combinatorial possibilities. Rather, players are meant to be artisans, tasked to create ornate, beautiful windows evocative of the game's namesake in the Basílica de la Sagrada Família. Isolating mechanics or systems as units of transposition in game adaptation misses important linkages to the communicative aspects of games' underlying mechanisms.

In *How Pac-Man Eats* (2020), Noah Wardrip-Fruin formalizes two closely related concepts to help understand both how games work at a fundamental level and how they convey meaning. The first is *operational logics*, which 'combine an abstract process and a communicative role, each refined through implementation to drive an ongoing state presentation and play experience' (2020: 7). One such logic is collision, which operationally defines when two objects are coincident with one another, that is when they 'touch'. But collision implementation varies significantly by platform, period and programmer. Sometimes it is driven by discrete circuit logic, as in the *Magnavox Odyssey*, often it is defined algorithmically in software and other times it is a hybrid of these forms. Likewise, what collision means in a given game varies according to its computational objects' specific representational implementation. In *Pong*, the game's audio-visual-haptic state presentation communicates that I am manoeuvring a paddle to intercept a ball, and thus collision means that I have made a successful deflection. In *Pac-Man*, I pilot the titular sentient mouth around a maze strewn with pellets. When I collide with these pellets, I do not deflect them – I eat them. So, as Wardrip-Fruin argues, '[w]e can only understand a logic such as "collision" by seeing it as something that communicates ("virtual objects can touch") and something that operates algorithmically ("when two entities overlap, do something")' *at the same time* (2020: 222).

Along with collision, Wardrip-Fruin catalogues the following 'major families' of adjectival operational logics that are foundational to a wide array of video games: camera, chance, control, entity-state, game mode, linking, navigation, pattern matching, persistence, physics, progression, recombinatory, resource and selection (2020: 49). These logics then 'compose together' to form a second foundational concept, *playable models*, that Wardrip-Fruin describes as learnable and actionable 'procedural representations of particular domains' (2020: 10–11). In *Metroid Prime* (2002), for example, navigation, physics, linking, entity-state, progression and camera logics combine to represent a playable model of interconnected three-dimensional spaces that players can explore along multiple concurrent axes. In contrast, the tile-based board game *Betrayal at House on the Hill* (2004) aggregates linking, pattern matching, chance and recombinatory logics to procedurally represent a bounded but modular two-dimensional space, wherein players explore and construct the interior of a haunted mansion.

Wardrip-Fruin, along with the colleagues who helped refine these concepts (Osborn 2017), conceived operational logics and playable models primarily to describe digital games, but they are not exclusive to that domain. Analysing which logics and models are shared across analogue and digital games – along with how material conditions shape their implementation – is critical if we want to refocus Hutcheon's theory of adaptation on an alternative unit of transposition. To work through these concepts and demonstrate how they can sharpen our critical analysis, we'll employ a single digital game – *Super Mario Bros.* (1985) – as a case study in adaptation encompassing multiple games, formats and decades.

Adapting *Super Mario Bros.*

Super Mario Bros.' longevity within popular culture, attributable in equal parts to the game's innovative design and Nintendo's targeted recycling of its characters and concepts through sequels, spin-offs and merchandising makes it an ideal candidate for comparative adaptive analysis. *Super Mario Bros.* has few peers in the domain of game adaptations, as Mario and the Mushroom Kingdom have been transposed to all manner of board, card and tabletop games, spanning the decades from the 1980s to present day. Of course, a game need not be popular to be adapted nor do we need multiple adaptations to analyse that process, but such cultural objects do provide unique insights into the perceived 'core elements' of a given game and how those elements are transposed into different material forms. And as we examine each transposition in turn, we find that story-, world- and even mechanics-centric adaptive theory fail to explain the full spectrum of analogue game adaptations.

For all of *Super Mario Bros.*' design innovations, its story remains its least distinctive – or least developed – feature. The NES instruction manual devotes only seven sentences to the game's archetypal fairy tale, which we can summarize with one: The malevolent turtle king Bowser and his Koopa tribe invade the peaceful Mushroom Kingdom, transform its inhabitants into inanimate objects and capture their Princess Toadstool, prompting the game's sibling heroes, Mario and Luigi, to embark on a quest to reverse Bowser's magic and save the Princess (Nintendo 1985: 2).[3] Once the stage is set, the manual's fifteen-plus remaining pages detail the real heart of *Super Mario Bros.* – interaction – through play instructions, button assignments, descriptions of game modes, explanations of power-ups and tips and tricks to help the player navigate the Mushroom Kingdom.

Interspersed throughout the manual are details about the game's heterocosm. 'The Mushroom Kingdom is made up of a number of worlds', it reads, adding, 'In order to rescue the Princess, Mario has to make it to the castle at the end of each world within the given time. Along the way are mountains, pits, sea, turtle soldiers, and a host of traps and riddles' (Nintendo 1985: 5). Likewise, four and half pages are devoted to images and descriptions of the game's characters. But what is being told and shown here has little relation to narrative. Rather, the manual's text, illustrations and screenshots build an interactive image of the Mushroom Kingdom and its inhabitants. The cast is characterized through actions and properties rather than feelings or motivations, all described in the language of play. Bowser, for instance, is described as follows: 'He comes at you spitting fire. There are several ways to kill him, but you only get points if you use fireballs' (Nintendo 1985: 14). These caricatures make sense for the Mushroom Kingdom, because Mario's heterocosm is fundamentally designed for play, not storytelling. The world and its characters become real through interaction.

So what interactions are possible? *Super Mario Bros.* is a now-canonical example of a two-dimensional platformer, a genre of game wherein players navigate a character through a series of spatial obstacles, typically by running and jumping across platforms. And indeed, most of the manual describes the game's primary platforming mechanics – running, jumping, crouching, swimming, throwing fireballs – as well as a set of related secondary mechanics – bumping blocks, collecting coins, using power-ups, kicking and stomping enemies, springing off jumping boards and grabbing flagpoles. In the interest of secrecy, the designers chose not to catalogue all of Mario's possible actions in the manual. A few secondary mechanics, like ducking into pipes and climbing vines, were left up to the player to discover, and these 'hidden' actions, along with a number of intended and unintended in-game secrets, cultivate an air of mystery and wonder surrounding the Mushroom Kingdom. It was a world that couldn't simply be seen or read – it required the player to bump and shatter its landscape to reveal its secrets.

Super Mario Bros.' barely there narrative explains why so few story-centric game adaptations exist. The closest example is Futabasha's trilogy of *Super Mario Bros.* game books released in Japan in the mid-1980s as part of their Famicom Adventure Game Book series. Futabasha game books follow the general structure of branching fiction established in the 1970s and 1980s by series like *Choose Your Own Adventure* or *Fighting Fantasy*. Each page in the game book is subdivided into one or more numbered text blocks that include a few sentences of exposition followed by instructions that direct the reader to another numbered block found elsewhere in the book, typically based upon a simple choice (e.g. proceed north or south) or a given game state (e.g. a particular item is in your inventory).

The first two *Super Mario Bros.* game books are fascinating examples of adaptive designers working with limited story resources. Scaling seven sentences to two hundred pages requires substantial expansion, and both books take divergent approaches. Volume 1's subtitle, *Save Mario from Evil!* (Studio Hard 1986a), immediately signals a shift in the player-reader's perspective. The game's prologue begins with you – a young boy – rushing home after school to play *Super Mario Bros.* After setting a personal best score, the TV screen mysteriously blanks out, and you hear Mario's voice in your head pleading for help. You then blank out yourself, awakening moments later in the Mushroom Kingdom, standing on a familiar runway of bricks and blocks. From here, the book turns into a meticulous first-person *Super Mario Bros.* play commentary, asking you to make decisions about whether you'll bump a block in your path or how you'll dodge a menacing Hammer Brother. Selected screenshots sit alongside the text to provide visual context. Some are even doctored to better fit the text descriptions, pasting enemies where they would not normally be or squeezing pipes together to provide more branching choices. Complementary illustrations assume Mario's perspective, further fusing you, the reader, to the game's hero. Beyond this reader-as-Mario framing, the game book follows the general arc of the game's story, but it reads more like an interactive Let's Play than a work of fiction.

Futabasha's play-by-play adaptive style only lasted for one book. Volume 2, subtitled *Defiance from Devil Neo-Kuppa* (Studio Hard 1986b), takes a sci-fi turn, outfitting Mario, Luigi and the Koopa tribe with cybernetic armour and laser weapons. The game dispenses with in-game screenshots and 'first-person' illustrations and adds a few more stat-tracking elements – like an item inventory and rudimentary player attributes – as well as some simple mazes and crossword puzzles to help make the reader's decisions feel more game-like. However, in this volume, you are not a young boy who loves playing *Super Mario Bros.* – you *are* Mario. You still interact with the video game's familiar cast of characters, aim to bring down King Koopa and strive to rescue the Princess, but you navigate a wholly original fiction.

What are we to make of these adaptations? Following Hutcheon, we might say that the gap between modes of expression forces a disconnect between the source game and the adapted text. This is true in the sense that the Futabasha game books are trying to tell what the video game lets us play, and since there is so little to tell, the books must either resort to detailed play commentaries or stretch far beyond the video game's narrative bounds. But this line of analysis raises questions about the apparent boundaries between modes of engagement. Games and other interactive media commonly operate across multiple modes of expression, and often simultaneously. The *Super Mario Bros.* video game oscillates between telling (via the instruction book, packaging and in-game text), showing (via instruction book illustrations and screenshots and non-interactive interstitial animations) and interaction (via play). But this kind of multimodal expression is not exclusive to digital media. The Futabasha game books juxtapose text, screenshots, illustrations and mini-games, often on the same page, to create their playable models. Modes of expression are equally intertwined in board and card games. Each format combines text, image and interactive components in playable aggregates, tasking players to 'switch modes' between reading, looking and interacting.

At this point it might make sense to abandon story in favour of mechanical comparison in order to provide a better analytical distinction between video game and analogue game. Even if we were to be liberal with our definitions – for instance, claiming that 'jumping' from page to page through the game book somehow correlated with Mario's physics-based video game jump – there appears to be little to no mechanical congruence between the *Super Mario Bros.* video game and game book. But that is not formally accurate. Nearly every primary and secondary mechanic in the video game appears, via description or illustration, in the game books. Players even enact several mechanics through reading, recording and making choices. Mario 'moves' through the world, for instance, as the player reads. Players 'collect' coins by making branching selections, and they maintain an inventory of items and power-ups by hand in a ledger at the back of the book. And in the second volume, readers play simple mini-games and puzzles to generate their next destination. At a mechanical level – and especially so in *Save Mario from Evil!*'s commentary format – readers are 'playing' *Super Mario Bros.* in a book. And that fundamental lack of mechanical distinction between unlike media demonstrates why operational logics become so critical in adaptive analysis – they provide the underlying support for mechanics and help structure our understanding of how a game world works.

Consider a duo of more recent *Super Mario Bros.* board game adaptations. In the past five years, there have been two different versions of Mario-branded *Monopoly* games: *Monopoly: Super Mario Bros. Collector's Edition* (2016) and *Monopoly: Super Mario Celebration!* (2020). As with many of the franchises that *Monopoly* has licensed over the decades, Mario's world is transposed with impressive fidelity, including many of the game's characters, locations and items. In *Celebration!* we even find reproductions of the game's sound effects, thanks to a button-activated Question Block component.

Although USAopoly's adaptation focuses solely on *Super Mario Bros.*, while *Celebration!* contains the original game as part of what we might call a franchise adaptation, both play nearly identically. The former touts that you can 'Buy, Sell & Trade Locations From All 8 Worlds', and the latter explains how 'Players can buy, sell, trade, and scheme to win it all with this Monopoly board game inspired by iconic Super Mario artwork, characters, and themes' (Hasbro 2020). Despite swapping Rich Uncle Pennybags' property blocks for Mario's heterocosm of plumbers, pipes and piranha plants, playing either adaptation is still procedurally identical to playing classic *Monopoly*. Re-painting *Monopoly* as a *Super Mario Bros.* game not only imports a bizarre set of mechanics into the latter's world but also forces anachronistic and illogical alterations, like the Go To Jail space that is adjacent to World's 6-4 and 7-1 in *Collector's Edition*, or the multiples of Princess Peach's castle that substitute for *Monopoly's* hotels in *Celebration!*

Wardrip-Fruin offers a similar comparative analysis of classic *Monopoly* versus a few of its variations, arguing that these 're-skins' of the base game, whether *Monopoly: Bass Fishing Edition* (n.d.) or *Monopoly: The.com Edition* (2000), 'aren't actually about what they say they're about' because their underlying logics and models do not change and, more critically, are incompatible with the representational finery they try to adorn (2020: 210). According to Wardrip-Fruin, 'the primary foundation of *Monopoly's* real estate investment model is its resource logics, though a pattern-matching logic determines which properties can be further developed, and a chance logic triggers resource flows' (2020: 222). In other words, recasting a *Monopoly* hotel in the mould of Koopa's castle does not dislodge the resource and progression logics that undergird it. Instead, it asks players to treat the Mushroom Kingdom like a speculative real estate market and its characters like capitalist tycoons.

If we identify some of *Super Mario Bros.'* logics and models, we find a number of significant adaptive mismatches, not only in the obvious cases of *Super Mario Bros.*-themed *Monopoly* but likewise in other less parasitic adaptations. *Super Mario Bros.'* principal playable model (and one shared by many platformers), for instance, is movement through a continuous two-dimensional space, comprising navigation, collision, physics, control and camera logics. In addition, the same and other logics can reconstitute to support other playable models, such as *Super Mario Bros.'* rudimentary combat model – comprising control, entity-state, physics and collision – and upgrade model – comprising entity-state, physics and collision. What is conspicuously absent is any kind of resource or pattern-matching logic – that is those elements that form the core of *Monopoly's* principal playable model.

Extending our analysis to the Futabasha game books, we find similar fundamental mismatches of logics and models. Branching narrative texts of their kind commonly use linking and selection logics to model navigable spaces (both continuous and non-continuous) and entity-state, resource and progression logics to model character stat-tracking and inventories. These elements, while common in digital role-playing games, are absent in *Super Mario Bros.'* core design and reinforce how mechanics alone, as a fundamental unit of transposition, are not specific enough to distinguish between adaptations.

Again, both video game and book include a jump mechanic, but in the former, jumping involves a complex interplay of player input, computational processing and graphical updates regulated by a specific computer platform, whereas in the latter, jumping involves simple text selections regulated by the material form of a book. The first implementation certainly has more fidelity to a real-world jump, but neither is an objectively better mechanical implementation than the other. Operational logics allow us to drill down further and see how identical mechanics can differ at a compositional level. Control, physics, entity-state and collision logics support Mario's video game jump, while selection and linking logics govern his game book jump. The lack of any logical overlap explains why the game book adaptation feels like such a mismatch to its source. At a fundamental level, they share no logical relationships.

Material conditions of analogue adaptation

Up to this point, it may seem like we have plucked the low-hanging fruit of incongruent adaptations. The material differences between video games and games books alone force drastic creative license, and the *Monopoly* variants deserve some adaptive leeway since they do, after all, bear the *Monopoly* title – *Super Mario Bros.* only appears as a subtitle. So how do original adaptive analogue games fare when they are not bound to the constraints of a secondary game (like *Monopoly*) or medium (like books)? And how do operational logics themselves adapt when transposed from digital-to-analogue media?

Here it is instructive to compare one of *Super Mario Bros.*' earliest original board game adaptations, Bandai's *Super Mario Bros. Game* (1985), released exclusively in Japan, with one of its most maligned, Milton Bradley's identically titled *Super Mario Bros. Game* (1988). Bandai's adaptation was part of a long-running series of board games titled Party Joy, all low-cost, book-sized games aimed at school children and released with the regularity of other children's mass media, like magazines and manga (Altice 2019). Partly driven by the limited size of the Party Joy format, Bandai's designers eschewed a traditional board and instead broke the Mushroom Kingdom into a deck of thirty-six modular 'map panels', each depicting a small segment of a given world. Players constructed each World as they played, drawing from a shuffled deck of map panels and connecting them edge to edge. Each player piloted their own Mario pawn, and that pawn's current power-up status dictated its movement speed. Normal Mario, for instance, moved one space at a time, while Super and Fire Mario could move three spaces per turn. As players raced to the World-concluding castles in hopes of rescuing the Princess, certain spaces could trigger a card draw, netting players power-ups, speed boosts or battles with Koopa's minions.

Milton Bradley's adaptation, in contrast, forced players to alternate control of a single Mario pawn. While one player moved Mario, their opponents planted hazards along the course in hopes of arresting Mario's movement and regaining its control. The board itself comprised four separate strips, each representing a complete World. Although this seems like a scaled-down variation of Bandai's design, Milton Bradley's board panels could only be arranged in a single sequence, perplexingly undercutting the purpose for detaching them in the first place. Coins and power-ups littered the game board, but these were all resources meant to prolong a player's control of Mario since, in the end, the path to victory did not matter: the winner was the player who controlled Mario once he had leapt over Bowser to reach the Princess. No prior choices made a difference, only that final step.

At the level of story, heterocosm and mechanics, both adaptations are largely equivalent. Both games adhere to the 'Mario saves the Princess from Koopa' archetype, and both use official and original artwork to present credible facsimiles of Mario and the Mushroom Kingdom. Likewise, both games cover the video game's mechanical bases, including movement, jumps, coin collection, 1-UPs, power-ups, enemy interaction and even pipe and vine traversal. Faced with such adaptive equivalency, what foundations do we have for comparative analysis? We might appeal to some best practices in game design, assessing whether each game affords adequate player choice or engaging systems to interact with. But again, both are ostensibly racing games, designed for children, that rely primarily on chance rather than choice or strategy.

Shifting our critical view to logics and models provides a more focused conceptual lens to analyse how either game functions as an adaptation, both in isolation and in comparison. Milton Bradley's adaptation, for example, is a game whose logics and models are at odds with its own materiality. Splitting the board into segments offers the potential of recombinatory and linking logics, which could then be combined with either selection or chance logics, to construct an explorable model of two-dimensional space similar to that of *Betrayal at House on the Hill* (2004). But the game's rules, material structure and graphical presentation foreclose those possibilities. Players are only allowed to link the boards in one prescribed order, confusingly using a linking logic to represent a *static* model of two-dimensional space. Even if players chose to circumvent this rule, there are only four boards to recombine, and the artwork is clearly designed to only make sense in its prescribed configuration. Beyond those structural issues, consolidating player participation in a single Mario pawn creates a round-robin model of player control – one directly transposed from the *Super Mario Bros.* video game – that contradicts the game's structural objective: a winner-take-all race to the finish.

Bandai's *Super Mario Bros. Game,* in contrast, recognizes a key distinction in affordances between board and video games, namely that the former are bound to material constraints (both physical and economic) governing the size, shape and substance of their in-game spaces. *Super Mario Bros.* is decades old, driven by severely constrained processing capabilities, but it already contains a world of sufficient scope and size that any board game adaptation aiming to replicate it would either have to condense or cut its spaces significantly. In lieu of replication, Bandai's adaptation opts to expand the use of linking logics – that is those that support the video game's warp pipes and climbable vines – and augment them with recombinatory and chance logics. Slicing the Mushroom Kingdom into discrete segments allows players to construct thousands of World configurations, all similar in function and form but variable in layout. Likewise, Bandai modifies the video game's control and game mode logics to expand, rather than collapse, the number of players. Instead of round-robin control, it is possible to have four individual Marios competing in the same space, a feature that the *Super Mario Bros.* video game series did not replicate in digital form until fifteen years later.

At this level of analysis, Milton Bradley's and Bandai's respective adaptations are not equivalent at all. The former game uses logics and models that are internally contradictory, structurally frictional and materially misaligned. These elemental inconsistencies manifest in play like an out-of-key note in a consonant chord. There is an internal dissonance that feels like the game is both at odds with itself and with its source material. The latter game recognizes the affordances of its source and target platforms, whether computational or cardboard, and uses logics and models that complement their material foundations. The resulting adaptation is not only complementary but additive – it manifests, as Hutcheon would say, 'the comfort of ritual combined with the piquancy of surprise' (2013: 4), one of the key pleasures of adaptation.

Delving deeper into digital-to-analogue game adaptations reveals that there is still much critical work to be done. Reckoning with the myriad adaptations of *Super Mario Bros.* equipped solely with stories, heterocosms or mechanics offers limited conceptual purchase for comparison or analysis, and *How Pac-Man Eats* lays out a compelling framework for refocusing adaptive analysis to logics and models. However analysing digital-to-analogue transposition also foregrounds some necessary adaptations to logics and models themselves. As Hutcheon points out, 'the materiality involved in the adaptation's medium and mode of engagement – the kind of print in a book, the size of the television screen, the particular platform upon which a game is played – is part of the context of reception and often of creation as well' (2013: 143). Put another way, the material conditions of adaptation matter not only for an object's creation or reception but for its logics and models as well. Some logics, like collision, for example, don't map neatly to the myriad ways that analogue, that is real-world, objects touch, overlap or occupy proximal spaces and the mechanisms to which these interactions give rise. Recognizing these material distinctions will help broaden the catalogue of operational logics and playable models and refine their definitions across both digital and analogue games. More importantly, doing so will illuminate shared foundations across material forms, bridging the gulf between analogue and digital game studies, sharpening our critical vocabulary, and inspiring novel combinations of logics and models, all in an effort to tell new stories, fashion new worlds and build new mechanisms to play.

Notes

1   The same held for computer games, too, perhaps even more so among hobbyist programmers, as recounted in Donovan: 'There were countless versions of tic-tac-toe, hangman and roulette, dozens of copies of board games such as Battleships and swarms of games that challenged players to guess numbers or words selected at random by the computer' (2010: 58).

2   Hutcheon describes a 'dice game adaptation of Jane Austen's novel, *Pride and Prejudice*' but does not name it (2013: 50). (It is likely *Pride and Prejudice: The Game* [2002].) Similarly, she notes that 'Tolkien's novels spawned *Dungeons and Dragons* board and computer games' but does not identify any specific adapted titles (2013: 136).

3   This brevity is not a quirk of translation. *Super Mario Bros.* US manual is a sentence-for-sentence translation of the original Japanese manual. For a comparison, see Mandelin (2018).

References

Altice, N. (2019), 'Joy Family: Japanese Board Games in the Post-War Showa Period', *Proceedings of the 2019 DiGRA International Conference: Game, Play and the Emerging Ludo-Mix*, Kyoto, Japan.

Altice, N. (2020), 'Super Mario Bros. vs. Super Mario Bros. vs. Super Mario Bros', *ROMchip*, 2 (1).

Anthropy, A. and N. Clark (2014), *A Game Design Vocabulary*, Boston, MA: Addison-Wesley.

Betrayal at House on the Hill (2004), [Board game], Designer: B. Glassco, R. Daviau, B. McQuillan, M. Selinker and T. Woodruff, USA: Avalon Hill Games.

Bloodborne: The Board Game (2021), [Board game], Designers: E. M. Lang and M. Shinall, USA: CMON Global Ltd.

Bram Stoker's Dracula (1992), [Film] Dir. F. F. Coppola, USA: Columbia Pictures.

Brathwaite, B. and I. Schreiber (2009), *Challenges for Game Designers*, Boston, MA: Course Technology.

Calvin, A. (2016), 'Warner Reveals 1m UK LEGO Marvel Sales as Sequel Looms', *MCV/Develop*. Available online: https://web.archive.org/web/20160302062139/https://www.mcvuk.com/news/read/warner-reveals-1m-uk-lego-marvel-sales-as-sequel-looms/0161198 (accessed 29 May 2021).

Dark Souls: The Board Game (2017), [Board game], Designers: D. Carl, A. Hall, M. Hart and R. Loxam, UK: Steamforged Games Ltd.

Dealessandri, M. (2016), 'Digital to Physical: The Rise of Video Games-Themed Board Games', *MCV/Develop*. Available online: https://web.archive.org/web/20161023135020/http://www.mcvuk.com/news/read/digital-to-physical-the-rise-of-video-games-themed-board-games/0171694 (accessed 20 May 2021).

Defender (1982), [Board game], USA: Entex Industries Inc.

Demaria, R. (2019), *High Score! Expanded: The Illustrated History of Electronic Games*, 3rd edn., Boca Raton, FL: CRC Press.

Donkey Kong (1982), [Board game], Designers: J. Breslow, D. Rosenwinkel and J. Zaruba USA: Milton Bradley.

Donovan, T. (2010), *Replay: The History of Video Games*, Hove: Yellow Ant.

Doom: The Board Game (2016), [Board game], Designer: J. Ying, Czech Republic: ADC Blackfire Entertainment.

Double Dragon: The Board Game (1989), [Board game], USA: Tiger Electronics.

Dragon's Lair (1984), [Board game], USA: Milton Bradley.

Gradius (1986), [Board game], Japan: Bandai.

Hasbro (2020), 'Monopoly Super Mario Celebration Edition Board Game.' Available online: https://monopoly.hasbro.com/en-us/product/monopoly-super-mario-celebration-edition-board-game:E43F80F5-6A97-4412-8F13-16EF1D2C3848 (accessed 27 May 2021).

Hutcheon, L. (2013), *A Theory of Adaptation*, 2nd edn., New York: Routledge.

Kent, S. L. (2001), *The Ultimate History of Video Games*, New York: Three Rivers Press.

The Legend of Zelda (1986), [Video game], USA: Nintendo.

Mandelin, C. (2018), 'Legends of Localization Super Mario Bros. - Manuals.' Available online: https://legendsoflocalization.com/super-mario-bros/manuals/ (accessed 13 June 2021).

Metroid Prime (2002), [Video game], USA: Nintendo.

Minecraft: Builders & Biomes (2019), [Board game], Designer: U. Blum, Germany: Ravensbuger.

Monopoly: Bass Fishing Edition (n.d.), [Board Game], USA: USAopoly.

Monopoly: The .com Edition (2000), [Board Game], USA: Hasbro.

Monopoly: Super Mario Bros. Collector's Edition (2016), [Board Game], USA: USAopoly.

Monopoly: Super Mario Celebration! (2020), [Board Game], USA: Hasbro.

Myst (1998), [Board game], USA: University Games.

Nintendo (1985), *Super Mario Bros. Instruction Booklet*.

Osborn, J. C., N. Wardrip-Fruin and M. Mateas (2017), 'Refining Operational Logics', 12th International Conference on the Foundations of Digital Games. Available online: https://dl.acm.org/doi/10.1145/3102071.3102107 (accessed 15 November 2021).

Pandemic (2008), [Board game], Designer: M. Leacock, USA: Z-Man Games.

Parlett, D. (1999), *The Oxford History of Board Games*, Oxford: Oxford University Press.

Plague Inc.: The Board Game (2017), [Board game], Designer: J. Vaughan, USA: Ndemic Creations.

Sagrada (2017), [Board game], Designers: D. Andrews and A. Adamescu, USA: Floodgate Games.

Sellers, M. (2017), *Advanced Game Design: A Systems Approach*, Boston, MA: Addison-Wesley Professional.

Sicart, M. (2008), 'Defining Game Mechanics', *Game Studies*, 8 (2).

Sim City: The Card Game (1994), [Card game], Designers: D. Bromley, L. Rexing, and T. Wham, USA: Mayfair Games.

Stoker, B. (1897), *Dracula*, London: Archibald Constable and Company.

Street Fighter: The Miniatures Game (2021), [Board game], Designers: A. Tune and J. Vargas, USA: Jasco Games.

Studio Hard Co. (1986a), *Super Mario Bros.: Save Mario from Evil!* スーパーマリオブラザーズ・マリオを救え！, Tokyo: Futabasha Co., Ltd.

Studio Hard Co. (1986b), *Super Mario Bros.: Defiance From Devil Neo-Kuppa* スーパーマリオブラザーズ Vol. 2・大魔王ネオクッパの挑戦, Tokyo: Futabasha Co., Ltd.

Super Mario Bros. (1985), [Video game], USA: Nintendo.

Super Mario Bros. Game スーパーマリオブラザーズゲーム (1985), [Board game], Japan: Bandai.

Super Mario Bros. Game (1988), [*Board game*], USA: Milton Bradley.

This War of Mine: The Board Game (2017), [Board game], Designers: M. Oracz and J. Wiśniewski, Poland: Awaken Realms.

Wardrip-Fruin, N. (2020), *How Pac-Man Eats*, Boston, MA: MIT Press.

The Witcher Adventure Game (2014), [Board game], Designer: I. Trzewiczek, USA: Fantasy Flight.

Wizard of Wor (1983), [Board game], USA: Ideal Toy Company.

XCOM: The Board Game (2015), [Board game], Designer: E. M. Lang, USA: Fantasy Flight Games.

Zubek, R. (2020), *Elements of Game Design*, Boston, MA: MIT Press.

Index

Aarseth, Espen   34–5
actor network theory   6
aesthetics   10, 22, 50, 51, 85–6, 91–3, 97,
        124–8, 130, 132, 143–4, 146,
        153, 155, 157
affect   67, 71, 74–5, 98
agency
    in games   1, 12, 25–6, 132, 149–51
    human   8, 9, 23–4, 108, 120, 124,
        125, 127–9, 133, 140
    nonhuman   3, 6, 7, 9, 24–5, 27–8,
        154–6
Ahmed, Sara   74
Alaimo, Stacy   10, 11, 149
Alam, Shahidul   145
Althusser, Louis   133
Analog Game Studies   3, 33, 43
analogue
    definitions of   4–5, 35–9, 48
    game industry   34
    game studies   2–6, 12–13, 33–4, 43,
        65, 222
    technology   41, 42, 207
Anderson, Benedict   124, 131, 137
animism   149–50
Anthropocene   22, 158
anthropocentrism   3, 12, 22–4, 131, 144,
        149, 155, 156
Anthropy, Anna   226
Apperley, Thomas H.   1–2, 5, 6, 11
Arnaudo, Marco   210, 212

Backe, Hans-Joachim   144, 149
Barad, Karen   6, 9–11, 22, 26, 28, 59–60,
        68–71, 77–9
Barthes, Roland   50
Bartlett, Alison   119
Bateman, Chris   55, 96
Bennett, Jane   2, 7–9, 11–13, 22, 27, 73,
        76, 77
Betrayal at House on the Hill   228, 235

Bienia, Raphael   3, 6, 54–5, 67, 70,
        71
biocentrism   149
biodiversity   154–8
biosphere   147–8, 151
BIPOC   34, 168–74, 176–7, 181–3
Bloodborne: The Board Game   223
Blood Rage   134
board, game   3, 13–14, 48, 54–5, 57–9,
        108, 112, 123–41, 152, 153, 157,
        192, 215, 217, 234–6
BoardGameGeek   170, 182
board game industry   33, 34, 85, 170–3,
        188, 191, 193, 194, 197, 206
Bogost, Ian   28, 126–7, 209
Bohunicky, Kyle   11
Boluk, Stephanie   26, 51
Booth, Paul   3, 14–15, 85, 95, 125, 128,
        169–70, 193, 210, 211
Bowker, Geoffrey   35
box, game   6, 34, 51, 54, 83, 130, 194,
        214, 215
Bram Stoker's Dracula   224
Bratich, Jack Z.   39
Brown, Bill   58
Brown, Douglas   4, 205, 211

Caillois, Roger   7, 90, 91, 106, 167
Candlekeep Mysteries   197–8
Carbon City Zero   144, 159
card games   32, 33, 57, 109, 189, 195–6,
        223, 231–2
Carter, Marcus   91
Catan   177–8, 191, 227
Chang, Alenda Y.   143, 150, 153, 159
Chartier, Roger   52
Chen, Mel Y.   66, 70, 73
chess
    the board game   93, 106, 128, 167
    Video Chess   223, 227
Chow, Rey   14, 124, 135–7

Clark, Naomi 226
Clark, Timothy 147, 158
climate
    action 143, 152
    crisis 11–12, 14, 15, 28–9, 143–8,
        150, 152, 153, 156, 157, 159, 219
    education 143, 149
Cluedo 191, 192
Cohen, Jeffrey J. 67, 69, 77
Colistra, Rita 211
colonialism 13–14, 29, 125, 132, 153
Commands & Colors: Napoleonics 57
Condis, Megan 128
Connect 4 188
Coole, Diana 1, 2, 8, 22
cooperative play 124, 138–40, 191, 194
coronavirus 14, 187, *see also* COVID-19
COVID-19 14, 187, 190, 195, 199, *see
        also* coronavirus
crafting 83, 85–90, 93, 95, 96
Critical Role 197
Cronon, William 146
crowdfunding 14, 85, 88, 206, 211–13
culture
    digital 5, 39, 40
    game cultures 3, 6, 11, 15, 85, 197,
        216, 218
    general 8, 21, 107, 129, 146, 148
    material 108, 119
    popular 229
Cvetkovich, Ann 74

Dark Souls: The Board Game 215, 222
Darwin's Journey 208
Dawn of the Peacemakers 138
Dean, Tim 66
Defender 223
De Koven, Bernard 51
Delap, Lucy 116, 120
de Peuter, Greig 123, 137
Derrida, Jacques 70, 77, 79
Deterding, Sebastian 80
dexterity games 56–7, 127, 138
digital
    definitions of 4–5, 15, 33, 37–42
    games 1, 2, 32–5, 38–9, 42–3, 84,
        169, 223, 226, 228, 237
    platforms 5, 14, 190, 195–8, 206,
        207, 209

technologies 3, 32, 35, 37–40, 42,
        207, 217
discrimination 11, 174, 175, 177, 178,
        181–3
diversity 11, 170, 171, 173, 183
Donkey Kong 223, 226
Donovan, Tristan 168, 237 n.1
Doom: The Board Game 222, 226
Double Dragon: The Board Game 223
Dragon's Lair 223
Duggan, Eddie 58
Dungeons & Dragons 13, 67, 71, 196
Dunnigan, James F. 96
Duvall, Kevin 211
Dyer-Witheford, Nick 123, 137
Dyhouse, Carol 114

Eco, Umberto 49, 50
ecocentrism 149, 152, 156
ecocriticism 22–3, 29
Ecosystem 155–9
ecosystems 147, 149–51, 154, 156–7
Edney, Matthew H. 123, 124
Eisenack, Klaus 144, 145
Elias, George Skaff 50, 209
Ellis, Erle 150
embodiment 38, 78, *see also* play,
        embodied
Engelstein, Geoffrey 57, 105
entanglement 3, 9–11, 15, 22, 24–6, 28,
        67–8, 70–1, 74–5, 80, 145, 148,
        150, 157
environments, game 10, 48, 124–33, 140,
        176, 178
ethics 11, 14, 22, 27, 140, 143, 148–9,
        170

feminism 105, 118–19, 149
Fjællingsdal, Kristoffer S. 145
Fleming, Dan 90
Forests of Pangaia 153
Fort 196
Fox, Jesse 169
Freedom: The Underground Railroad 124,
        138–41
Fritsch, Melanie 50
Frost, Samantha 1, 2, 8, 22
Frosthaven 198, 205
FunEmployed 197

Gaia   147–8, 158
Game of Life, The   112, 127
Games Workshop   69, 71, 85, 90, 95
Garfield, Richard   50, 209
gender
    constructs   106
    discrimination   175–6, 178, 183
    experiences of   13, 106, 107, 113–14,
        120
    identity   169, 170, 174–5
    inequality   166, 181
    representations of   43, 168, 211
Germaine Buckley, Chloé   7, 67, 71
Gibbs, Martin   6, 57, 84, 85, 91, 92, 194,
        195, 206–8, 210, 211
Gilbert, Michael   169
Gilbert, Scott F.   150
Gloomhaven   167, 198, 205, 217
Goffman, Erving   25, 92
Gradius   223
Graeber, David   29
Gray, Peter   96
Grosz, Elizabeth   71
Groves, Christopher   145
Guerra, Douglas A.   10
Gutschera, K. Robert   209

Haraway, Donna   14, 67, 89, 143, 146
Harman, Graham   7
Heidegger, Martin   14, 124, 131, 135,
        141 n.3
Heron, Michael   56
Hnefatafl   58–9
Huizinga, Johan   7, 27, 28, 52, 53, 123,
        138, 167
Hunicke, Robin   50, 144
Hustak, Carla   79
Hutcheon, Linda   223–6, 228, 231, 236,
        237

idealism   2, 146
ideology   109, 131–3, 137, 138, 191
Ideology: The War of Ideas   124, 134, 135
imperialism   13, 123–4, 133
Ingarden, Roman   13, 47–55
Ingold, Tim   22, 145, 148, 157
inhumanism   66
Inis   134
interactive media   39–40, 225–6, 231

interactivity   39, 40, 49–50, 116, 128,
        225–6, 229–32
Iovino, Serenella   8, 12
Iser, Wolfgang   49–50

Järvinen, Aki   48, 50, 55, 56, 125
Jayemanne, Darshana   1, 2, 5, 6, 11, 21
Jenga   53–4
Junk Art   56
Juul, Jesper   7, 8, 48

Kankainen, Ville   85, 92, 98
Kantor, Tadeusz   55
Keep Cool   144
Kemet   134
Kickstarter   5, 14, 85, 88, 198, 205–19
Kirkman, Robert   187
Kirschenbaum, Matthew G.   152
Kocurek, Carly A.   166, 168
Kromand, Daniel   56
Krukowski, Damon   37, 38
Kushinski, Alysse Verona   73
Kwok, Roberta   145

Ladder of Academic Success, The   106,
        111–16, 119
Lahsen, Myanna   145–6
LaRell Anderson, Sky   1
Latour, Bruno   6, 146–8, 158
LeBlanc, Marc   50, 144
Legend of Zelda, The   225
LeMieux, Patrick   26, 51
LGBTQiIA+   168–71, 174, 178, 181, 183
Liu, Alan   41–2
live action role-playing   3, 7, 32, 38, 71
Lords of Hellas   134
Lovelock, James   147, 158
Luciano, Dana   66, 73
Lugones, Maria   25–6, 28, 29

MacCallum-Stewart, Esther   3–5, 8, 14,
        205, 211
McGlotten, Shaka   66, 68, 79
McKeown, Conor   9
magic circle, the   7–8, 124
Magic: The Gathering   166, 195–6
Mahaffey, Mark   126, 127, 129, 133
Manovich, Lev   35, 40
Marder, Michael   155

Margolies, Eleanor   55
Margulis, Lynn   147
Marks, Laura   65
Martinez, Xiuhtezcatl   152
material feminisms   149
material turn, the   1, 5–8, 10–15, 22, 66, 188
MDA framework   144, 151
mechanics   6, 13–14, 65, 107, 109, 115, 120, 123, 143–51, 153–9, 226–7, 229–30, 232–6
Medhurst, Andy   114
Merleau-Ponty, Maurice   56–7
Mert, Aysem   144
metagaming   26, 50, 51, 156
Metroid Prime   228
Minecraft   11, 223, 227
miniatures   3, 6, 13, 83–99, 127, 206–9, 212, 214, 219
Monopoly   32, 57, 58, 127, 138, 188, 191, 192, 232–4
Montfort, Nick   40, 209
Morning Leader, The   110
Morton, Timothy   145, 147, 148
Muñoz, José Esteban   80
Murray, Janet   55, 59
Myers, Natasha   79
Myst   223

Nancy, Jean-Luc   69, 70, 77
narrative   6, 12, 13, 50, 57, 89, 92, 94, 108, 128, 225, 229–31, 233
nature   8, 11, 12, 14, 38, 143, 145–9, 151, 153, 155–7, 159–60
naturecultures   146–7
New Game of Emulation or the Road to Knowledge, The   16
New Game of Human Life, The   116
new materialisms, the   5, 66
Nintendo   229
nonhuman, the   3, 8–10, 12–14, 22, 25–9, 56, 59, 60, 66–7, 143, 149, 150, 159
Norcia, Megan A.   124, 125, 132

Ockelbo Runestone   58–60
ontology   5–7, 9, 12, 13, 15, 34, 36, 40, 77, 144, 149

Opperman, Serpil   8, 12

Pandemic   124, 138–41, 190, 226, 227
Pank-a-Squith   13, 107–10, 113, 116–19
Parikka, Jussi   73
Parlett, David   54, 222
performance
   performativity   9, 53, 57, 109, 132, 134
   play as   13, 25, 47–60, 78–80, 128, 133
phenomenology   23, 37, 50
Photosynthesis   150, 152–6, 158, 159
Plague Inc.: The Board Game   223
Planet   158–9
platform studies   5, 209
play, embodied   14, 167–8, 183
Pobuda, Tanya   14, 34, 43
posthuman   9
procedural rhetoric   126, 140
prop   55, 96

Quachri, Trevor   36
queer   10, 13, 65–80

race, representations of   43, 168, 174
racism   118, 176–8, 181
Ramankutty, Navin   150
relationality   22, 206
Renature   146, 157
Rhino Hero: Super Battle   56
RISK   14, 123–4, 127, 129–35, 137, 139, 140
Rogerson, Melissa J.   6, 194–5, 206, 208, 210, 211
role-playing
   games   2, 3, 6, 8, 14, 32, 33, 84, 91, 165, 189, 199, 200, 226, 233
   as a mode of play   13, 65–80
   platforms   198
rules   25–6, 33, 47–50, 54, 65–6, 84, 91–3, 96, 108–9, 112, 128, 131, 143–4, 146, 147, 151–7, 159, 190, 194, 212, 226–7, 235

Sagrada   227
Salen, Katie   7, 49
Samantrai, Ranu   115

Sapp, Jann   150
Sax, David   4
Schneider, Rebecca   70, 71, 74, 75, 80 n.2
Scott, Leslie   53, 54
Scrabble   191, 192
sexism   181
sexuality   65, 77, 80
Shalev, Isaac   57, 105
Sicart, Miguel   10, 12, 13, 24, 51, 144, 151, 226
Sihvonen, Tanja   65
Simard, Suzanne   150–1, 154, 155
Sim City: The Card Game   223
Singh, Julietta   74
Small World   134
Smith, Wally   6, 57, 194, 195, 206–8, 210, 211
Sofer, Andrew   55
Sotamaa, Olli   199
space
    gaming spaces   14, 34, 57, 166–70, 172, 174, 176, 181–3
    in-game   57, 236
Spirit Island   138, 208, 209
Star, Susan Leigh   35
Stenros, Jaakko   65
Sterne, Jonathan   37–8
Stoker, Bram   224
Street Fighter: The Miniatures Game   223
Strong National Museum of Play, The   21
subjectivity
    digital   40–2
    in general   12, 13, 56–7, 154, 158
Suffragettes In and Out of Prison   110–11
Suits, Bernard   53
Super Mario Bros.   222, 228–37
sustainability   144–5, 148, 159
Sutton-Smith, Brian   95
systems, game   48, 50–1, 56, 127, 128, 134, 136, 143–4, 150, 158–9, 227, 235

Tang, Wai Yen   169
Tauber, Alfred I.   150
Terror in Meeple City   193
This War of Mine: The Board Game   223
Thomasson, Amie   54

Thomlinson, Natalie   118
Tiny Footprint   144, 159
Tipping Point   144
tokens, game   47, 48, 55–6, 67, 83, 91–3
Tokyo Highway   56
Torner, Evan   3, 4, 33, 43
touch   4, 13, 54, 56–8, 65–80, 190, 193–4, 199, 219, 228
toys   13, 21–3, 51, 85, 87, 90–5, 97, 192
Trammell, Aaron   3–4, 12–14, 167, 206, 207, 211, 212
transcorporeality   10, 11
Tsing, Anna   149
Turnhout, Esther   146
Twilight Struggle   124, 134–6, 139
Twister   58
Two Rooms and a Boom   193
Tyni, Heikki   199

Van der Hel, Sandra   144
Vasel, Tom   56
video games   5, 9, 25, 33, 144, 153, 158, 166–7, 169, 222, 224–6, 228, 234, 236
virtual, the   4–5, 68, 76–9, 138
virtual worlds   14, 68, 124–9, 137
Votes for Women   108

Wake, Paul   6–7, 13, 145, 193–4, 217
Waldron, Emma   3–4, 33, 43, 67
Walking Dead, The   187
Walton, Kendall   55, 96
Wardrip-Fruin, Noah   40, 227–8, 233
wargames   14, 35, 57, 71, 84, 96, 123–4, 128–30, 132, 134, 152, 158
War of Whispers, A   57–8
Wasserman, Joe A.   48, 93, 210
Wells, H. G.   133
Werewolf   193
Werning, Stefan   14–15, 205–11, 215
Wingspan   146
Witcher Adventure Game, The   222
Wizard of Wor   223
Wizards of the Coast   189, 195–8
Wohlleben, Peter   153–4
Womanopoly   115–19
women's suffrage   107–11
Woodard, C. Jason   5

Woods, Stewart   3, 6, 151–3,
     193
wood wide web   151

XCOM: The Board Game   222

Yu, Dale   56

Zagal, José   80
Zimmerman, Eric   7, 49
Zubek, Robert   50, 144, 226

www.ingramcontent.com/pod-product-compliance
Lightning Source LLC
Chambersburg PA
CBHW050415280326
41932CB00013BA/1872